UNDIVIDED

UNDIVIDED

coming out, becoming whole

and living free from shame

VICKY
BEECHING

**WILLIAM
COLLINS**

William Collins
An imprint of HarperCollins*Publishers*
1 London Bridge Street
London SE1 9GF

WilliamCollinsBooks.com

First published in Great Britain in 2018 by William Collins

First published in the United States by HarperOne in 2018

1

A catalogue record for this book is available from the British Library

ISBN 978-0-00-818214-4 (hardback)

Designed by Yvonne Chan

Set in Filosofia

Printed and bound by CPI Group (UK) Ltd, Croydon CR0 4YY

MIX
Paper from
responsible sources

FSC
www.fsc.org   FSC™ C007454

This book is dedicated to the memory of Lizzie Lowe, a fourteen-year-old British girl who tragically took her own life in 2014 because she feared telling her Christian community that she was gay.

Research statistics show that lesbian, gay, bisexual, and transgender (LGBTQ+) young people are far more likely to self-harm, suffer from mental-health issues, and contemplate suicide than their heterosexual peers.

For Lizzie and the countless other LGBTQ+ young people who have ended their lives out of fear and shame: We will remember you. Your stories matter. We carry you in our hearts.

CONTENTS

PREFACE

This is a book about me, and also *not* a book about me.

It's a memoir about the battle I've fought to make peace with who I am and to unlearn a lifetime of shame and fear. In my case, this centered on the vast tension between being gay and being Christian.

When I asked on social media, "What would you like me to include in my memoir?," hundreds of you responded. A common theme was: "I identify as part of the LGBTQ+ community too. I wish there were more books I could relate to about growing up dealing with identity struggles. Reading those would make me feel less alone." Others of you said, "I'm straight, but I want to understand what it's like to be gay, so I can be a better ally. Your story could provide one example of that."

Some messages I received said, "I believe the Bible teaches that same-sex relationships are sinful. Can you explain how you understand the Bible on this topic?" Others said, "I'm nonreligious and work in the corporate world, where I'm championing diversity. Your memoir could shine a light on the harm it does when you can't be your authentic self at work. It could encourage businesses to take better care of their staff's well-being."

I decided that all of these suggestions were important, so I chose to use them as my guide. Also, I decided that unless I was going to get vulnerable enough in the writing process to wonder whether I should really be putting certain things in print, the book was unlikely to help anyone. So prepare for me to share (and perhaps overshare) about the highs and lows of my teens, twenties, and thirties; about how I finally found the courage to come out, leaping into the unknown; and about what life has been like since.

Some of you, I hope, will feel a resonance—a sense of "me too." Others of you reading this who believe that LGBTQ+ equality goes against the teachings of Bible, thank you for giving this book a chance. I hope you'll keep the door of your heart open as you travel through its pages.

Right now, the issue of same-sex marriage threatens to split the global church. In news headlines, in political campaigns, and on social media, people with polar views are debating this heated topic. It's reaching boiling point. Juggernauts like the Anglican Church, with its 85 million members worldwide, teeter on the edge of a split. This book is only a drop in the ocean of that vast situation, but it's my attempt to show that LGBTQ+ people of faith, and same-sex marriage, should be fully affirmed.

S o, yes, this is a book about me and my story.
But it's also a book that's *not* about me. At least, *not only* about me.

It's about something far bigger and wider—about themes that are woven into all of our human DNA: our need to find a place to belong, our fear of becoming vulnerable, our longing to be authentic, the shame we feel about aspects of who we are, and the way others' criticisms can paralyze our ability to live and love.

So, this might be a story about you too. About the ways you feel awkward about, embarrassed by, or ashamed of parts of your identity, or the way fear holds you back and stops you from attempting to dream big. Diversity can be tricky: the very things that make us stunningly unique can also be the things we hide in the closet because they cause us to feel different from the crowd.

The shapes these differences take are as diverse as we are. Perhaps it's that you can't talk about your struggles with mental health; you're dealing with anxiety or depression and don't want colleagues at work to know. That part of your identity is firmly locked in the closet, even though deep down you wish you could be open about it.

Or maybe you've always known you are trans, but haven't dared tell anyone, fearful that no one in your life will understand. Or maybe your battle is similar to the one I faced; you're gay and terrified to come out.

Or perhaps it's about neurodiversity. You're on the autistic spectrum and don't want to mention it for fear that people will treat or think of you differently. Maybe it's about gender roles; you might be a teenage boy who dreams of becoming a ballet dancer (like the fabulous Billy Elliot), but you're afraid your friends (and enemies) would endlessly tease you and make life unbearable if you chased that dream.

Of course, it's totally fine to keep these things private if it feels safer; only you know what's right for you. Not everyone needs to "come out," and you can be perfectly happy, healthy, and whole without taking that step. What is crucial, though, is this: we need to love and accept who we are. *It's about making peace with ourselves.*

It's about finally feeling comfortable in our own skin, not allowing others to make us ashamed or embarrassed of things that are part of our beauty, our diversity and uniqueness. When we take those pieces, shattered by shame, and dare to be ourselves, we find healing. We're not forced to choose between aspects of our identity. We become whole and "undivided."

sn't this just a bunch of selfish navel-gazing?" critics may ask.

No, it's quite the opposite. *We can only love others well when we live from a place of wholeness.*

The Christian faith teaches: "Love your neighbor *as you love yourself*"—the implication being that we must learn to love ourselves first, in order to love others from a place of health and well-being. Otherwise, it's like pouring a glass of water from a broken jug; our fragmentation affects everyone.

Entrepreneur and inventor Steve Jobs, in his 2005 address at Stanford University, said, "Your time is limited, so don't waste it living someone else's life . . . Don't let the noise of others' opinions drown out your own inner voice . . . Have courage."

He's right. When fear and shame push us to copy the crowd, we risk living someone else's life. Everyone loses when that happens; we won't be the best family member, coworker, or friend we can be unless we're authentic and whole.

So becoming "undivided" is not just about us: *When we make peace with ourselves and are no longer fearful or defensive, it changes how we engage with the world.* If enough of us do this, the ripple effect will go far and wide, from neighborhoods to nations.

Often, we humans run away from what we can't relate to, from people who seem different to us. It might be someone from a different political party, a refugee from a far-flung nation, someone from a different socioeconomic background, or someone who is LGBTQ+. We build walls, bunker ourselves away, and allow stereotypes to govern the way we view the people we don't understand. This is rife in global politics and in the church right now and requires urgent change.

Fear of the "other"—fear of the person who is different from you—is something I've felt personally and painfully. One moment I was seen as an insider in my evangelical Christian world; the next, I was treated as an outsider. People I'd known my entire life suddenly saw me as different, because my orientation did not match theirs. I felt their suspicion and coldness as they stepped away. They didn't see *me* anymore—they just saw someone who was different from them, and they relied on broken stereotypes and judgments. Experiencing this firsthand has fueled my desire to see society change.

So, as well as becoming "undivided" on an individual level, I hope we can break down the walls that divide us societally. If we exchange our fear of others' differences for a love that transcends stereotypes, it could have vast impact.

I'll bring this preface to a close and let you dive into the book itself. As you read on, whoever you are and whatever the reason this book came to be in your hands, my hope for you is this: May you find the courage to be yourself in all your uniqueness. Then, free from fear and shame, may you live and love from that place of healing and wholeness.

Never underestimate the change you can bring to the world around you. Authenticity and vulnerability have a powerful domino effect. If enough of us try to live in an authentic and vulnerable way, who knows what might happen. The world could become a very different place.

1

Blinking in the bright lights, I stared out at twenty thousand people. The stadium was filled to capacity, and they sang along to one of my songs, "Yesterday, Today and Forever," at the top of their lungs. I was in my late twenties and living in the US, and although I'd been recording and touring for a decade, I still treasured every time I was able to play and sing.

The volume of so many voices always takes my breath away. It sounds like a waterfall—thunderous. Crowds that big have an energy all their own, and emotion hangs in the air like a tangible mist.

I motioned to my band to bring the music down to a softer volume and, taking the microphone, I asked for the arena lights to be dimmed. I then invited the crowd to get out their phones and hold them up. Doing this creates a beautiful moment at any concert; each phone shines a tiny speck of light, and they join together to illuminate the darkness, like thousands of glowing candles, or stars in the night sky.

I'm sure all songwriters feel deeply moved when they hear people using their lyrics and melodies to express themselves—I certainly always have. It meant even more to know that people were using my songs to connect with God, as the events I played at were faith based.

I stood back, watching the sea of faces and listening to the beautiful thunder of twenty thousand voices. Every hair on the back of my neck stood on end as I captured the moment in my mind: every voice, each harmony, every sparkling light. They sang and sang, and I listened, soaking it all in. I could've watched them forever. It was like visiting a loved one for the last time, knowing you'll never see that person again; you struggle to take note of all the details in an effort to ward off the inevitable dimming of the precious memory with time.

I knew that someday very soon I would lose all of this. Something in me was breaking, and I couldn't keep going much longer. There were things I needed to say—and doing so would bring it all crumbling down.

But in that brief moment, my heart was at peace. The crowd and I were one as we sang in the darkness.

If I close my eyes, even now, I can still hear them singing.

One week after that stadium event, I sat on an overnight flight to England, headed to a Christian conference where several thousand people gathered every year. Despite trying, I hadn't slept a wink as my mind raced with emotion. My body ached from months of touring and constant jet lag, but far more painful was my inner world: I was heartbroken because the girl I'd secretly fallen in love with had just got married.

I say *secretly* fallen in love with, because she never knew about my feelings—no one knew. Nobody in my life had the faintest idea that I was gay, as I'd never dared talk about it, despite the fact I was now in my late twenties. So, unknown to anyone but me, these feelings had grown the more I'd got to know this smart, vivacious, and creative American girl.

We'd become close friends over the years, so I was the first person she called when she met the guy she'd ultimately marry. I got to hear every detail of their relationship whether I wanted to or not—their first date, their first kiss, and a year later the evening he got on one knee and proposed. Wanting to be a good friend to her, I'd been there to watch the couple walk down the aisle in a New York church. As they drove off at the end, headed for their honeymoon, my heart was shattered at the loss.

I was grateful that a UK trip had come up; I knew it would be a helpful distraction from the pain. The sleepless flight wasn't helping, though, as memories of the wedding played on my mind all night. Jammed into my coach-class seat, staring out the window into the darkness, I felt my heart free-falling into nothing, as lonely and endless as the cold midnight sky.

A lifetime of secret sadness was washing over me. This certainly wasn't my first heartbreak. I felt stuck in a recurring cycle of unexpressed feelings, repeatedly watching the women I'd fallen for walk away with someone else. It wasn't that they'd rejected me—they'd never even known how I felt because I couldn't tell them. I couldn't tell anyone.

Since childhood, the church had taught me that homosexuality was an "abominable sin." As a result, I couldn't accept my own gay orientation. As an adult, my only survival solution was to shelve my feelings, keep them entirely private, and assume I'd never be able to date or marry. This way I could still belong to my faith community, keep my livelihood—the church-music career I loved—and not risk losing everything and everyone.

I was only twelve or thirteen when I first realized I was different, and knowing how "sinful" these feelings were caused waves of shame to crash over me. At that age, I'd felt shame before—when I'd lied to my parents about something small or failed to do school homework. But the feelings around my sexuality were different. This wasn't shame about anything I'd *done*; it was shame about who I *was*.

I'd first fallen in love around my fourteenth birthday, and, in the way of teenagers, I fell hard. Everything she said was magical. Everything she did captivated me. Our class had been together for a couple of years already, but as with most kids, puberty brings a totally new perspective on people you've been next to every day and never noticed.

Suddenly, I realized how incredibly blue her eyes were, how gracefully her body moved, and I could pick out the sound of her voice from another room. I wanted to be around her, to matter to her, to hear her thoughts on everything and anything. It was unlike anything I'd ever felt before and definitely a world away from the platonic emotions I had for boys.

One fateful day she confided in me that she'd met an amazing guy and that they were dating. The moment I heard this, it felt like all the lights in my world went out. I went home that night and sobbed into my carpet, utterly heartbroken and weighed down by the shame of my "sinful attractions." After hours of crying, my thoughts kept turning to suicide. I told God I'd rather end my own life now if I had to continue to live with the tension of being gay and Christian; it was just too much to bear. If this was just the first of many such broken hearts, I could tell it would eventually leave me in pieces too shattered to mend.

There was a lot of pressure on me during those formative years from another source too—my profile as a young Christian leader. In my late teens I was already singing in front of hundreds of people at worship gatherings. As that grew to national and international exposure, the pressure increased. I was a role model—parents encouraged their kids to buy my CDs, and pastors told their youth groups to follow my example. I was terrified at the thought of disappointing them all. What if they knew who I really was? Being put on a pedestal felt as much like a prison as it did a privilege.

Year had followed year, and heartbreak had followed heartbreak as reliably as the changing of seasons. I sensed the future held more of the same, and if that was the life ahead of me, I wasn't sure I wanted to live.

My peers were now marrying and starting families as we all progressed through our twenties. They were moving forward with their lives, celebrated at every step by their families and their faith communities—bringing a partner to church for the first time, getting engaged, getting married, announcing a pregnancy, baptizing a child. Every heterosexual social milestone was met with smiles and church ceremonies.

I felt frozen in time. No one would have celebrated my feelings, had I expressed them. No one would have celebrated my milestones if I'd gone on dates, brought a female partner to church, gotten engaged or married. For straight people, finding a spouse and starting a family were viewed as blessings from God. For anyone gay, these exact same steps were seen as sinful and something to be ashamed of.

Because of this, I'd never acted on my feelings for girls—not so much as even the briefest kiss, despite the fact I was nearing thirty. All of it was locked away inside as I tried to impeccably do the right thing by my Christian values. As I saw it, I'd chosen God instead of these attractions, pursuing holiness instead of sin. I'd boxed my feelings up and put them on a high shelf in my psyche, leaving them there—I believed—permanently. But I had no idea how deeply it would damage me.

Slowly but surely, over the years, all my emotions began shutting down and switching off, like a giant factory closing up until every machine is still and every light is out. My heart stood like an abandoned building. Empty and echoey. Uninhabited, unvisited, with doors and windows all boarded up. A monument to someone I used to be—or maybe could have been. I felt like a shell of a human being.

My life seemed a monotonous drone of work with no one to come home to. I kept my friends and family at arm's length, because my core identity was something they couldn't know about, and most likely wouldn't understand. I asked my music manager to book gigs on as many holidays and special occasions as possible, so I never had to be home alone—especially on my birthday, Valentine's Day, and New

Year's Eve. Since I was always on the go, my undecorated apartment was simply the place I did laundry, repacked my suitcase, and left again.

Weighed down by these thoughts, I stared out of the plane window as we descended into London's Heathrow airport and taxied on the tarmac. Soon I was inside, lugging my equipment off the baggage carousel. I slung a heavy guitar case over my shoulder and wheeled a large suitcase behind me, heading toward a train bound for central London.

Fifteen minutes later, the Heathrow Express train pulled in to Paddington station. One more quick journey on the Underground, and I'd meet the conference runner who would take me to the event. The idea of stepping into the busy, upbeat energy of a worship conference felt utterly overwhelming—I had cried all night; I could barely speak, let alone sing.

On the Underground platform, the first train to arrive wasn't going to my destination. It rushed in at breakneck speed, and I felt the whoosh of air as it sped toward me. People boarded, and then with a release of energy it sped away into the blackness of the tunnels.

I dropped my luggage next to a bench and sat with my head in my hands. My mind kept returning to the same question: "What's the point anymore?" This frightened me to the core. I was usually a stable, balanced person, but this inner struggle with my sexuality and the incessant cycle of brokenheartedness had brought me to the point of breakdown. Embarrassed to cry in public, I tried to brush the tears away as they fell down my cheeks, but no one was watching anyway. Busy, faceless commuters stared into space, lost in their own worlds as they rushed past.

I was so incredibly tired. Every cell in my body, every fiber of my being was exhausted from carrying this emotional weight since my teens. Growing up, I hadn't known a single gay person and had had no LGBTQ+ role models; social media didn't exist back then in the early 1990s, so finding solace in YouTube's coming-out advice videos—as young people do today—was a universe away from my teenage experience. I'd felt utterly isolated back then, and all these years later, I still felt the icy grip of loneliness; the passing of time only made it harder to bear.

I stood up, rubbing my bloodshot eyes and my tear-stained cheeks, and walked to the edge of the platform. *This could be it,* I thought. *I don't have to do this anymore. I don't have to live this cycle of heartbreak, shame, fear, and isolation over and over. I don't have to do this anymore—it could be over so easily.*

I moved my feet forward inch by inch on the concrete floor, stepping past the line of yellow paint that marked the safety point. I looked down into the tunnel and saw distant lights. Tears were streaming down my face again. I knew if I moved another inch forward, at just the right second, I could step out onto the tracks as the train thundered into the station. It could all be over.

The lights blinded me as the train approached. My feet moved another inch closer to the edge. But just before I stepped out, I thought: *The last hands that touch me and carry my body will belong to total strangers. My whole life I've felt alone. If I die here, it'll be with people who don't even know my name.*

Dying that way, falling onto the hard steel of the train tracks, to be carried away by total strangers, seemed too lonely to go through with. In that split second, I'd found a thought more painful than carrying on with life, and it had distracted me long enough for the train to thunder into the station with my feet still firmly planted on the platform edge.

I staggered backward, returning to the bench where I'd sat before. My heart was racing. I tried to slow my breathing and recover from the shock of what I'd almost done. No one noticed. Hundreds of pairs of feet continued to rush past, on their way to their next appointment. Surrounded by this chaos, I sat, and breathed, and cried as relief washed over me. I don't know how long I stayed there; it could have been minutes or maybe hours. I just sat and sat, until my breathing relaxed and my heart rate finally slowed.

Eventually, feeling as though I were moving in slow motion, I took a deep breath, grabbed my belongings, and boarded the next train. I had only minutes to pull myself together before I'd arrive at the worship conference and be plunged into a busy week of meetings and rehearsals. There would be no one safe there to confide in—any confession of being gay would be a one-way ticket to the end of a career. I just had to hide my pain and keep going.

Desperate for change, my heart ached. I couldn't seem to die, but I also couldn't seem to live.

PART I

Beginnings

2

Baby photos are supposed to be treasured keepsakes, showing you at your very best: wide-eyed, angelic, and utterly adorable. Unfortunately, in my first baby photo I resemble a small, startled alien. My hair stands straight up in jet-black spikes as though I were auditioning for an infant rock band. I'm told that I'd been fast asleep when the hospital photographer arrived. In a hurry, he'd clapped his hands loudly to wake me up, and the moment I'd stirred, he'd snapped the shot. Thanks to him, the photo of the startled spikey-haired alien has been displayed on my parents' living-room wall ever since.

My early years were carefree. In my favorite childhood photo, I'm six years old, wearing a bright-red t-shirt and yellow dungarees, and grinning like a Cheshire cat. My hair is cut in a bowl-shaped bob, and my green-gray eyes have a mischievous twinkle. Back then, my favorite hobby was reciting the latest joke I'd memorized from my collection of joke books. Making people laugh was one of my favorite things, and more often than not I had a big smile on my face.

I grew up before the wonders of the internet. My family lived in the countryside, so instead of PlayStations or Xboxes, my days were filled with playing in tree houses, building forts, damming rivers, and running through fields. It gave me a love for wide open skies, the smell of forests after rainfall, and the rustle of wheat as you run your fingers over it like a golden, waist-high carpet. If I'd owned Mario Kart or Zelda back then, I probably never would have left the house.

Perhaps everyone grew up more slowly before cyberspace came along. Today, kids' minds can be exposed to wonderfully diverse ideas and perspectives at the click of a button. But back then, education and socialization happened organically, not digitally. I learned everything from the small radius of my everyday life, from teachers, schoolmates, family, and the other huge influence in my life: church.

My family lived in a small village of four hundred people. The local school was tiny too, with only forty pupils, aged four to eleven. Always a tomboy, I saved my pocket money until I could afford my first skateboard. My sister, Jo, two and a half years younger than I, also loved skateboarding and riding bikes, so it was brilliant to have a comrade to play with.

Along with my sister, my other childhood partner in crime was the boy who lived across the road. We spent our evenings and the gloriously long summers walking his dog in the nearby woods, practicing skate tricks, and sneaking into the local farmer's hay barn and climbing all the way to the top of the bales, where we'd lie giggling and coughing in the clouds of straw and dust. Sometimes, if it was raining, I'd hide up in the hayloft on my own with a good book and read, listening to the raindrops drumming on the steel roof.

Two threads wove through my earliest years: one was faith and the other was music. Our local church felt like a second home to me, and I was taken to my first service within days of being born. My grandparents on my mother's side, who had left their careers in England and moved to Africa as missionaries, were well known throughout our Pentecostal denomination. They came back from Africa once a year to visit us, often around Christmastime. They'd tell us stories of life in Harare, Zimbabwe, showing us photos of the Bible school they ran and of land-marks like Victoria Falls.

While home in England, they'd gather spare clothes and shoes from everyone in our church and ship them back to Zimbabwe to distrib-ute among those in need when they returned. Hearing their stories prompted my earliest dream: to be a missionary in some remote part of the world, preaching, teaching, and pastoring. I remember, around the age of six, when my teacher asked our class, "What do you want to be when you grow up?" Most children replied, "A footballer," or "A film star," or "A doctor." Not me. I answered resolutely, "I want to be a mis-sionary." My grandparents had become heroes to me, and I wanted to follow in their footsteps and make them proud.

Christian faith felt as natural to me as breathing. It was not a rigid, cold, distant religion, but a genuine heartfelt relationship with God. Prayer never seemed formal either—for me it was just a conversation. At five years old, I walked around the schoolyard chatting with God about my day so far, sharing the highs and lows of my little life. God felt like a friend and a confidant. When I looked out my window at night and saw the moon and stars, my small mind spun with questions about where heaven was located, what angels looked like, and whether I'd ever see my recently deceased (and much-loved) hamster again someday.

Our church, part of the Pentecostal tradition, was always relaxed and upbeat, with music played on guitars, drums, and keyboards and everyone wearing casual clothes. It was a world away from the choirs, pipe organs, incense, and people wearing their Sunday best, found in more formal places of worship.

There were always new faces each Sunday, and everyone was made to feel at home. Refugees from other nations, students who'd moved away from their parents to study at Kent University, homeless men and women, elderly folks in need of a hug and a chat—all received a warm wel-come. Our lunches buzzed with the energy of connection as lonely peo-

UNDIVIDED

ple found community and hungry people received a meal. It was church doing what church is meant to: loving people with grace and kindness.

My mum led the musical part of the worship service every Sunday at church and at weekday prayer meetings. She was a prolific songwriter, penning something new every week without fail. After the sermon, there would be a time of reflection and she would play her latest song—it was her way of serving the church community, using her gift to help others.

Mum worked on her new song during the week at home, in the snatched moments that any parent makes use of while raising kids. So while I was building with Lego blocks or arranging my stuffed animals in rows, she would grab ten minutes to craft her latest song. As soon as I could shake a tambourine or rattle a maraca, I joined in on Sundays, toddling up to the front to stand next to her and trying to keep time with the song.

Our church taught that the Bible was literally true, word for word, so Adam and Eve were considered actual humans who historically existed. The talking snake in the book of Genesis was considered historical too, as was the speaking donkey in the book of Numbers. Everything had happened exactly as it was written.

A few members of the church went out with presentations about Creationism in their spare time, trying to disprove the scientific evidence behind evolution. Medicine was suspect, as people believed in God's healing power, and we heard stories of people like Kathryn Kuhlman, Smith Wigglesworth, Aimee Semple McPherson, and Benny Hinn, who (allegedly) healed thousands by the power of prayer.

There was a firm belief that God still did miracles today, so when the pastor gave an altar call, people would come forward and stand at the front to be prayed for. Many spoke in tongues—something described in the New Testament as an unknown language given to believers by God. Sometimes, when prayed for at the altar, these people would fall down—"slain in the spirit"—when the Holy Spirit was thought to have powerfully touched them.

When I was four years old, my first job at church was to carry a small

14

basket of cloths. These were known as "modesty protectors." If during the altar call a woman was "slain in the spirit" and fell down, I would carry my little basket of cloths to where she was lying. If her skirt or dress had accidentally found its way above her knees, I would lay one of the cloths over her legs to protect her "modesty." I felt very adult and responsible as I trotted around and carried out this important task.

For most of the service, we children had our own meeting in a different part of the building: kids' church. It was a place for the under-twelves to go while the adults listened to the sermon, as the preaching often lasted for forty-five minutes. In kids' church we had our own teachers, songs, and picture books; it was a lot of fun.

One thing baffled me though. The picture-book Bible that was read to us had some very disturbing images and stories. The double-page illustration of Noah and the flood left me bewildered about why so many people were pictured in the throes of death, flailing in the foaming waters. The next page showed Sodom and Gomorrah burning to the ground with hundreds of people, charred and frightened, running to escape the flames.

We were told Sodom and Gomorrah were destroyed because of the "sin of homosexuality." When a bold child piped up, asking, "What is homosexuality?," the only reply given was "We can't talk about that until you're older—just know that it's something very bad." In my tiny mind, this instilled the knowledge that whatever homosexuality is, it must be terrible indeed.

The picture-book Bible also told the story of Moses and the Israelites fleeing captivity in Egypt. God had struck the Egyptians with various plagues when they refused to release the Israelites from slavery, culminating in the murder of every Egyptian firstborn boy. The artwork showed parents sobbing, holding their dead children in their arms, as Moses led his people out of captivity toward the promised land. It was a lot for a child to take in.

Another page showed Abraham sacrificing his little son, Isaac, as God had asked him to. He'd tied the boy up with ropes and raised a knife over the child, ready to kill him. The story ended with God telling Abraham, at the very last moment before he stabbed the child to death, not to murder the boy after all; it had been a test of his faithfulness. This too seemed an extremely violent and frightening story.

Even as a child, I had a hundred questions. What about all the people who drowned in Noah's flood—did they really need to die? What about everyone who was burned in Sodom and Gomorrah? What about the Egyptian baby boys who were slaughtered—how could that be fair? How did Isaac ever recover from the trauma of being tied up by his dad and almost knifed to death? Why was all of this portrayed as okay? And how could these stories be the work of a loving God? My mind spun. It didn't feel safe to ask any of these questions at kids' church, and I felt bad for thinking them in the first place.

Many of our worship songs were about love and forgiveness, but others contained military language and reminded me of the more violent Bible stories. Hymns had lyrics like: "Onward Christian soldiers, marching out to war, with the cross of Jesus going on before. Christ, the royal Master, leads against the foe; forward into battle see his banners go. Like a mighty army moves the Church of God."

More modern songs also reflected these themes: "The victory is the Lord's; we've just begun to fight," "The Lord is a warrior," and "Our God is mighty in battle, our God is mighty in war." I found the aggressive language of these songs a bit confusing and unsettling. Although I understood, as much as a child could, that they were based on the Bible, they still seemed at odds with the Jesus who was pictured in my kids' Bible holding a baby lamb in his arms and smiling at a crowd of children in a field of flowers.

If God really was as angry as those violent stories suggested, I didn't want to be on the receiving end of his punishment, or on the wrong side of a church "marching out to war." I never wanted to feel like the people drowning in the floodwaters as Noah sailed past. It was confusing. Was God the person standing with the lamb, the children, and the flowers, or was he an angry warrior destroying people?

I brushed these thoughts away from my mind, as they were too much for me to figure out at that tender age. My simple childhood faith was one rooted in God's love and kindness, so I tried to focus on the stories that emphasized those qualities. Besides, I had no reason to believe I'd ever be "out of the club." After all, I was part of God's army, not someone his people were fighting against. I was "inside the ark" and always would be—not someone left outside to drown. At least, that's what I imagined back then.

Another thing that stood out at church was that God was always described as male. Jesus was male too, of course, and our senior pastor and elders were all men. God was called Father, not Mother. It gradually dawned on me that girls and women were seriously underrepresented.

When anyone preached about marriage, St. Paul's teaching was quoted: "The husband is head of the wife just as Christ is the head of the church." Boys and men were in charge at church, and men took the leading roles in the exciting Bible stories, whereas women were almost always the supporting characters. I wasn't used to challenging "what the Bible clearly said" as a child, but something about it didn't sit well with me. I guess I felt shortchanged for being female, and sad that maybe I couldn't be part of the action.

Back then, in the mid-1980s, most UK churches weren't ready to give women the freedom to lead. Singing or teaching kids' church was allowed, but being a senior pastor or priest-in-charge was not. It was a stained-glass ceiling, a layer of promotion through which women could not pass.

The Church of England wouldn't see its first female priests ordained until 1994, when I was fifteen, despite the campaign for this change spanning back to the time of the suffragettes at the turn of the century. The first female bishop wasn't consecrated until just recently, in 2015, when I was thirty-six.

At school, I tried to express my faith passionately, especially as I had dreams of becoming a missionary like my grandparents. I told other children in my class about God, hoping they might get converted. At the age of four, I had a very serious chat with a classmate about the fact she was going to hell unless she accepted Jesus and became a Christian. All of this happened while playing in the sandbox, an unlikely setting for such severe theology. Several of my friends came to church with me a few times—possibly because of my fire-and-brimstone preaching in the sandbox, or perhaps because the elderly women in our congregation handed out jelly babies and fruit gums to us kids after the meeting.

I was well-meaning at heart. Even in those early years, God had become a genuine presence in my life. He was a constant companion and friend, and I wanted to share that, in my simple childhood way, with everyone I knew so they could experience it too.

When I reached the age of eleven, our family moved from the Pentecostal denomination to a small Anglican church in our village. Our goal was to help revive it, as its numbers were shrinking and many smaller parish churches like this were at risk of closure.

The Church of England congregation was far more moderate in its theology than our previous church, but the longer we were there, the more it started to reflect our charismatic evangelical values. My mother and I started playing guitars and keyboards on Sundays, rather than the traditional pipe organ, and enlisted a drummer and saxophonist when we could find volunteer musicians. My parents hosted small meetings at our home one evening a week, where people studied the Bible, sang songs, prayed for the sick to be healed, spoke in tongues, and prophesied over one another. We also organized trips to conferences so the people in our new church could hear well-known evangelical and Pentecostal speakers.

Alongside all this, I continued to go to local youth events linked to my previous church too. So, despite moving to a more moderate denomination, little changed for me. I retained the beliefs that had been woven into me during my formative years and, rather than growing out of them, I held on to them with even more passion.

3

As most British kids do, I started high school at the age of eleven, and it was a shock to my system. My village elementary school with only forty pupils seemed tiny now as I entered a huge building containing a thousand students in the nearby city of Canterbury. It was a girls' school with an associated boys' school a mile down the road. Single-sex education seemed great at first, but it would bring me some unique challenges as the years went by.

Once I acclimated to the size and scale of the new environment, I thoroughly enjoyed it. The high school had an entire wing dedicated to music: several private rooms with their own pianos, plus a drum kit and a cupboard full of acoustic guitars. Every lunch break I'd try and get one of these rehearsal rooms, where I would make up piano compositions or learn new guitar chords.

Sometimes my classmates and I would go there and sing. We'd take our lunch boxes with us and spend an hour making up songs and harmonies as we ate and talked. More often, though, I'd head over to one of the music rooms alone. With the security of a locked door, I found a privacy for my singing and playing that I'd never experienced before. I began writing very personal songs—mostly about faith and spirituality. Before long, I'd filled several notebooks with compositions.

My mum overhead me playing them at home in my bedroom and encouraged me to share them at church sometime. The idea terrified me—standing up there in front of so many people—but after months of her encouragement, I agreed to give it a go. I vividly remember that teenage debut. My mum was leading worship, and I was playing guitar. I'd agreed to play one of my songs during the service, and I became increasingly racked with nerves as the evening progressed.

With my eyes clamped shut so no one could see how nervous I was, I stood in front of the fifty or so people in the congregation and sang into the microphone. To my amazement, when I finished and opened my eyes, people looked visibly moved and tearful. Several of them were quietly praying. Somehow, my simple song had helped them connect with God.

What could be more rewarding than that? I pondered, on an emotional high as I packed my guitar into its case at the end of the church service. That first experience made me want to write more songs that would help people to worship. That day, and that song, set the course of my career.

My first experience singing in church, and the positive welcome it had received, had been formative. As the months went by, I wrote and sang more songs, and my shyness slowly went away. I was growing up, discovering my place in the world, finding my voice. But, simultaneously, all that growing up and self-discovery was revealing other aspects of who I was becoming—and not all of them were easy.

As my classmates began nervously giggling about which boy they "fancied," I was experiencing something totally different. I kept noticing girls. And I was increasingly embarrassed each time it happened. By this time, I'd found out what the word "homosexuality" meant (the older kids at school liked to try and educate us about anything and everything), and I'd made the connection between the Bible stories of my childhood, the punishment of Sodom and Gomorrah, and my attraction to girls.

All these feelings had come totally out of left field for me. It baffled me; I knew I wasn't choosing them. The conversations I'd overheard among Christians about gay people being sinful all centered around it being a *willful choice*, but I knew what I was experiencing was involuntary. Even if I didn't want those thoughts and feelings, they kept happening regardless. It was as normal and natural for me as my friends giggling and getting butterflies over their latest opposite-sex crush.

Female school friends started noticing boys' bodies were changing. They remarked about how our male friends' voices were deepening and their skinny arms were turning to muscle. Sometimes the local boys' school used our gym or outdoor track in addition to its own, and our school erupted with whispers of "Check him out!" as an especially tall or muscled male student walked through our hallways on his way to meet his teammates.

In contrast, I was far more aware of the changes happening in the girls around me. Puberty was hitting all of us, and I blushed anytime I found myself looking too long at someone across the school dining hall or tennis courts. I would catch a glimpse of someone I liked across the classroom and feel butterflies in my stomach. I would daydream about how amazing it would be to hold her hand or kiss her cheek, wishing I could ask her to the school dance, and wanting to help with her English essay just because I would get to spend time with her.

I remember one awful moment when a girl a year ahead of me was changing for sports and walked in front of me in her bra. My eyes fell on her for a couple of seconds longer than would have seemed normal, and she snapped, "What are you staring at?" Blushing terribly, I stammered, "Nothing, sorry. I was just thinking about something else . . . It was nothing to do with you . . ." This wasn't about lust or ogling anyone—I was just struck by how beautiful she was.

A similarly awkward moment happened when, at a school assembly, a group of girls from an older class decided to perform a Madonna song. I had been sheltered from dance parties and clubs as they were considered to be unwholesome by the Christians I knew, so it was a shock to my system when the girls emerged onto the school stage dressed in revealing clothes and danced to the pop track.

My classmates clapped along to the music, loving it, but I felt extremely uncomfortable. I stared at the floor, with no idea where to look. The girls who were performing seemed like the most stunning humans I'd ever cast eyes on, but surely those feelings were not right— God would not be pleased. *What on earth is wrong with me?* I thought, as I blushed with ever-increasing embarrassment, hoping no one around me had noticed my discomfort.

Outside of school, it was the same. Every now and then, often when I least expected it, these thoughts would break into my consciousness. I went with my family to watch a local performance of the musical *South Pacific* and was embarrassed when I realized how gorgeous I thought the female lead actress was.

Once at a Christian conference I attended, I was distracted by one of the female singers in the worship band; her voice and personality were so captivating. Whenever these things happened, I felt a wave of shame and did all I could to drown out the thoughts in my mind, especially in a place like church. These were just the normal, run-of-the-mill moments of attraction that would take place in any straight person's mind each day and be dismissed without a second thought. But for me, as a gay person, each one of them was laced with anxiety and left me feeling dirty and ashamed.

I was certain I couldn't hide these thoughts forever. Someone would figure me out, I worried. Acting on any of these attractions wasn't an option for me—I might have daydreamed about it, but I shut down those thoughts as, to me, they were off-limits and wrong. But I feared my accidental gazes at girls might make people suspicious, and it felt awful.

Honestly, I hoped it was just a phase—I wanted to fit in with my Christian friends and my church; I just wanted to belong. Sneaking away from my parents once at the local library, I found a book about teenage psychology. Flicking to a section on sexual development, I read that lots of young people experienced attraction to people of the same gender for a while and then they grew out of it.

After reading that, my prayers every night—offered with urgency—begged God to help this "phase" come to an end, so that I could stop these sinful thoughts and start living a holy life. The guilt these feelings generated was leaving me feeling paralyzed. I had nowhere to go with them and no one safe to confide in. Would God still love me if I was attracted to girls? I was pretty sure the answer was a resounding no.

"Go on, Vicky. It's just for a weekend," a school friend said, handing me a paper invitation. "You'll love it—loads of us are going."

Despite my increasingly solitary behavior at school, one Christian classmate invited me to a weekend event for church youth. Lately, I'd felt miles away from everyone, behind an invisible wall, trying to navigate the tensions in my life created by this new awareness that I was attracted to girls and not boys. All my friendships had grown distant as I spent my free periods alone in the library writing in my journal or with my Walkman plugged into my ears.

I didn't feel like being social, but since this would be a conference to develop young adults in their Christian faith, I thought I'd give it a try. It would be held in a beautiful old property in a nearby town and was a Catholic event—something outside my usual Protestant tradition. I was curious and intrigued. "Okay," I said. "Count me in."

The weekend arrived, and my initial nerves about being with a roomful of strangers dissipated when someone grabbed a guitar and led worship songs that I was familiar with. I enjoyed the talks, the meals, and, most of all, the singing. But, as always, nagging shame and fear plagued me as I thought about my orientation, knowing that everyone on the weekend would see me in a totally different light if they knew I was gay. Their friendliness would have turned to disapproval and judgment, and I would certainly not have been viewed as an "up-and-coming young faith leader," as they were describing me there that weekend.

Every time we prayed, and each time we sang a slow song encouraging inner reflection, my mind played the same broken record that beat me up mentally and emotionally for being broken and sinful because of my orientation.

I wondered if maybe, somehow, I could get help that weekend. *Perhaps in this more anonymous setting, one of the Catholic leaders could help me?* I thought. Whispering a prayer, I asked God for a breakthrough.

On the final afternoon, the event leaders announced that something different would be happening. A priest was visiting for a few hours and would be performing private confessions in a small room down the hall. Any participants wanting to go to confession, to repent of whatever sins they had committed and receive the priest's absolution (official forgiveness from God), could make their way to that small room and wait their turn.

The Church of England didn't offer one-on-one confession, and neither had my earlier Pentecostal denomination. This was something new to me and I wondered if it might be the key to getting free from my feelings for girls.

Summoning all the courage I had, I made my way down the hallway to the small room and knocked on the dark mahogany door. The sound of that knock seemed to echo for miles, and I blushed, hoping none of my friends knew I was going to see the priest. It could only mean I was struggling with something. And for an "up-and-coming" young Christian leader like me, that was not the impression I wanted to give anyone.

The whole exchange was unfamiliar to me, but the old Catholic priest was friendly and put me at ease. With a smile, he gestured to an empty seat opposite him. After reading some liturgy, the priest wanted to make it more teen-friendly, so he spoke in everyday language: "Are there specific things you'd like to repent of, to say sorry to God for? If there are, just speak them out now, and we'll give those things to God."

I listed some minor things—like getting angry, using bad language, and forgetting to do my daily Bible readings. When I left a long pause after this, he sensed that there was something I hadn't mentioned, the real reason I was there.

"Is there anything else?" he interjected.

I gulped and felt my chest tighten. Desperate for change, for the first time in my life I tried to voice the words: "Um . . . Yes . . . I am having feelings for other girls . . . like gay feelings . . . and I want to be forgiven for that, and set free from it as I know it's sinful."

I hung my head, red-faced, as heavy tears began streaming down my cheeks. It was a shock to hear those words come out of my mouth for the first time.

The priest gave me a kind look and said, "That was very brave. Well, let's pray, shall we?" Then he read the prayer of absolution, offering my repentance to God and pronouncing his forgiveness over my life. I heard the words, but mostly I was lost in a moment of shock that I'd told someone.

The prayer ended, and he thanked me for dropping in. Surely, I thought, God would see how brave I'd been in speaking out this deeply held secret. Surely, the Catholic priest, with his spiritual authority and the powerful words of the liturgy, would have the ability to change me.

Stepping out of the room, I closed the heavy wooden door behind me. I heard it shut with a loud thud and believed I'd left my sins—my gay feelings, my gay identity—behind that door. Forgiven and set free, I'd stepped out of an old life and into a new one.

But it didn't take long for me to realize nothing had changed. The feelings remained and with them came the rush of embarrassment and fear. I was crushed—my prayer hadn't been answered. My moment of courage and honesty with the priest had been for nothing. Perhaps God had forgiven me, according to the priest's absolution, but he certainly hadn't set me free.

My head spun with questions, but I had no one to go to with them. That priest had been from another town, and I had no idea how to contact him; to be honest, I was so embarrassed about telling him that I hoped we'd never cross paths again.

I must be so rebellious and sinful, if just hours after the confession I've had my old thought patterns return, I thought tearfully. *God must be so angry with me.* I felt utterly alone and saw no chance of an end to all of my struggles. If even a priest couldn't break off these chains of sinful feelings, who could? It seemed to me that I must be too broken for even God to fix.

4

Transfixed, I stood in the music store, gazing at the most beautiful electric guitar I'd ever seen. It was red and white, modeled after the famous Fender Telecaster—a cheaper version but still stunning to me. The gregarious salesman grabbed a stepladder and got it down, the weight of it surprising me as he handed it over. I plugged it into an amplifier and began to play. My face lit up, and my mother, watching from nearby, could tell I was desperately hoping we might take it home.

We'd only planned to buy a basic, cheap classical guitar that day, something for me to learn on instead of always stealing my mum's acoustic. But she could tell my heart had attached itself to this red-and-white electric. I agreed that I'd gladly have it as birthday and Christmas gifts all rolled into one. So we left the store with that gorgeous instrument, plus a small practice amp, a tuner pedal, a capo, and all the cables and plectrums I could wish for.

With this new guitar waiting for me each evening when I returned home from high school, I practiced even more than before. Once homework was done, every night I'd close my bedroom door and play, teaching myself from a book and asking Mum for help if I got stuck.

One evening, shut away in my room playing and singing, something unusual happened. Usually I only made up worship songs, taking my lyric ideas directly from parts of the Bible, like the Psalms. But that evening, rather than singing about faith, I found myself writing a love song. And it was about a girl.

After five minutes, I blushed, stopped, and put the guitar away. It felt as though I'd used my musical gift for something wrong and dirty; I'd polluted the beautiful talents God had given me. I put the guitar down, switched off the bedroom light, pulled the curtains open, and stared out at the stars. "Sorry, God," I whispered. "I won't do that again. I promise to use my music for one thing only: to glorify you."

That was the last time I sang about a girl.

Music quickly evolved from a hobby to something more serious. I recorded my first demo during a high-school summer break—a cassette tape with eight of my songs on it. I borrowed the school's four-track recorder, a now-ancient device that can record four different layers of audio on one cassette. This was long before easily affordable laptops and music software came into being; as I look back, it feels like the technological Dark Ages.

Proficient in several instruments by then, I played guitar, drums, and piano and then layered vocals and harmonies on the four-track tape. Finally, I finished it off with synth pads and some harmonica.

My parents and sister could barely walk around our living room for weeks, as I'd filled it with cables, wires, amplifiers, and instruments. A piece of paper taped to the door, scribbled in my handwriting, read: QUIET PLEASE: RECORDING IN PROGRESS. I'm grateful that my family was infinitely patient and supportive of my musical quest.

Once the finished demo tape was in my hands, I sent it to one of the UK's biggest Christian record labels. It was a shot in the dark, but worth a go. To my amazement, they chose one of my songs out of thousands of submissions and featured it on a CD. A copy of the album arrived in the mail, and my family and I sat around and listened to it together. My crazy summer of cables, wires, and recording equipment had opened a significant door.

Spurred on by this, I worked on other songs, hopeful that they'd be published and recorded too. The following year, at one of the Christian youth camps I attended, the leader brought me up in front of five thousand attendees and spoke about how impressed he was with my songwriting. After that, other teenagers came up to me all week, saying hello or asking me to sign their copy of the CD. It was heady stuff for someone still in high school, but instead of making me develop an ego, it just fueled my desire to be the best Christian I could be. I didn't want to let anyone down.

I discovered that plenty of people made a living recording Christian music and touring across the UK, the US, and Canada. Once I knew this, I wondered if it could ever become my full-time career; I certainly hoped it might. It felt like my childhood dream of becoming a missionary, but through music. *I want to be a musicianary,* I joked to myself. This dream brought up lots of insecurities too—I worried that I wasn't good enough at singing or songwriting—but most of all it brought up embarrassment about my "secret personal struggles."

Amid the growing musical opportunities in my teens, my sexuality hadn't shown any signs of being a phase. My feelings for girls were real as ever. Daily, I played mind games with myself to silence the thoughts. *Who you're attracted to isn't a big part of life anyway,* I told myself. *I mean, it's just one small fraction of what it means to be human. I can shut it out, stay single, and have a perfectly happy and fulfilled future . . .* I was trying to compartmentalize my heart, and silence my emotions, but it was a struggle I couldn't seem to win.

Because of this, despite the exciting musical doors that were opening, I was feeling less and less enthusiastic about life. As I segmented my identity into good and bad parts, I felt like I was fragmenting. A dark cloud fell from the sky and settled over my mind and heart.

In my anxiety, I created long, detailed prayers that I would recite to myself each time I felt attracted to a girl. It was my own private liturgy—my internal confession booth—in which I told God how sorry I was ten times a day. My mind became a complex place, a far cry from the mind of the simple, happy child I had been before.

Friends in my class noticed a change in my previously carefree personality. I became aloof and felt awkward in my own skin; I slouched my shoulders and didn't look people in the eye. Mostly I had my Walkman headphones plugged in, shutting out the world, with my midnight-blue denim jacket buttoned all the way up to the top like a suit of armor.

I began throwing my packed lunches away and stopped eating during school hours. I didn't know how to relate to my body anymore. It seemed to be betraying me with its sinful desires, so I didn't want to give it food. My flesh and blood were now the enemy; I was fighting a battle against myself.

D o you think there's any chance he likes me?" one girl asked, looking hopeful, as she ate her sandwich. "I mean, he did sit next to me on the bus the other day—and I could've sworn he was looking at my hair and my outfit. I just can't stop thinking about him."

I never knew quite how to handle these conversations. I wanted to be part of the crowd, so I listened to my classmates sharing their latest stories. But when someone casually asked me, "So, Vicky, which of the guys do you like? Anyone you've got your eye on? Who have you been kissing lately?!" I felt totally stumped. Stumbling over my words, I would say, "Oh, no one really . . . ," but that recurring answer was only making people ask more frequently, as they were curious.

I'd had my first kiss somewhere around the age of twelve or thirteen. It was with a boy, of course, as girls were, in my mind, forever off-limits. In keeping with my outdoorsy, countryside childhood, it had happened when we were sitting in a field of tall yellow flowers; so tall that they stood far above our heads, swaying in the summer breeze. And the boy I'd sat in tree houses, splashed in rivers, and run through wheat fields with since we were nine was the one who'd decided to kiss me.

It was a first kiss that almost anyone would treasure, picturesque in location and with someone I cared for. But I felt nothing for him beyond the platonic friendship we'd always shared. My heart was wired differently, so I couldn't reciprocate his attraction. So my first kiss, despite being a happy memory because of our friendship, was not one I felt a romantic connection to. At the time, I wondered if maybe I would feel something for other guys; perhaps he was more like a brother than a boyfriend to me, I'd thought.

Several other interested boys came and went during my high-school years, mostly just friends I bonded with over guitars. My heart would sink if those guys began looking at me differently, as I knew what was coming. They'd tell me about their feelings, and I'd be forced to choose: try dating them and see if any feelings appeared or admit what I already knew, that I was gay and attraction to boys would never be there.

When one of these male friends tried to kiss me at a bus stop, nothing about it made my heart skip a beat or gave me butterflies—but I did feel all of those things when I looked at the girls I liked. Kissing somebody male felt unnatural and awkward to me, like playing a forced role in the film of my life, an understudy for the person I was trying to become. But it felt important to explore this—I was figuring out who I was, and I was desperate to fit in.

I said yes to dating a few of my male friends, but they were deeply hurt when I broke up with them only weeks into our fledgling relationship. I couldn't tell them the truth about why I had no attraction to them—so I was left grasping at clichés like "It's not you; it's me" or "You're more like a brother to me." It was an emotional car crash for both of us every time; we both walked away hurt, and they had a sense of confusion because my reasons for breaking up were never fully convincing.

As my female classmates and I arrived at the legal age of consent to have sex (sixteen years old in the UK), conversations about "fancying boys" became more serious and progressed further. Some of the older girls were claiming to have "gone all the way." I'm sure much of it was just bravado, but a number of my peers at school were now sexually active. This, in turn, would bring a new degree of heartache for me.

Once, on my way to a science lesson, the blue-eyed girl in my class whom I'd fallen for three years earlier and still couldn't seem to get over said she wanted to go on a walk with me at break time to tell me something. Getting to spend time with her alone was the Holy Grail for me, and I thought about nothing else all morning.

We met at lunchtime and walked across the school field to the secluded area where tall trees lined the edges. It was June and unseasonably hot with scorching sunshine, so we tied our sweaters around our waists and kicked at the dry grass.

Leaning against a tree, she looked around nervously, scanning for teachers, and reached into her bag. Pulling out a cigarette, she lit it and inhaled the smoke to calm her nerves. Perhaps one reason I liked her so much was because she was my polar opposite. Known as a troublemaker, she always seemed so sure of herself and willing to challenge the status quo. There was something beautifully dangerous about her.

She cleared her throat, preparing to tell me her news. Ever the optimist, I wondered if she was going to tell me that she liked me—that she was gay. (Of course, she had no idea that I was or that I liked her in that way, as I put immense energy into hiding it.) That lunchtime, as she looked into my eyes, nothing could have been further from her mind.

"So," she began, "I've decided . . . I mean, I think I'm ready to . . ." She paused to take another drag of her cigarette. "I'm ready to . . . have sex with him. I think I'm . . . in love with him," she said, her face flushed.

Her boyfriend had been keen to sleep with her ever since she'd turned sixteen, and here she was, telling me she was going to do it. I coughed and looked away. She thought I had cigarette smoke in my eyes and apologized, exhaling slowly in the opposite direction.

"So what do you think?" she asked. "I mean, I know your faith wouldn't condone it, but apart from that, what do you think, as my friend?"

"Friend" rang in my ears. That was all I would ever be to her. All I would ever be to any of these girls, now or ever. All I could mumble in response to her question was "Well, I guess only you can know when you're ready . . ."

My heart broke into a hundred pieces as I processed the news she'd shared. It wasn't that I wanted to sleep with her—my feelings were far more innocent than that, plus I believed that sex should only happen within marriage, as that's what my church had raised me to think. I just wanted some sort of emotional exclusivity with her, where I was the one she ran to when she was frightened or happy. I wouldn't have allowed myself the "sinful" behavior of kissing or dating her even if she had been interested, as my faith made that impossible for me. Liking her had felt much easier when she was single, but now that she was seriously dating a guy, it was a constant reminder to me that she was falling in love with him and not with me.

Anytime I found myself thinking of her in that way, I shut the feelings down at once, as guilt and shame rushed in. But as we stood there talking, I felt lost in her gaze. She seemed closer than ever, and yet now, based on this news, she'd never been further away.

"I guess we'd better go back for afternoon class," she said, stubbing her cigarette out on the trunk of the tree. We started our walk back, and when we reached the school entrance, I told her I'd see her later.

I made my way to one of the bathrooms, locked the stall door behind me, and stood with my back against it. Silent tears fell down my cheeks, creating a mess of black mascara. I slid down the back of the door until I was sitting on the floor and, pulling my knees into my chest, I sobbed into the thick blue wool of my school sweater.

5

July arrived and the heat wave continued, but to me it felt cold and overcast as I processed the news the beautiful blue-eyed girl had shared with me. A few weeks later, I found out she had gone ahead and slept with her boyfriend. I managed to avoid hearing the finer details from her, but was told enough that my heart felt stabbed by a thousand knives.

I couldn't wait for August and the long school vacation. The only glimmers of happiness on my horizon were the big Christian youth camps I attended every summer break, so I busied my mind by looking forward to those.

I'd had great experiences at those camps throughout my teens— several thousand young people all camping in tents, eating way too many hamburgers and donuts, gathering in a big venue to sing, and listening to energetic speakers firing us up about our faith. They were always a highlight for me, mostly because I was around other people like me: young, Christian, and passionate about God.

Those camps taught me a lot about developing into a well-rounded adult: about how to be a good leader, put others first, keep your word, dream big, and live a meaningful life. And they always had fantastic music with some of London's finest session players. Watching them during the meetings and sneaking in to see their rehearsals if I could, I grew leaps and bounds in my own understanding of how to play in bands.

Nursing my broken heart, I was glad when August finally arrived and I could head to Soul Survivor, a camp held in the southwest of England. It was as great as ever, and I came away feeling inspired and encouraged. After a few days at home to get clean laundry and catch up on sleep, I headed to my second camp, one that would be held in a large showground in Warwickshire, and I couldn't wait for it to start.

Initially, I was enthusiastic, joining in with the singing and praying, but somehow all my feelings of shame, heartache, and isolation caught up with me. The energy of the camp helped lift my spirits, but, underneath, my heart was still aching about the girl from school and my unrequited feelings for her.

One night this played on my mind so much that I couldn't stay in the worship gathering, so I walked out into the evening air, gazing up at a sky full of stars. I was a tenacious young person, but my resilience was being tested to the hilt. I was breaking under the weight of shame and anxiety, believing I had to keep this secret forever.

As the chill of the night gave me goose bumps, and I shivered in my thin t-shirt, I prayed: "God, you have to do something this week. You have to heal me. I need to be straight; you have to set me free from these feelings. All I want is your will—to be who you want me to be. You've always been first in my life—and always will be. So do something at this camp. Change me. I'm desperate, and I need your help."

Staring up at the starlit sky, I told myself that this time it would work. This time, God would answer and perform some kind of miracle. This week, I assured myself, would finally be the moment I got free from the orientation that was driving me to desperation.

I couldn't face going back into the meeting, so I headed to my tent. The voices of thousands of young people singing their hearts out in the main venue carried on the breeze. I felt so far away from it all at that moment—an outsider, both literally and figuratively, living behind a wall of shame and fear. Exhausted, I climbed into my tent and fell into a fitful sleep.

Two nights later at the camp, it seemed as if my prayer might have been answered. The sermon was about God's power, that Jesus could heal us and set us free from any form of addiction, sin, or shame. After the sermon, several young people my age were invited onto the stage to share their stories—or testimonies. One teenage boy said he had been "set free from alcoholism." He'd started drinking at thirteen and developed a major addiction. After being prayed for last year at this same summer camp, he had never drunk alcohol again.

Another teenage guy stepped up to the microphone saying he'd been "set free from the sin of pornography." After growing obsessed with porn magazines and videos (which the church saw as entirely inappropriate and sinful), he'd had prayer ministry last year and managed to break his habit entirely.

The last young person to speak was a girl with long curly red hair. She was, perhaps, a year or two older than me. Shyly, she said into the microphone that she'd been "set free from the sin of homosexuality." My cheeks flushed, and I squirmed in my seat. I looked at my friends nervously, hoping they hadn't noticed my face turn red.

The red-haired girl went on to say that, after being prayed for last year, all her feelings for girls had gone. She ended her testimony emphasizing how relieved she was "not to be gay anymore," so that she could now live a life that pleased God at last.

I felt as if I'd been punched in the stomach. Although I knew the Pentecostal and evangelical view on homosexuality, I'd never heard of anyone who'd been changed from gay to straight. The timing of it all felt so pertinent to the prayer I'd prayed two nights earlier.

The red-haired girl's bravery seemed amazing to me. I sat in awe of her as she stood there, in front of thousands of other teenagers, telling her story so confidently. She stepped down from the stage, and the preacher motioned for the worship band to play some soft music. Then came the moment of invitation—the altar call or ministry time, as it's known in charismatic circles.

The leader gave us an invitation: "Come up to the front of the auditorium if you want to get prayed for and be set free from whatever is holding you captive." As the band began to play, he added, "God can break the chains of any addiction; just step out in faith. People will be standing up here—well-trained adults—ready to pray with you. Just come forward and take the step tonight."

I knew I had to respond, but my face was crimson with embarrassment at the idea of walking to the front, with my friends and thousands of other young people watching. It seemed an impossible task.

The lights were dimmed a little, and everyone was encouraged to stand and sing. As people moved from sitting to standing, and under the cover of the dimmed lighting, I slipped out of my chair and began the long walk to the front of the auditorium.

Arriving at the front, I found a long line of ministry team members waiting, Christian adults who had been trained to pray with us. Other teens had arrived before me, and several were deep in prayer. Each had two adults, one on either side, speaking aloud as they asked God for healing and freedom.

I'd had great experiences with those ministry times before—the adults were always kind and sensitive, eager to help younger Christians grow in their faith. Unfortunately, that evening was different.

Two adults walked up to me and smiled. They put me at ease and said, "Well done for being brave enough to come all the way to the front." We exchanged smiles, although mine was fleeting and nervous.

"So what can we pray about for you? What would you like God to set you free from tonight?" they asked.

I wished I could invent something inane, like being scared of the dark, stealing my sister's pocket money out of her piggy bank, or being rude to my parents. But I had to deal with reality and face it head-on.

"Um . . . I think . . . I mean, I know . . . I'm . . . gay," I said in a whisper only just loud enough for them to hear. My already beet-red face turned purple.

The couple exchanged worried looks. Their eyes communicated something like "the severity of this situation needs more backup." With mild urgency, they waved other adults over to join us. This made me feel like a difficult case, as though I contained too much darkness for two people to tackle alone. At that moment, I wished I could run miles away, but it was too late. Shame swallowed me up like a rising tide.

"Let's pray," the adults said, as four or five of them surrounded me. As is our custom in charismatic churches, I closed my eyes and held out my hands with upturned palms. For us, this is a physical posture of surrender to God. The adults each placed a hand on one of my shoulders or on my back. This also is normal—it's the way we show each other we're standing together in supportive prayer. But as their prayers began, it felt anything but supportive.

One by one they started praying out loud. An impassioned man said, "These feelings are not from God—we stand against homosexuality tonight. Her heart is a battlefield, and the devil is not going to win."

Several voices all chimed in with loud agreements. One said, "Yes, Lord, this is going to be a red-letter day for her: the end of these feelings at last." Another said loudly, "We command the demons inside her to go. We bind the demons of homosexuality." Another woman shouted, "Satan, get out of her. Let her go. Release your grip on her life."

Other adults on the prayer team, having finished praying with other teens, joined our circle. They too raised their voices. People were shouting loudly now, and I was increasingly uncomfortable. "Release the demons!" they yelled, pressing on my back and shoulders. "We command these demonic feelings to leave. We tell every demon to go."

"She belongs to you, Jesus—set her free. Give her back her purity. Give her back her life and her freedom to love the right way." They continued to tell Satan and his demons to get out of my mind, heart, and body.

I stood frozen to the spot, my eyes clamped shut and my face flushed. Hearing their words was alarming to me. I knew being gay was sinful, but I'd never imagined that it was caused by demons or the devil. I felt more ashamed than ever, and now there was an added sense of fear as well. I was in the grip of a darkness I couldn't control or beat; I was full of demons.

My stomach turned, and I felt sick. I began to sob, punctuated with retching. Thinking this was a sign of demonic expulsion (people often vomit during exorcisms, which is when the demons are thought to leave), the adults didn't express concern, but shouted all the more loudly as they prayed.

By the time it was finally over, I was hunched on the floor, shaking and wishing the ground would swallow me up. As their impassioned prayers subsided, one of the team bent down and asked me, "Are you okay? Do you feel like God has set you free from homosexuality tonight? Do you feel different?"

I had no idea what to say, so in hopes that they'd stop and leave me alone I nodded and muttered a tearful "Maybe . . . I mean, yes." But I knew nothing had changed.

One woman handed me a fistful of tissues and helped me to my feet. An enthusiastic man patted me on the back and said, "Well, tonight was a powerful night for you. I'm sure you'll never forget the evening when you left those sinful feelings behind at the foot of our Savior's cross."

The woman with the box of tissues added, "You're set free now, by the power of Jesus, so go and live your new life. I hope I'll meet you someday in future with a husband and children of your own—you'll be a testimony to God's healing grace."

I began walking away, but one man called out with a final thought: "You know, the Bible says some demons only come out 'by prayer and fasting,' so if those sinful feelings come back, try fasting, as that is a powerful way to be set free by the power of Jesus."

"You mean not eating?" I replied, sounding worried.

"Yes," he said. "You know Jesus fasted for forty days, like the Gospels tell us. It's a proven way to get free from demons that won't go any other way. If you want God's freedom enough that you're willing to fast from food, you'll see your feelings change for sure."

I walked away, clutching the tissues. The auditorium was empty; they had prayed with me long after the meeting had ended. The band had stopped playing, and all the other youth had left the venue. I walked through the huge empty building, weaving my way through the rows of chairs and out into the night.

Rather than finding freedom, healing, and pastoral support from those adults, I came away feeling more ashamed and broken. Previously, I'd thought of my feeling for girls as emotional, biological, and psychological. But now panic set in: apparently I was not creating these desires myself—it was the sinister work of demons. This information, new to me, was extremely alarming.

I thought about the man's encouragement to fast too. I decided that, yes, I would go to any lengths to get free from my sinful desires, even if it meant starving myself. Food, body image, and self-worth are tricky for any young adult, and this set in motion a preference for punishing my body rather than caring for it.

My mind felt full to the brim. The hope I'd felt surging through me that evening as I'd listened to the red-haired girl and her testimony had fallen flat. That night, I fell asleep under the canvas of my tent, scared stiff that I was inhabited by dark powers that would never let me go.

I took what my Christian leaders had taught me at face value, and I didn't feel equipped to question it. I was an intelligent person, near the top of my class in most school subjects, but when it came to spirituality,

I wasn't used to thinking for myself. There were no LGBTQ+ people in my life, so I didn't have role models to tell me that same-sex feelings were, in fact, not the work of demons or that being gay *and* Christian was possible.

I'd summoned all my teenage courage that night and spoken out about my same-sex feelings, asking for help. Having had it go so badly, I couldn't imagine telling another soul about my secret ever again. As the writer Ian McEwan strikingly expresses in his novel *Atonement*: "A person is, among all else, a material thing, easily torn, not easily mended." After that night at summer camp, I would not be easily mended.

6

"This," he said, gesturing soberly, "is what happens when you have . . . sex." Looking at us with an intense gaze, the man at the front of the Christian youth event held up two pieces of white paper. He took a stick of glue and spread it liberally over both sheets. Then he pressed the sheets together, so they stuck firmly.

"Sex means you are literally gluing your soul to the other person; it's sacred. Something significant happens when two people become 'one flesh,' as the Bible describes it. It's not just about flesh and bone; part of you joins with that other person. It's a spiritual union that cannot be broken." He held the two pieces of paper in the air, showing us they were completely glued together.

"Now, see what happens if you have sex with someone casually—who you're not married to—and then you break up." His brow furrowed as he took the two pieces of paper and, starting at the top, tried to pull them apart. Of course, the glue had done its work, and this proved a difficult thing to attempt. Finally, he managed to separate them but was left with a mess: part of one piece of paper was left attached to the other and vice versa. In his hands the two sheets—once perfect—were now ripped to shreds and full of holes.

"This," he said, "is what sex outside of marriage does to your body and soul. You leave a part of yourself with that other person. You are both damaged by it. And you can never be whole again." All of us in that summer camp seminar were around the age of sixteen, and we exchanged worried glances.

"Save sex for marriage," he said, bringing his illustration to a close. "Wait for the partner God has chosen for you, the perfect husband or wife, who you'll be married to for life. If you don't wait, the consequences are very serious in God's eyes."

At the end of the seminar on sex and relationships, we all shuffled out of the venue looking shell-shocked. I knew a couple of my friends had already had sex, and I hated to think what emotions they were trying to process after seeing those ripped-up pieces of paper.

One friend who I knew had been sexually active whispered to me, "What am I going to do now? If I'm damaged, just like that piece of paper, who is ever going to want me?" Tears began trickling out of the corners of her eyes, and she wiped them away, smudging her makeup. "God must be so angry with me . . ." she added as she walked away in need of some privacy to cry.

Sex had become a regular topic at the Christian events I attended, as soon as my friends and I had hit sixteen. Some of the seminars did better than others at handling this sensitive topic, although even the best ones made it clear sex was only allowed within a heterosexual marriage to another Christian. It was an important evangelical teaching, an unmovable line in the sand. It was the only godly option—everything else was serious sin.

Many times in those talks, I heard St. Paul quoted: "Flee from sexual immorality. All other sins a person commits are outside the body, but whoever sins sexually, sins against their own body" (1 Cor. 6:18, NIV). We were taught that this placed sexual sin above others; it was the most grievous offense against God and against yourself. It frightened our teenage minds, which I think was part of the aim—to scare our hormones into obedience.

At one Christian camp, a visiting American speaker used a different illustration. She held up an apple and, taking a bite out of it, said, "This is an example of what happens when you have sex." She handed the apple to a person in the front row, instructing, "Take a bite." The teenager awkwardly chomped into the fruit. "Now hand it to the person next to you," the leader instructed. Once five people had bitten chunks out of the apple, there was little left but the core. "Hand it back to me," the leader said, holding out her hand.

"Now," she said, looking at us, "this is what happens when you give yourself away sexually to multiple people. All you're left with is this ugly core." She held what was left of the apple in the air. "Who's going to want you if you are left like this? What godly man or woman will want to give their life to you then? Stick to God's way for sex: save it for marriage."

This area of life was treated with severity in evangelical and Pentecostal churches. I'd heard of several married pastors in the UK who'd lost their job as a result of having an affair. A male youth leader in another city had been fired for sleeping with his girlfriend before they were married. Punishment was seen as helping the sinner get back on track.

Our youth meetings also brought up the topic of masturbation. We were told it was sinful and not something Christians should ever do. Sex and the feelings that went with it were for marriage, not for selfish pleasure. We shouldn't be "harboring lustful thoughts," so masturbation had no place in the life of a follower of Jesus. It was a lot to process for all of us, leading to repetitive cycles of guilt, repentance, and more guilt.

American influences were increasingly making their way into British church culture, especially in Pentecostal circles. Speakers and musicians frequently traveled between the two countries, so ideas cross-pollinated. As I attended conferences, listened to tapes, and watched Christian documentaries, I was discovering more of them.

A movement called True Love Waits—also known as the purity movement or abstinence movement—was sweeping the States, and it didn't take long for it to reach me on British shores. Various authors, speakers, and singers taught an impassioned message insisting not only on no sex before marriage, but also on avoiding any physical affection at all between dating couples.

I watched several documentaries featuring American Christian teens who were choosing not to kiss until their wedding day. "I'm choosing to put Jesus first," one of them said to the camera in a documentary, "that means choosing the way of the Spirit, not the way of the flesh." Another said, "Physical intimacy—even a quick kiss—is a slippery slope toward sex, and I'm worried I'll go too far. Better to avoid anything besides holding hands until marriage. I know it's what God wants, and I want to please him with my life."

Spokespeople for the abstinence movement described it as follows: "True Love Waits promotes sexual purity not just in a physical way, but also in a cognitive, spiritual, and behavioral way." It was all-encompassing; thoughts of sex, sexual feelings, and any physical affection between young people were seen as potentially dangerous. Sexual desire was the enemy, and life was a battlefield where we must wage war against it.

A major book on this theme, *I Kissed Dating Goodbye*, by Joshua Harris, was published in January 1997, when I was seventeen. His book sold 1.2 million copies worldwide. Harris was a homeschooled, twenty-one-year-old Christian when he wrote it, and he was proud to be a virgin.

The book opens with a story about a young Christian couple, Anna and David, who are soon to be married. One night, Anna has a dream about their wedding day, but gradually it turns into something of a nightmare. In this dream, as she walks down the aisle to David, other girls suddenly start standing up and walking toward him too, taking his hands and standing next to him.

"Who are these girls, David?" Anna asks in the dream, feeling tears welling up.

"They're girls from my past," David answers, looking ashamed. "Anna, they don't mean anything to me now . . . but I've given part of my heart to each of them." Anna was devastated and David was deeply ashamed as this strange scene unfolded. It left both of them ashamed and uncomfortable, turning a beautiful wedding day into a scene of tears and shame. This was just a dream, but by using it in the opening of the book, Joshua Harris hit home his message about the fallout that not being sexually abstinent could create for any of us. Our own wedding days might turn from a dream to a nightmare.

Reading this was enough to shock any churchgoing teen. It left us anxious and horrified. Harris wasn't just talking about sex in his analogy; it was about David giving his heart to other girls *emotionally* too. Emotional closeness was something that should be saved for marriage as well.

Not only were sex and kissing off-limits, according to Harris, but so was dating itself. Dating, he argued, was a selfish approach to relationships. It treated them casually, as something you could start and finish at will. Dating was "a training ground for divorce," as teens would learn to walk away whenever relationships became difficult.

Harris proposed a different model, known as courtship. This meant spending time with the person you liked only in groups, not one-on-one, and having family members present as much as possible. Also, a guy and girl should only begin courting if they believe it is likely to progress toward a lifelong marriage.

The book contained stories of various young couples who had "strayed" into sex before marriage and (apparently) dealt with debilitating guilt, trauma, and damaged future relationships as a result. It was distressing stuff.

For me, this extreme ideology was strangely appealing; if any Christian teen was keen to distance themselves from the effects of puberty, it was me. Hormones seemed like the ultimate enemy, as they were causing my feelings for girls.

Perhaps, I thought, *I can make up for those secret feelings by being a perfect example when it comes to my morals around saving sex for marriage. Someday God will change me, I'll fall in love with a guy, not a girl, and when I do, we'll save everything beyond a brief kiss for our wedding night.*

The purity movement was encouraging young adults to buy "purity rings" and wear them as a sign of their commitment to stop dating and to save sex for marriage. When I attended a concert that preached this message and sold these rings on a merchandise table, I bought one and put it on.

True Love Waits was igniting a generation of Christian youth, mostly in the US, but also around the world. Other resources followed, to keep us all reading and learning. Josh Harris's flagship book was still flying off the shelves, and he followed it with sequels, including *Not Even a Hint: Guarding Your Heart Against Lust* and *Boy Meets Girl: Say Hello to Courtship*.

Well-known Christian artist Rebecca St. James wrote the foreword to Harris's first book and, a few years later, released her hit song "Wait for Me," a prayer for her future husband to remain a virgin until they met and were married, and a promise that she would do the same. The song was nominated for a Dove Award (Christian music's equivalent of a Grammy) in 2002. Following the song's success, Rebecca published a book, *Wait for Me: Rediscovering the Joy of Purity in Romance,* which sold over a hundred thousand copies. The abstinence movement was gathering huge momentum.

Ever a perfectionist and never one to go half measure, I fully embraced the ideas of True Love Waits. Not all of this was entirely bad, but it was certainly extreme, and it damaged my perspectives on sexuality and the body. Seeing my sexuality as the enemy, leading me away from God, provided a religious reason to completely distance myself from my own body.

Slowly, I felt less and less of a connection to my emotions too, and dissociation became my norm. This brought some relief—I now had fewer feelings for girls. But it had far broader consequences; it became harder to feel anything at all. At a high-school parents' evening, when a teacher praised me in front of my mum and dad for an essay I'd written, I couldn't even crack a smile. I didn't feel happiness, or pride, or encouragement. I felt nothing.

"Vicky, you can look pleased if you want," the teacher remarked jokingly, taken aback by my blank expression. I tried to look happy, but I felt numb and unaffected.

On my sixteenth birthday, when other girls were picking out the shortest dress they could get away with to go on a date with their boyfriend, my parents had asked me, "Vicky, what would you like for your birthday?"

My response? "I'd like two Bibles, please." I had my eye on two specific versions at our local Christian bookstore in Canterbury. One was a study version—*The Spirit-Filled Life Bible*—complete with commentary, maps, and translations of Greek and Hebrew words. The second was a contemporary translation—*The Message*—that put the Bible into everyday language. These were genuinely what I wanted—a way to deepen my faith.

Delighted, I unwrapped and pored over those books, filling them with underlining and notes. I loved God deeply, but faith was starting to get out of balance in my life and becoming a form of escapism. I thought about, read about, and spoke about little else. Prayer and worship provided me with a different reality to live in—a spiritual one. This otherworldly, ethereal realm was easier to focus on than the physical world I was finding so tough to navigate.

Like many evangelical Christians, I got up early each morning and did devotions for an hour, following a daily Bible reading plan. Gradually those morning devotions became more self-critical; I adopted a practice used by John and Charles Wesley, the founders of Methodism, who used to get together for meetings that they called the Holy Club. During those gatherings the Wesleys painstakingly assessed themselves using twenty-two accountability questions that explored how well they'd lived up to God's standards each day. They listed the good character traits they wanted to see in themselves and examined where they'd failed to live up to them.

Inspired by the Wesleys, in a big blue journal I wrote out accountability questions each night. My perfectionism caught every flaw. I felt I had so much to make up for in life, because I believed I was inherently broken due to my gay feelings.

Alongside all of this, I was getting a steady stream of invitations to play and sing at churches and youth events, and the numbers attending were larger and larger. Other churches had started using my songs in their services too. "Hundreds of young people your age are looking up to you now—make sure you give them a great example to follow," I was told by well-meaning people. It was exciting to see my music reaching bigger audiences, but responsibility weighed heavy on my shoulders, as did fear and shame.

I wanted to be a Christian musician and a worship leader. I wanted to set a great example and make those around me proud. I wanted to serve God and use the musical gifts he'd entrusted me with. It was terrifying to think of letting everyone down. If my church music career was to grow, I'd need to keep a perfect moral track record. The pressure was on.

On top of this, major change was ahead. High school was nearing its end, and in a year or so I'd be heading to university. Church leaders had warned me that many eighteen-year-olds had gone to university and lost their faith, which alarmed me. I had no idea what sort of ideas or people I would encounter in this future chapter of my life. I'd be away from my family, my church, my youth group; it would be a whole new start—which excited and scared me in equal measure.

PART II

Oxford

7

September sunshine bathed the sandy-brown Oxford buildings in a magical light. The stones seemed to glow, illuminated with golden warmth. Oxford is one of the oldest universities in the world, with its foundations dating back to 1096. That rich history seemed etched on every cobblestoned pathway, leaded window, and lofty spire.

My parents and I had packed our car to the hilt and made the three-hour drive from Canterbury to deliver me to my new student dormitory. I never imagined I'd attend such a well-respected university. My perfectionist tendencies had helped me study intensely for my exams and, somehow managing to get good grades, I'd secured a place. Still passionate about my faith, I'd decided my degree would be in theology (religious studies).

I was grateful that all UK universities charged the same fees, regardless of how prestigiously they ranked. I knew that in some countries, like the US, education at an Ivy League–like institution cost vastly more than at others. My family was not wealthy, so there was no way I could've afforded that. Thankfully, UK universities charged one standardized fee at that time, and which university you attended depended solely on your grades.

The initial semester was intense as we knuckled down to produce four-thousand-word essays every week. But there were lighter aspects of life too. I loved the traditions, quirks, and pageantry of the university. One of these was called matriculation, the official induction ceremony.

We had to buy specific clothing known as "subfusc," from the Latin *subfuscus*, meaning "of dark, brown, or sober hue and color." Shepherd & Woodward, a shop on High Street that had been selling academic gowns and robes to Oxford students for more than 150 years, was the go-to place.

As I look back now, it feels like when Harry Potter went shopping for school supplies in Diagon Alley. We needed a "gown made of black material with the style of a turned-over collar." It could not have sleeves, but had to have "a streamer on each side with square pleating and hanging to the full length of the gown, which covers the normal lounge coat." It was basically a black sleeveless cape with two long, trailing tails of material that streamed behind us when we walked.

Once all the Hogwarts-style clothing was taken care of, the rest was simpler. The matriculation ceremony was held in the Sheldonian Theatre, a circular building dating back to 1664. The round stone walls and domed roof looked stunning enough from outside, but walking in, we were treated to an even more amazing view. Cricking my neck to stare upward, I gazed at the exquisite ceiling fresco that depicts a wide-open sky, giving the sense that there is no roof at all.

Once we'd been matriculated, life mostly took place in our colleges. Oxford University is made up of thirty-eight individual colleges that function as halls of residence where students spend most of their time. Undergraduates had to choose which college they wanted to live in when they applied to Oxford, and I'd found that choice a simple one. A creature of habit, when I'd heard there was an evangelical college called Wycliffe Hall, I'd applied there. It struck me as perfect: I could live with fellow evangelicals and also be an undergraduate at Oxford.

Wycliffe had no bar—very unusual for an Oxford college, as most undergraduates spent their evenings chatting over pints of beer. To me this felt safe and familiar, and made leaving home feel less scary, as I was entering a culture very similar to the one I already knew back home.

Wycliffe Hall's primary role was to train priests for the Church of England, putting them through Oxford theology classes. Wycliffe had never accepted eighteen-year-old undergraduates until the year I applied. Three boys also sent applications, so there were four of us straight out of high school. The vast majority of Wycliffe students were thirty or forty and training for a life in the priesthood.

My student days would be vastly different from those of the average Oxford undergraduate. Rather than broadening my worldview, my years there would reinforce everything I already believed. Some students and tutors at Wycliffe Hall believed women shouldn't be allowed to preach or enter the priesthood, and on the issue of homosexuality the college was staunchly traditional. But back in 1997, when I walked through the college doors for the first time, those evangelical values were comfortingly familiar to me, and I fitted in quickly.

Most people at Wycliffe were friendly and well-balanced, and it was clear the college was producing good priests who would serve in churches around the world. But even during my first year, as a rather naive eighteen-year-old, I was taken aback by the ways some people weren't practicing what they preached when it came to sexual morality.

A priest from overseas sat next to me at dinner one evening during my first year. To my shock, he sexually assaulted me under the table.

Because we were sitting on long wooden benches in the dining hall, packed tightly next to one another, there was no chance for me to move away. "Do you have a boyfriend?" he'd asked me quietly, as his wandering hands found their way up my legs. My face turned deep red, and I felt a mixture of shame, anger, and panic.

When this happened, I had no idea who on earth to tell. I wasn't brave enough to talk to the college staff, fearful that I wouldn't be believed. Days later, the same man pinned a female student against a wall, pressing himself against her and trying to kiss her. Soon afterward he was sent home. I heard of several incidents like this, involving trainee male priests, happening to others during my three years of study, and it left me shell-shocked.

Within the college, lots of unmarried seminary students were having sex, and a handful of married students were having affairs with other students. The shiny façade of evangelical morality seemed to be crumbling in front of my eyes. This was not what I'd expected to see at an evangelical college.

Going to university hadn't made any difference to my sexual orientation; I knew that I was still gay, and I still believed it was sinful and wrong. It felt increasingly strange, though, trying so hard to perfectly uphold Christian moral standards when those around me didn't seem to.

The more aware I became of seminarians having affairs and premarital sex, the angrier I felt toward the college and the wider evangelical world it represented. It was a part of the church that stood on moral high ground, condemning gay relationships as sinful, yet I was seeing with my own eyes that it was failing to live up to its own standards.

During my time at Wycliffe Hall, two male priests in training were asked to leave because they had (allegedly) been involved in sexual activity with other men. Both cases were handled under a shroud of secrecy, and the subject remained taboo within the college. *How can evangelicals judge gay people so confidently when they aren't practicing what they preach?* I often wondered, through tears, as I tried to process it all.

I quickly found a church in Oxford that I loved, called The Vineyard. It was a denomination founded in California by a man named John Wimber, who was passionate about faith healing and God's ability to do miracles today. It felt a lot like the Pentecostal church I was raised in.

Vineyard congregations were springing up all across the UK, known for their contemporary-style worship music, informal atmosphere, and the fact that they served donuts and coffee after every service.

This particular Vineyard congregation believed that women should not be allowed to preach or be senior pastors. Its view on homosexuality was equally traditional. Its outer aspects looked very contemporary—guitars and drums, casual clothes, and plates of donuts—but on the inside its belief system upheld the views I'd been raised with. While other Oxford students were playing sports, joining clubs, sitting at the bar, and generally getting a wider experience of life, my extracurricular activities only involved attending church or spending time with other Christian students at Wycliffe. Somehow, I'd managed to re-create my Christian bubble in a new city.

One thing proving very difficult was watching my fellow students pairing up. When I thought back to high school, those days seemed simple in comparison. Mine had been a girls' school, so dating had only happened outside of the classroom. Now, at Oxford, it was happening all around me.

Every university event seemed to involve inviting a "plus one." Coupledom reigned. There were dinners and dances and summer balls, and I wanted to go, but nobody went alone. I could attend with a male friend, but they would often end up getting the wrong idea and the friendship would be ruined. Heteronormativity (the assumption that heterosexuality is the only societal norm) was everywhere, and I was realizing it more and more.

I did go on a few dates in Oxford. When a charming trainee priest named Will invited me out for dinner, I was curious to see how we'd get along. He was popular—tall, blond, sporty, and passionate about his faith. Will and I went out for dinner and had a great time. It was clear that he was one of the nicest guys on the planet. But even with someone this intelligent and attractive, the feelings I thought I might experience just weren't there.

Other male students asked me on dates: picnics in the park, boat rides on the river, and long evenings of fascinating conversation over coffee. I certainly couldn't have been accused of not trying. Friends said, "Don't worry. You just haven't met Mr. Right yet." But deep down I knew it wasn't about that—I knew I was gay. Men were great company—in fact I often preferred male friends, because they shared my tomboy interests. I never felt anything beyond platonic affection for them, though.

Unknown to me, another world was only streets away. St. Hilda's was, at that time, the university's all-female college, and it attracted a large number of gay women. One of them, who would study in the year below me, was Ruth Hunt. Ruth would go on to be CEO of the UK's largest LGBT organization, Stonewall. We never met during our student days; I only got to know her when I was thirty-four. Looking back, I've often wondered what might have happened if I'd met her back then and been introduced to her circle of friends and the university's LGBT Society. She would, I'm sure, have shown me a different way of viewing things. Who knows what my life's path would've been then? It's funny how near, and yet how far, we can be from monumental change.

I would manage to go my entire three-year degree course without talking to or getting to know anyone who was openly LGBTQ+. This wasn't hard as, in my first year, I was creating a pattern that I would maintain, and it kept me locked away among my evangelical community. I was either at Wycliffe Hall with the seminarians and priests, or at The Vineyard church, or in lecture halls where students barely spoke. If I had been introduced to any lesbians or bisexuals, I'd probably have run a mile in the other direction, concerned they would lead me into temptation. In my mind, it was a battle to fight, a slippery slope, a risk of being led astray—so the further I stayed away from it all, the better.

I knew nothing of LGBTQ+ history and the steady pace of change happening in the UK and beyond. I had no clue that there were thousands of other people out there like me, and that they were gathering together and challenging the status quo. Only years later would I read the rich history of the global LGBTQ+ rights movement and learn how many people had been fighting for my rights before I even arrived on the planet.

I would learn that, on a hot summer night in 1969, ten years before I was born, police raided the gay bars in New York on a mission to shut down those "rogue" establishments. An LGBTQ+ fightback took place at the Stonewall Inn that would give birth to the modern-day LGBTQ+ rights movement. One year later, in commemoration, five thousand people marched down Sixth Avenue, beginning the tradition of Pride marches that continue around the globe today.

Before 1962, homosexuality was classed as a felony in the US in every state. A few states had shifted on this by 1979 (the year I was born), but by no means had they all. In 1980, it was decriminalized in New York and Pennsylvania. By 1992, it had become legal in another handful of states. In 1996, homosexuality was decriminalized in Tennessee—a place I would later live and work in my twenties.

In the UK, some progress had been made with the 1967 Sexual Offences Act, but as one influential campaigner noted:

> The criminalisation of homosexuality in the UK did not in fact end until 2013. . . . Not only was homosexuality only partly decriminalised by the 1967 act, but the remaining anti-gay laws were policed more aggressively than before by a state that opposed gay acceptance and equality. In total, from 1885 [to] 2013, nearly 100,000 men were arrested for same-sex acts.
>
> The 1967 legislation repealed the maximum penalty of life imprisonment [for gay sex]. But it still discriminated.[1]

The 1967 act applied only to England and Wales, not to Scotland or Northern Ireland, and they adopted it only in the 1980s, so it was slow progress.

In 1988, when I was nine years old, Parliament passed the notorious antigay law known as Section 28. This stated that local authorities must "not intentionally promote homosexuality" or "provide teaching" on "the acceptability of homosexuality as a pretended family relationship." At that time, Section 28 received strong political support from Christians in the UK who saw it as defending God's standards for sex and marriage.

The act applied to all local authorities, including councils and the schools they were responsible for. Many teachers saw Section 28 as a ban on talking about gay relationships in their classrooms. As a result, at high schools like mine, same-sex relationships were never mentioned in any classes on biology or social education. It felt like an outlawed and taboo subject.

Because of this, if students thought they might be gay or bisexual, it was unlikely they'd feel safe confiding in staff or talking about it at school. From the teaching many of us received, it seemed like there was only one model of acceptable romantic relationship: heterosexuality.

Section 28 wasn't repealed until November 2003, when I was twenty-three years old. So my formative teenage years were spent in a country where homosexuality was not just a taboo subject but one that parts of society were prohibited from discussing. During the process of repealing Section 28, Christians were a strong force behind the campaign to retain it as law.

Thankfully, in London, activists like Ian McKellen, Peter Tatchell, Michael Cashman, Lisa Power, Sue Sanders, Pam St. Clement, Isaac Julien, and Christine Burns were working tirelessly to get laws like these changed. Their tenacious work and that of many others led to the eventual repeal of Section 28 and a brighter future for everyone.

It would take until 2001, when I was twenty-one, for same-sex marriage to be legalized anywhere; the first country to do so was the Netherlands. In 2014, same-sex marriage legislation came into force in England and Wales, and the US legalized it nationwide in June 2015 as a result of the *Obergefell v. Hodges* case in the Supreme Court.

Those radical shifts all lay ahead. But for me, living in my evangelical hall of residence in Oxford, LGBTQ+ history wasn't something I'd even heard of. My mind was shaped solely by church teachings, and thanks to Section 28, my high-school years hadn't taught me anything different. The internet was in its infancy—I got my first email address when I arrived at university and we all thought it was groundbreaking stuff—but none of us spent time online, and social media didn't yet exist.

I wish I'd allowed myself to socialize with students from other colleges in the city who could have told me about LGBTQ+ rights and introduced me to a more diverse social circle. University could have been an enlightening opportunity for me—a place of healing and self-acceptance, where both my faith and my gay orientation could have been affirmed. Instead, I just ignored my feelings, buckled down, and focused on my academic work. The pace was intense, and before I knew it, my first year at university was over.

8

One afternoon during my second year at university, the phone rang abruptly, interrupting the writing of my latest essay. I was sitting cross-legged on the floor of my student room, surrounded by a huge pile of books. Knocking papers everywhere as I rushed to grab the receiver, I was surprised to find the voice on the other end was American.

It was Vineyard Records, an international record label founded by the church denomination I attended. They were well known for producing worship CDs that flew off the shelves in the States.

The man on the phone said I was invited to a training retreat for Christian songwriters who showed great potential. Thirty of us from around the world would be given a week of input and teaching to take our songwriting skills to the next level—we'd also get the chance to pitch our newest compositions to Vineyard Records representatives.

The entire trip would be fully paid for by the label in the hopes of discovering fresh talent. It was a lot to take in; I couldn't stop smiling as he talked. The best news of all was finding out where this training would take place: Los Angeles, California. I'd always wanted to visit the US, and now I finally would.

Hanging up the phone, I was delighted and stunned. I'd been singing a lot in my Oxford church and at national Christian conferences, and now this trip to the States felt like a sign that exciting opportunities were ahead. My goal for getting a theology degree wasn't a career in academia—I still wanted to be a professional musician, singing and playing in churches—so I was encouraged to see doors opening nationally, and now also internationally.

The dates of the trip fell during a university vacation, so my parents and tutors wouldn't mind. It would be a much-needed break from my studies, and it would introduce me to a country that, in the coming years, would become a huge part of my life.

As the plane descended toward LAX airport I watched the grid-shaped streetlights of Los Angeles coming into view. When I stepped out of the airport into the Californian evening, the hot, dry air hit me like a wall. The sky was a smudged, pastel mess of pinks and blues, with rows of tall palm trees rustling overhead. A black SUV collected the other songwriters and me, and as we drove along the coastal road, the turquoise ocean filled our view, with the sun lazily melting into the horizon.

I didn't know the other songwriters on the trip, and they were older than I was, but they took me under their wing. Our days consisted of sharing our newest compositions, chatting with record label executives, and then sitting around fire pits at night, playing guitar and toasting marshmallows. I adored it.

I got to put my toes in the Pacific Ocean for the first time. I tried fish tacos and root beer soda, neither of which we had in the UK. Most of all, I loved experiencing the warmth of American culture; people were so friendly. After that week, part of my heart belonged to the US and always would.

The Vineyard, the church denomination I attended in Oxford, had begun in Anaheim, about twenty-five miles south of Los Angeles. Since then, it had established fifteen hundred separate churches around the globe. During my LA trip I was taken to visit the flagship church, where it had all started. It was my first experience of a megachurch—a fascinating phenomenon, with very few parallels in the UK.

Anaheim Vineyard's six thousand members met in a huge purpose-built auditorium. It was a facility to rival any high-end theater in London, nothing like the traditional churches in England with ancient stone walls, pews, and steeples. This had cinema-style seats, a huge stage, and state-of-the-art sound and lighting systems. A giant screen filled the front wall, and high-spec projectors beamed song lyrics and videos onto it.

I walked around the massive venue, struck by its size. It had its own coffee shop and, within the same facility, an entire bookstore selling publications by its pastors and musicians. I shook hands with some of the staff and noticed how many there were. Back home in the Church of England, one full-time priest was the norm. But here there were multiple leaders, all salaried—including a worship pastor, a teaching pastor, a youth and kids pastor—and various administrators, maintenance staff, and coffee-shop and bookshop staff—a whole crowd of people.

I was stunned by how vast the overhead expenses must be to have bought a building like this, equip it with such amazing technology, and employ so many people. I found out that megachurches are funded by "tithing" or donations, the collections taken at each service. People's generosity kept the bills paid.

That first visit to an American megachurch was eye-opening indeed. I felt like a tourist taking in the new sights. I had no idea that these vast buildings would be where I'd spend most of my twenties. There was an endless network of huge churches, just like this one, ready to book and pay worship leaders to come and sing, and that very soon would become my livelihood.

The trip seemed to pass in the blink of an eye. As I took off from LAX airport, I knew I was leaving part of my heart there and hoped it wouldn't be long before I'd visit again.

B ack at university, I reflected on how much I loved the innovative culture I'd experienced in California. Everything about it seemed huge, shiny, and new. But going there had also given me a fresh appreciation for the history and architecture in Oxford.

Walking to and from my classes, I was aware that every stone staircase echoed with the footsteps of centuries past. It was amazing to sit in The Eagle and Child pub, where C. S. Lewis and J. R. R. Tolkien had held the Inklings society meetings and read aloud their drafts of *The Lion, the Witch, and the Wardrobe* and *The Lord of the Rings*, or to walk around the Iffley Road sports ground, where Roger Bannister, back in 1954, became the first person to run a mile in less than four minutes.

So many world-changing people had passed through the university buildings—authors Aldous Huxley and William Golding; poets W. H. Auden, Percy Bysshe Shelley, John Donne, and Oscar Wilde; suffragette Emily Wilding Davison; philosopher John Locke; and the explorer Sir Walter Raleigh, just to name a few.

Their achievements—and their faces in oil paintings—stared down at me as the months went by. Somehow, the way they'd challenged limitations and forged new ground was waking me up. I began to think perhaps anyone could take a stab at changing the status quo, if they had enough grit and daring.

This sense of waking up grew and grew the more time I spent around the exceptional lecturers and professors who taught us. I was learning a great deal from them. Plenty of them were Christians and passionate about their faith. Using their minds—revering and exploring the sacred text of the Bible, its historical context, and its layers of meaning—was, to them, part of their worship of God. Many of these academics and professors were ordained as pastors or priests as well, and I loved the congruence between their academic work and their vibrant personal faith.

The church I'd grown up in spoke about the Bible as though it had been hand-delivered last year in contemporary English and with a glossy hardback cover. It was seen as a familiar book with an obvious and unmissable message. "The Bible clearly says . . ." was a phrase I'd heard endlessly.

The more I learned in Oxford lectures, the more I saw what a rich, complex, and vast journey the Bible had been on. After its infancy as oral tradition (stories passed on by word of mouth), it had been written onto early scrolls in Hebrew, Aramaic, and Greek and then later translated into Latin and finally into various versions of English. It had been through thousands of years of evolution, and the people in its pages lived in cultures startlingly different from ours, yet the book had found its way into our hands.

Understanding the complexity of the Bible, especially how translators made varying (and sometimes conflicting) decisions about what the Greek or Hebrew words actually meant, didn't devalue scripture in my eyes. I gained even *more* respect for how the book had traveled through the centuries. This was an important shift for me; I was around academics, many of whom were passionately committed Christians, who were saying the texts could be interpreted in different ways and that the context and culture in which they were written had to be taken into account.

Thanks to hours of homework, I could now read the Bible in its original languages of Greek and Hebrew, and I had a strong understanding of the cultures in which it was first written. I could see it was a far more complex book than I'd imagined.

It felt like being given the keys to drive a car, when formerly you thought you were only allowed to sit in the backseat. I had been handed the necessary skills for serious study of this ancient text. My new perspective was enlightening but also frightening. Honestly, it felt safer to just sit in the backseat. I wondered what tackling the tricky aspects of the Bible for myself would lead to—and whether I was ready for it.

I knew my biggest questions related to what the Bible actually said about same-sex relationships, but I dreaded challenging the status quo of my church, of Wycliffe Hall, of my friends and family, and of the people at the American Christian record label, Vineyard Records, whom I hoped to work with after I graduated. What if the arguments in favor of same-sex marriage convinced me? What would I do then?

I wanted to explore these questions, but I feared doing so would come at too high a price. I'd adored my visit to California, and my heart was set on that career path. My family and close friends loved the songs I was writing, and they felt God was using me to touch a lot of people's lives.

As I wrestled with these huge questions, the psychological damage that had begun in my teens was continuing through my years at Oxford. I felt trapped and fearful. Part of me longed to find a soul mate, as loneliness was a constant and painful reality. But I couldn't give up my community, my conscience, or my future career. It was a cruel choice for anyone to face, and as the years went by, the toll it was taking on my life grew and grew.

"Why do I have to choose between such core aspects of my identity?" I often asked myself, sobbing into my pillow at night. "Why can't I pursue my Christian music career and also be able to date and marry someone of the same sex?" It seemed immensely unfair that straight people didn't have to make these vast, cruel choices, and it felt like being ripped in two.

9

Magdalen College stands proudly above Oxford's High Street. It's the place C. S. Lewis worked for almost thirty years. A herd of deer is kept on college property and are a beautiful sight to behold; Lewis wrote that he could stare out of his window and watch the stags running majestically in the early morning mist.

One of Lewis's favorite habits was to travel a sixteenth-century pathway known as Addison's Walk through the grounds of Magdalen College, past the deer, and down along the banks of the river. He reminisced in his letters about walking there with Tolkien, so I loved going there, knowing they had trod the same ground. Addison's Walk became my favorite place to escape the indoor world of libraries and lectures, and I'd sit on the banks for hours, watching the river flow past.

At that point in my studies, we were learning about church history. Attending classes and doing my own reading, I was fascinated to see a recurring pattern. Each generation of Christians had wrestled with particular ethical issues they saw as insurmountable. In every case, they'd said it would be *the issue* that would split the church into pieces. But with prayerful consideration and the passing of time, they always found a way through. Usually, this involved admitting they were wrong and adopting a better approach. It was intriguing to see this play out, again and again, in the history of the church.

One warm afternoon I strolled through Magdalen College, past the deer, and down Addison's Walk to the river. Choosing a grassy spot, I put down my backpack of books and laid out a blanket. That day I would be doing some research on an important topic—how the church had handled the question of human slavery.

The river sparkled in the sunshine, and I began reading.

I discovered that in centuries past the church had argued that the Bible "very clearly" defended slavery as part of God's ordained structure for society and that people of certain nationalities were divinely preselected for slavery. Genesis 9:18–27 was seen as definitive proof of this, so I flicked through my Bible and read those words myself:

> The sons of Noah who went out of the ark were Shem, Ham, and Japheth. Ham was the father of Canaan. . . .
>
> Noah, a man of the soil, was the first to plant a vineyard. He drank some of the wine and became drunk, and he lay uncovered in his tent. And Ham, the father of Canaan, saw the nakedness of his father, and told his two brothers outside. Then Shem and Japheth took a garment, laid it on both their shoulders, and walked backward and covered the nakedness of their father; their faces were turned away, and they did not see their father's nakedness.
>
> When Noah awoke from his wine and knew what his youngest son had done to him, he said, "Cursed be Canaan; lowest of slaves shall he be to his brothers." He also said, "Blessed by the LORD my God be Shem; and let Canaan be his slave. May God make space for Japheth, and let him live in the tents of Shem; and let Canaan be his slave."

Noah clearly thought slavery was an acceptable burden to place on a human being—and even on his own offspring. That in itself was a lot to take on board. Also, I was baffled how this part of the Bible was used to justify enslaving a certain demographic of people; I could see no specific link to race or skin color in these verses, despite the fact that they had been the foundation of Christians' belief that slavery was ordained by God for certain nationalities and not others.

I later found a BBC article that explained the way this link was formed:

> *Africans were said to be the descendants of Ham, the son of Noah, who was cursed by his father after looking at his naked form. Moreover, in Genesis 10, the "Table of Nations" describes the origins of the different races and reveals that one of the descendants of Ham is Cush-Cush, and that the Cushites were people associated with the Nile region of North Africa. In time, the European connection between sin, slavery, skin color and beliefs would condemn Africans.* [1]

An op-ed in the *New York Times* also summarized this succinctly:

> *In the biblical account, Noah and his family are not described in racial terms. But as the story echoed through the centuries and around the world, variously interpreted by Islamic, Christian and Jewish scholars, Ham came to be widely portrayed as black; blackness, servitude and the idea of racial hierarchy became inextricably linked.* [2]

I was horrified at how offensive, and how lacking in biblical evidence, this argument was. My mind spun as I thought of the vast damage done in the name of this so-called theological truth. Fellow Christians who loved and worshipped Jesus had defended this, and it was heartbreaking to realize that.

I read on. The Old Testament book of Leviticus was also used to support slavery. God said to Israel:

As for the male and female slaves whom you may have, it is from the nations around you that you may acquire male and female slaves. You may also acquire them from among the aliens residing with you, and from their families that are with you, who have been born in your land; and they may be your property. (25:44–45)

Exodus 21:21 was brought in as scriptural evidence too: "The slave is the owner's property."

Based on these verses, everything existed in the binary categories that God had (allegedly) created: there were Jews and Gentiles; there were free people and slaves. Using these Old Testament scriptures, the church had argued throughout history that God had made it this way, and that to change things would disrupt his design for social, political, and family life.

I was curious to find out whether they had used the New Testament to defend slavery too. They had. According to 1 Peter 2:18–21:

Slaves, accept the authority of your masters with all deference, not only those who are kind and gentle but also those who are harsh. For it is a credit to you if, being aware of God, you endure pain while suffering unjustly. . . . For to this you have been called, because Christ also suffered for you, leaving you an example, so that you should follow in his steps.

Not only was slavery portrayed by St. Peter as acceptable, but even slaves who were mistreated were supposed to stay quiet and put up with it. It sounded as though he was condoning abuse. Maybe, I hoped, the subject had come up at one of the major councils of church history as an issue that needed reexamining? Not so.

The Synod of Gangra held in 340 CE issued this statement: "If anyone shall teach a slave . . . to despise his master and to run away from his service, and not to serve his master with goodwill and all honor, let him be anathema."[3] So, any Christian opposing slavery was "anathema," literally meaning "cursed," which in practice meant being declared heretical and, most likely, excommunicated by the church.

What about some of the influential thinkers from church history? I wondered. What about a famous theologian like St. Augustine? St. Augustine of Hippo (354–430 CE), in his book *The City of God*, argued that slavery "is appointed by that law which enjoins the preservation of the natural order and forbids its disturbance. . . . Therefore the apostle admonishes slaves to be subject to their masters, and to serve them heartily and with goodwill."[4] Augustine believed slavery was a result of the Fall, so he didn't see it as God's ideal state for humans. Despite that, he didn't reject it as immoral. Instead, he regarded it as an unavoidable part of society and taught Christians to accept it.

Did Thomas Aquinas (1225–74 CE) think along these same lines? A Doctor of the Church, Aquinas believed that all humans were inherently equal, and that slavery was a consequence of the Fall. But he was still willing to teach that "slavery belongs to the right of nations" and that it should not be challenged by the church.[5]

What about the popes? Did they provide a better view as the years went by? Apparently not. Pope Gregory IX (1145–1241 CE) decreed:

Slavery, in which a man serves his master as his slave, is altogether lawful. This is proved from Holy Scripture. It is also proved from reason; for it is not unreasonable that just as things which are captured in a just war pass into the power and ownership of the victors, so persons captured in war pass into the ownership of the captors. All theologians are unanimous on this.[6]

His last phrase echoed in my head. "Unanimous." I could imagine people back then saying, "But we've always done it like this . . ."

What about more recently? In 1866, Pope Pius IX stated: "Slavery itself is not contrary to natural and divine law. There can be several just titles of slavery, and these are referred to by approved theologians and commentators of the sacred canons."[7] It amazed me that these views were held by Christians only a hundred years before I was born.

A set of notes from an 1861 Presbyterian gathering in Georgia reported: "The Presbyterian Church in the United States has been enabled by Divine Grace to pursue a . . . thoroughly scriptural policy in relation to this delicate question [slavery]. It has planted itself upon the word of God and utterly refused to make slaveholding a sin."[8]

They argued that the church should not interfere with the state on the topic of slavery, as "God has not entrusted to the Church" the ability to change the "construction of government" or the "allotment of individuals to their various stations."[9] Instead, they were to focus on "the real tyrants which oppress the soul—sin and Satan."[10] Washing their hands of any moral judgment on the matter, they said: "We are neither the friends nor the foes of slavery . . . we have no commission either to propagate or to abolish it" and "we have no right, as the church, to condemn it as a sin."[11]

As I read about this, it seemed like a classic case of the church sticking its head in the sand. Faced with a divisive political matter that ignited arguments among its members, they absented themselves from any responsibility and just sat on the fence. It was astounding to me that they could claim, in good conscience, that slavery was a governmental issue with no relevance to the spiritual well-being of humans. Rather than speaking up for the freedom and human rights of the enslaved, the church claimed it only dealt with so-called spiritual matters, turning a blind eye to what was going on and the obvious suffering and degradation that slavery caused. Their silence, and their refusal to stand up for truth and justice, only perpetuated the existence of the slave trade.

So what finally happened to shake things up and set things right? Enter William Wilberforce (1759–1833), an English Christian and Member of Parliament who argued that God valued all humans equally and people should not be bought and sold as property. As he raised these radical views, he had to contend with Christians who waved Bibles in the air, saying that anyone who took the Bible seriously knew slavery was "clearly" endorsed by scripture.

Eventually the tide began to turn, as people realized the truth of Wilberforce's interpretation of the Bible and sympathized with his passion for equality. He was instrumental in that shift, but it came at great personal cost: his health began to fail. He died three days after hearing that legal changes would take place and that his work had finally succeeded. One month later, the Slavery Abolition Act, which declared all slaves in the British Empire free, became law.

As I continued to study all of this, sitting on the riverbank that warm afternoon, one thing became undeniably clear to me: Christian interpretations of the Bible *do* shift over time. The adage "We've always done it this way" was neither true nor a good moral compass. With regard to slavery, God seemed to have been at work in the trajectory of positive change, helping the church develop a more compassionate and intelligent perspective.

Later, I walked back along the river and into the grounds of Magdalen College, watching the deer playfully chase each other around the meadow as the liquid-orange sun got lower and lower in the evening sky. I thought about C. S. Lewis watching them out of his window, all those years ago. He'd had some of his own powerful spiritual moments on Addison's Walk and in the adjoining college. I knew his conversion story almost word for word, as I'd read it so many times over the years:

> You must picture me alone in that room in Magdalen [College, Oxford], night after night, feeling, whenever my mind lifted even for a second from my work, the steady, unrelenting approach of Him whom I so earnestly desired not to meet. . . . In . . . 1929 I gave in, and ad-

*mitted that God was God, and knelt and prayed: perhaps, that night,
the most . . . reluctant convert in all England.*[12]

That feeling of being a "reluctant convert" resonated with me. Not
with regard to faith itself, but to new ways of seeing the Bible. I was
slowly realizing my part of the church had got things very wrong in the
past and it was hard to come to terms with. I'd never heard a sermon
about this in any evangelical meeting; it seemed to have been swept
under the carpet. We considered ourselves the ones who accurately interpreted scripture and led the social justice movement within Christianity, but we definitely had a checkered past. My studies were opening
my eyes—and once you see something, you can never unsee it.

10

The cobbled streets were lit with twinkly lights, and festive trees covered in tinsel stood on every college green. Invitations for the Oxford Christmas Ball were pinned on notice boards across campus, and I was awkwardly declining invitations from male friends who hoped we could attend together and move our relationship from platonic to romantic.

It was lovely to walk down St. Giles Street, past The Eagle and Child pub, accompanied by a soundtrack of carol singers on the corner. I was on my way to return a couple of books to a friend named Mike at a nearby college. Visiting other halls of residence was always a pleasure, as they seemed so different, and I was curious to experience what Oxford life was like for other undergraduates, away from the priests and seminarians of Wycliffe Hall.

Entering through the wooden doors of Mike's college, I crossed the immaculate lawn, or "quad." Its statues and fountain gleamed in the fading evening light. Winding up an old stone staircase, I found my way to his hallway. Turning a corner, I saw an unexpected sight. Two people were standing outside a dormitory door, locked in a tight embrace. In the low-lit corridor they hadn't seen me, so I paused in the shadows. My heart missed a beat as I realized something—they were both women.

They laughed quietly under their breath, sharing a joke. Then one of the girls touched the other's face with infinite tenderness and, leaning toward her, softly kissed her. I blushed, aware I was watching someone else's intimate moment. I'd never seen two people of the same gender expressing any kind of romantic affection before.

The love between them was tangible, and they stood there for what seemed like an eternity whispering, laughing, kissing, and running their fingers through each other's hair. Eventually, their silhouettes parted, they said good night, and one of them left down the opposite stairway. The girl who remained in the hallway turned around.

Realizing she'd seen me, I began walking toward her, so I could get to Mike's room. Awkwardly, it turned out they were only a few doors apart. As I knocked and waited for Mike to answer, I stood a short distance away from the girl as she fumbled in her backpack for her keys.

He opened his door, and light spilled out into the dark corridor. Looking back at the girl in the hallway, I caught my breath. Now I could see her. She had long, curly red hair and a very familiar face. It was the girl who'd stood on the conference stage years earlier and shared her testimony about being set free from homosexuality. She was here at Oxford University, and just moments ago she'd been kissing another woman. My brain and heart tried to take it all in.

The sound of her door closing jolted me out of my thoughts. She'd found her keys and disappeared into her room. Now that I could see the outside of her door clearly, I noticed it had a sign on it: "I am the College LGBT Representative: Knock if you'd like to chat about anything related to gender or sexuality. I'm always here to listen."

It was a lot to process. She was the only example I'd ever seen of a person who'd been "set free" from homosexuality. Now I knew it was not true after all. Here she was, openly gay *and* an LGBTQ+ college representative, giving advice and support to other students.

Hearing her speak from that conference stage, when I was in my teens, had made a huge impact on me. Knowing that God had, apparently, turned her from gay to straight had left me believing I could expect the same transformation. I'd been hanging on to it all these years; she was the only tangible form of proof I had.

I felt so disoriented as I tried to take it all on board, and my mind spun with questions about her: I wondered how she'd found the courage to step away from the traditional beliefs we all held. I felt a mix of shock and devastation, but also admiration.

I felt like Truman from *The Truman Show*. I'd glimpsed a huge crack in the "set" that was the backdrop of my life. Everything wasn't as secure or stable as I'd thought. The red-haired girl's experience of "healing" hadn't worked. God hadn't changed her sexual orientation. Instead, she'd chosen to follow her heart and be in a relationship with a woman—and tonight she'd looked a hundred times happier and healthier than she had on that conference stage.

11

Intrigued by all I'd learned about the church and slavery, I moved on in my studies to explore another topic: Christianity and women's equality. Inside the Radcliffe Camera, a huge dome-shaped stone library, I sat in the shadowy lamplight and read. I hoped Christians in years gone by had behaved better on this issue, as I was still staggered by all I'd learned about their endorsement of the slave trade. Unfortunately, as the days passed and I did my research, I found it had been a bleak and disappointing battle.

Women had mostly subservient roles in the Old Testament, and the Ten Commandments seemed to categorize women as property: "You shall not covet your neighbor's wife, or male or female slave, or ox, or donkey . . ." (Exod. 20:17). But it was St. Paul's teachings that were most often quoted when Christians argued against women's voting rights or suitability for the priesthood.

In 1 Timothy 2:12, he writes: "I permit no woman to teach or to have authority over a man; she is to keep silent." In the nineteenth century, that verse was used by Christians as key evidence, as were Ephesians 5:22 and 1 Corinthians 11:3.

Their point seemed unchallengeable back then, and yet today, few evangelicals would command women to "keep silent" in church. Our understanding of how St. Paul's teachings should be interpreted has clearly changed, based on context, culture, and consideration of the broader witness of scripture.

Huge animosity existed toward those who wanted equality. The nineteenth-century priest Justin Fulton said, "Who demand the ballot for woman? They are not the lovers of God, nor are they the believers in Christ. . . . Those who contend for the ballot for woman cut loose from the legislation of Heaven . . . and drift to infidelity and ruin."[1]

Those arguing that women should be subordinate appealed to God's "design" or "order" within creation, as many had done in the slavery debate. God had made things a certain way, and that order should not be messed with. As one campaigner said in 1911, women should remain "in their places . . . attending to those duties that God Almighty intended for them. . . . Woman is woman. . . . Let her be content with her lot and perform those high duties intended for her by the Great Creator."[2]

This was disheartening reading, and, after days of research, I found myself staring at the ceiling of the Radcliffe Camera library, desperately wishing church history were different. *Surely it was just male Christians arguing this way,* I thought. But I was wrong. In 1870, Susan Fenimore Cooper wrote an influential piece titled "Female Suffrage." Her views made for difficult reading: "Christianity confirms the subordinate position of woman . . . the submission of the wife to the husband, and allots a subordinate position to the whole [female] sex while here on earth."[3]

What did she think of those who joined the suffragettes? "We have arrived at the days foretold by the Prophet, when 'knowledge shall be increased, and many shall run to and fro.' . . . We dare not blindly follow that cry [of 'Progress!'] . . . The tyranny of the present day . . . is the tyranny of novelty."[4] Those words seem eerily similar to what had been said in the slavery debate and then seemed to be said every time the church faced a new issue of social justice: "It's a tyranny," "It's about novelty," "It's a sign of the end times," "We've always done it this way."

So what happened to bring change? A few men and women rose up, fighting long and hard to shift those views. Suffragette Emily Wilding Davison was among those who died for the cause, knocked down by King George V's horse when she staged a protest at the Epsom Derby in 1913. She was a passionate Christian and did her utmost to challenge the status quo of the church and nation, believing that the biblical texts about women had been misinterpreted over the centuries and did not prohibit a right to vote and have a voice in society.

The Church League for Women's Suffrage was a powerful voice for change, founded by an Anglican priest. Similar groups existed among Catholics and free churches too. Those campaigning groups helped new ways of understanding the Bible to break into public consciousness. Eventually, centuries of quoting St. Paul as evidence to keep women in their place made way for a more compassionate and nuanced interpretation of scripture. As with slavery, victory came slowly, and at great cost. But it did finally arrive.

I ended my research feeling frustrated and disappointed at the ways the church had held back such crucial progress for women, and the way they'd used the Bible to back up their arguments. Yes, eventually, things had improved, but so many had paid for it in heartache and suffering—for some it had even cost them their lives.

The Radcliffe Camera library was now my favorite study haunt. It wasn't the best place to be in December, though—the ancient library heating system was faulty at best, so during the winter I often sat in there wearing a woolly hat, a thick scarf, and fingerless gloves to avoid freezing to the bone. It felt ridiculous, but many students were doing the same. We exchanged empathetic smiles, adding layer on top of layer, until we gradually resembled academic versions of the Stay Puft Marshmallow Man from the movie *Ghostbusters*.

Looking at the way the church had changed its mind on slavery and then on women's rights had gotten my brain spinning. I was curious about similar issues; had this happened on other topics too?

One afternoon, I pulled a book from a high dusty shelf. It was about the Italian physicist and mathematician Galileo (1564–1642 CE). I discovered that in the seventeenth century a heated debate had taken place over whether the sun revolved around the earth or vice versa. Galileo believed the earth moved around the sun. The church, however, argued that the sun must revolve around the earth, as that's what scripture said.

Christians quoted Psalm 104:5: "[The Lord] set the earth on its foundations; it can never be moved" (NIV). Ecclesiastes 1:5 was also used: "The sun rises and the sun goes down, and hastens to the place where it rises" (RSV). The book of Joshua was another key piece of evidence, as Joshua had prayed for the sun to "stand still," and it "stopped in the middle of the sky and delayed going down" (10:13, NIV). In the seventeenth century, to take the Bible seriously meant to believe this as literal truth.

Galileo's ideas were considered dangerous. The church said his theory was absurd and heretical, because it explicitly contradicted, in many places, "the clear meaning of Holy Scripture." He argued that the Bible could be interpreted in a way that fitted comfortably with a heliocentric view of the universe, but his theology was rejected. The Catholic Church placed Galileo under house arrest and threatened him with torture in an attempt to break him. He remained in his home for the next nine years until he died of heart failure at age seventy-seven.

Of course, in time everyone realized the earth did indeed revolve around the sun. Galileo was just too early. It cost him his place in the church, caused him a huge amount of trauma, and finally led to his death. I was seeing a pattern emerge from history: those who saw a new paradigm were treated appallingly by fellow Christians and then finally accepted as correct, but far too late, after the damage had been done. The church learned, but it seemed to learn painfully slowly.

In the lamplight of the Radcliffe Camera library, I discovered books on the civil rights movement too, in which developments followed very similar patterns.

In 1954, the US Supreme Court declared that racial segregation in schools was unconstitutional. Responding to this, a popular Southern Baptist pastor preached against it from his pulpit in 1958. He argued that if the government "had known God's word and had desired to do the Lord's will," the attempts to integrate people of different races "would never have been made." He warned: "When God has drawn a line of distinction, we should not attempt to cross that line."[5]

Thankfully, the American Baptist minister Martin Luther King Jr. (1929–68) showed up and fought for justice. He interpreted the Bible differently and gave his life to challenge the status quo. King was seen as a heretic by many Christians who saw civil rights like interracial marriage as sinful and unsuitable for followers of Jesus.

The popular Southern Baptist pastor emphasized this in his sermon, saying: "A friend of mine tells me that a couple of opposite race live next door to his church as man and wife. This will destroy our race eventually."[6]

King finally won, but not without pushback from those who quoted the Bible against him.

All my research was proving to be enlightening and frustrating in equal measure. Why did the church keep getting things so wrong, over and over, constantly finding itself on the wrong side of justice? It had been wrong about the solar system, slavery, women, interracial marriage, and other civil rights.

Thinking of these historical patterns, my mind kept returning to one question: was the church perhaps also wrong in its condemnation of same-sex relationships? History showed there was a decent possibility. My spiritual home, the evangelical church, always presented a position of certainty on theological issues, but I had to accept that it had consistently gotten things very wrong in years gone by.

January arrived and a new semester began. The new year brought with it a generous downfall of snow. The streets looked like something out of a fairy tale. I cycled past a tall black lamppost surrounded by snowdrifts. A few yards away was a door with a carving of two golden faun-like creatures carrying panpipes—the location thought to have inspired C. S. Lewis to dream up Narnia, where it was "always winter but never Christmas."

Arriving back at my hall of residence, I saw an amusing sight—countless students and a few staff out on the snow-covered lawn throwing snowballs at one another. As I neared them, one of the boys from my dorm hallway landed a huge wet snowball right on the side of my head. I laughed and threw one back, missing him by a mile.

Cold and rather soggy, I headed into the building to warm up. I'd left a pile of papers in our college reading room earlier and needed to collect them. I preferred to work in the Radcliffe Camera, but it was quite a trek to get down there, so sometimes it was easier to use the small library within our building. Walking in, I found it deserted. It seemed the whole student population had joined the snowball battle outside. I'd never had that library to myself—a luxury for a bookish geek like me—and I walked up and down the aisles savoring the privacy.

A thought entered my head: *I wonder whether there are any books in here about . . . being gay and Christian.* I blushed as the thought emerged; the topic still filled me with shame and awkwardness. I had huge respect for spiritual leadership, but my recent studies had shown me that even the most senior church leaders had got things wrong in the past, despite their best attempts. It gave me the desire to keep exploring the Bible for myself and to read more widely.

Checking to see that I was the only one present, I found a section marked Sexual Ethics and followed the alphabetical shelves to H and Homosexuality. I grabbed a few paperbacks and started scanning them. The volumes I'd pulled out were written by "liberal" theologians, the sort my church back home had warned might lead me astray during my university studies. I felt as though I was betraying God by even looking, and I could feel my heart in my chest, much louder than usual.

Leaning against the shelf, ready for flight at any minute if someone returned and saw me, I explored the books with caution. The authors suggested that for centuries we'd mistranslated and misunderstood the Bible passages thought to relate to same-sex relationships. These writers explained that the Greek word in scripture thought to describe same-sex relationships was *arsenokoites*, a term that hadn't occurred in any previous historical documents. St. Paul may well have coined the term himself, they said. As a result, translating it was partly guesswork.

Arsenokoites was a word made of two parts: "arsen" (male) and "koites" (bed). Beyond that, nothing was known about what it actually meant to Paul. In the King James Bible it was translated as "abusers of themselves with mankind." It surprised me that such a key verse, used to utterly condemn same-sex relationships, hung on a word no one could accurately translate or cross-reference for contextual meaning. Many scholars studying Paul's writings had apparently questioned whether this term referred to something quite different: to temple prostitution and pederasty (sexual relations between a man and a boy). Based on how unknown the true translation of *arsenokoites* was, many scholars believed it had nothing to do with equal, loving, same-sex partners. It also seemed to appear in places where Paul was focused on economic sins, not sexual sins, suggesting it was about power imbalance and coercive abuse, not monogamous, loving relationships.

Reading further, I found the books addressed the story of Sodom and Gomorrah—from which the word "sodomy" originated. My thoughts drifted back to kids' church and the picture book with vivid drawings of those cities burning to the ground, while fire and brimstone rained down from the sky. My eyebrows rose as I read several scholars who claimed the story of Sodom and Gomorrah had absolutely no connection to homosexuality. Rather, they said, it was about the sins of gang rape and inhospitality.

I grabbed a Bible and scanned through the story in Genesis 19:1–11. Lot, the main character in the story, was visited by people from out of town. That night when he and his guests were inside the house, "all the men from every part of the city" had appeared at his door, insisting Lot surrender his visitors, so they could forcibly "have sex with them" (NIV). I flipped back to the scholarly book that pointed out that if "all the men from every part of the city" wanted to rape the visitors, it wasn't about their orientation, but about something else. Why? Because it wasn't logically possible for an *entire city* to consist only of gay men. Rather, they explained, in that ancient culture men raping male strangers was a common demonstration of power and dominance.

Another interesting point was drawn from Lot's response to the angry mob. When Lot tried to calm them down, he made them a counteroffer. He said they could have his two virgin daughters instead. In addition to being an appalling act toward his daughters, this suggested he knew the mob could be pacified by women. Lot lived in the city, so he knew these men well. If he'd known them to be gay, the last thing he would have done is offer them a sexual opportunity with anyone female.

I wondered, "Why *was* Sodom judged by God?" The men's thirst for violent gang rape seemed one reason at least—and had nothing to do with homosexuality. I followed a few footnotes and found the book of Ezekiel shed helpful light on it. Ezekiel directly states that the "sin of Sodom" was inhospitality and a lack of social justice, as the people "did not aid the poor and needy" (16:49–50). The same reason was echoed in the book of Hebrews, which assumed that readers would be familiar with the story of Sodom and the angelic visitors: "Do not neglect to show hospitality to strangers, for by doing that some have entertained angels without knowing it" (13:2).

Suddenly the library door creaked open—a few snow-covered students had made their way back into the college to resume work. I shoved the books back onto the shelf, not keen to be spotted in the Sexual Ethics section of the library in case it raised questions, and headed out.

12

The next morning, I pulled my dorm-room curtains open to see heavy snowflakes were still cascading out of the stone-gray sky. I'd had a night of disturbed sleep, as my mind was racing with questions about the books I'd read the evening before. "I'm getting sucked into the sort of ideas my church friends back home warned me about . . ." I worried to myself, as I pulled on jeans and a hoodie, ready for another day of university.

I tried to work on an essay all day in the library, but was hoping everyone might leave so I could sneak over to the Sexual Ethics section again. The dinner bell rang, perhaps the fastest way to summon any gang of hungry students. *Maybe,* I thought, *if I skip the evening meal, I'll have the place to myself.* And I did.

Lurking beside the H for Homosexuality shelf, I grabbed a book and started reading about Romans chapter 1, the crucial New Testament text thought to condemn same-sex relationships. This theologian argued Romans 1 had nothing to do with being gay and Christian. "Hmm," I said under my breath, "I'm not so sure . . ." He pointed out that St. Paul specifically addressed people who had "traded the worship of God for the worship of idols"—they had rejected God completely. On that basis, it could not apply to LGBTQ+ Christians who were putting Christ first in their lives.

The book also noted that what St. Paul criticized was "unnatural relations." Paul's viewpoint would have been heavily influenced by his culture, where relationships between people of the same gender were seen as the result of insatiable lust, practiced by those who could have been content with heterosexual sex but were looking for novel experiences with motives of excess and greed and an absence of self-control. So the activities he referenced were about excess and treating others like functionaries, not about equal partners, and not about people who followed Jesus. The book's author pointed out that for gay people, a committed same-sex partnership wasn't an outlet for "uncontrolled lust"—it was an opportunity to "sanctify their desires" in the context of a covenantal union.

I was fascinated to learn St. Paul used the same Greek word—translated as "unnatural"—elsewhere. In 1 Corinthians 11:2–16 he declared that men having long hair, and women praying without their heads covered, were both "unnatural" and therefore a "disgrace." Using that same word for hairstyles and head coverings suggested that there were cultural values at work here rather than fixed, timeless moral imperatives. No women wore head coverings in any church I'd been a part of, and no one told men they were sinning if they grew their hair past their shoulders.

Leaning against the library shelf, I took all of this information in. The author certainly seemed to have done his research—and it made a surprising amount of sense. I felt as though I'd cracked open Pandora's box and it unsettled me immensely. I needed to get some head space to think.

Wycliffe Hall had a beautiful chapel, with a wooden ceiling and wonderful echoey acoustics, so I headed there. It was empty, so I sat down at the piano. In the silence, my mind kept returning to the books I'd been reading and how well researched the scholars seemed. They appeared to have strong, robust answers to my difficult questions. Could I, someday, dare to be openly gay and Christian? Based on these new ways to understand the biblical texts, perhaps I could. But making that decision would turn my life upside down in ways that terrified me, and my conscience was still skeptical about "liberal" theology.

For now, all I knew was one thing: I wanted God to be my priority. Whatever conclusions I would reach on this difficult issue, I wanted him to be first in my life. Obedience to him mattered more to me than anything else.

My fingers ran over the black and white piano keys, and I started to make up some lyrics. After a while they took shape, and I scribbled them into a notebook.

ABOVE ALL ELSE

Jesus, my passion in life is to know you.
May all other goals bow down to this journey of loving you more.
Jesus, you've showered your goodness on me,
Given your gifts so freely,
But there's one thing I'm longing for.

So, hear my heart's cry
And my prayer for this life:

Above all else, above all else,
Above all else,
Jesus, give me yourself.

Savior, the more that I see your beauty,
The more that I glimpse your glory,
My heart is captured by you.

Jesus, you are my greatest treasure.
Nothing this world can offer ever compares to you.

So, hear my heart's cry
And my prayer for this life:

Above all else, above all else,
Above all else,
Jesus, give me yourself.

The song summed up the way I felt as I sat there in the chapel that night. Nothing meant more to me than my faith. As I tried to figure out what to do with the new theology I was reading, God was still my highest priority and my greatest love.

I introduced the song a few weeks later at church, and people easily caught on to the simple chorus. Vineyard Records showed interest in it too, saying, "Send us a demo of that song—we'll record it on a future CD," which they did.

As doors opened for me to sing at Vineyard national conferences, it became my most requested song so far. And every time I played it, I remembered the evening in Wycliffe chapel when I wrote it as a prayer. It expressed my commitment to follow God, even through all the confusion I was battling.

As the snow melted and another spring rolled around in Oxford, I received the news that I would be taking a new class: Contemplative Spirituality. My tutors would be two globally renowned thinkers in this field, a nun called Sister Benedicta Ward and an Eastern Orthodox bishop named Kallistos Ware.

What I would learn from them would introduce me to a deep and ancient world—the roots of Christianity in the monastic tradition. It would expose my obsession with having a faith that felt watertight—one where everything neatly added up—and remind me that faith should be rooted in mystery and wonder rather than in sterile claims of certainty.

Walking underneath spring's cloudless skies, I headed to my first tutorial with Sister Benedicta. She was known around the world as the leading translator of the writings of the desert fathers and mothers, a group of Christians who in the third century withdrew to the deserts of Egypt to seek God. When I arrived, my eyes scanned Sister Benedicta's study. Her shelves were lined with books that looked older than I was. A few simple religious icons hung on the walls. Peace was tangible in the room and I felt my shoulders relax. I sensed she was a person who knew God deeply and welcomed the curious minds of her students; this was a safe place to ask questions.

As Sister Benedicta led me through the writings of the desert fathers, they struck me as highly relevant to twenty-first-century faith. One in particular jumped out. It was an ancient story about Abbot Anthony, later revered as St. Anthony the Great and considered the father of all monks. Renowned for his wisdom, Anthony was often visited in the desert by those wanting to learn from him. One day a group came to see him that included one of his respected students, Abbot Joseph. The story went like this:

> Some elders once came to Abbot Anthony, and there was also with them Abbot Joseph. Wishing to test them, Abbot Anthony brought the conversation to the Holy Scriptures. And he began, from the youngest, to ask them the meaning of this or that text.
>
> Each one replied as best he could, but Abbot Anthony said to them: "You have not understood it yet."
>
> After them all, he asked Abbot Joseph: "What about you? What do you say this text means?"
>
> Abbot Joseph replied, "I do not know what it means."

> *Abbot Anthony said, "Truly Abbot Joseph alone has found the way, for he replied that he knows not."*

When I read the final sentence of that story, an unexpected smile crept across my face. *Truly Abbot Joseph alone has found the way, for he replied that he knows not.* It was so refreshing that Joseph was praised for *not* knowing the answer. It stood in stark contrast to my conservative faith, where we prided ourselves on having every difficult theological question figured out.

But here in the desert fathers' story was a different system of measurement, one in which embracing the mystery of God—and admitting we could never fully figure out the answers—was seen as praiseworthy and mature, not as weak and lacking in faith. It felt like inhaling lungfuls of fresh air.

I met with Sister Benedicta week after week and relief crept over me. For years, I'd lived under the heavy burden of obsessively needing to get every theological question answered and tied up with a neat bow. She was gently helping me to see how absurd that was—God could not be placed in a box or fully understood by our limited human minds. In the depths of her relationship with God, I could see a far richer way of approaching faith—one rooted not in anxiety and arrogance, but in wonder and mystery.

That semester, the Contemplative Spirituality course introduced me to some of the best-known Christian "mystics": St. John of the Cross, St. Teresa of Avila, and Julian of Norwich and a text called *The Cloud of Unknowing*. All of them wrote about mystery within the Christian faith, that we had to do a lot of "unknowing" as we let go of our unrealistic, fixed ideas about God. These ideas felt refreshingly honest. God was vastly beyond human minds, so faith should never be treated like an algebraic equation that must perfectly add up.

The second tutor in my Contemplative Spirituality course was Bishop Kallistos Ware, one of the most revered Eastern Orthodox theologians in the world. I loved his deep sonorous voice and long white beard, and couldn't help thinking that he resembled the academic equivalent of Santa Claus. Bishop Kallistos explained:

> In the Christian context, we do not mean by a "mystery" merely that which is baffling and an insoluble problem. A mystery is, on the contrary, something that is revealed for our understanding, but that we never understand exhaustively, because it leads into the depth or the darkness of God. The eyes are closed—but they are also opened.[1]

The more I pondered it, the more absurd it seemed that theology could be neatly explained in a theology textbook. Of course it couldn't— but this was a big departure from the culture of certainty I'd been raised in. The obsession with fixed answers felt increasingly wrong to me: if God can fit into a box, it's no longer God we are dealing with but someone made in our own image.

Perhaps, I thought, *it even had resonance with the commandment not to make "graven images."* Evangelical theology seemed to paint a picture of God—a graven image of sorts—and tell everyone else it was the *only* likeness of him that existed. As the biblical scholar Peter Enns points out, rather than being a sign of mature faith, this approach could be seen as committing "the sin of certainty."[2] It was interesting to think it all over, and I found myself agreeing.

Bishop Kallistos introduced me to a new perspective on what it meant to be faithful to Christian history. We weren't diminishing it by changing our minds on certain things; that was all part of the journey. As he put it, "Holy tradition is not static but dynamic, not defensive but exploratory, not closed and backward-facing but open to the future."[3]

He patiently explained: "Tradition is not merely a formal repetition of what was stated in the past, but it is an active reexperiencing of the

Christian message in the present. The only true tradition is living and creative, formed from the union of human freedom with the grace of the Spirit."[4]

This made me think of my studies on slavery and women's equality and how stunned I'd been that the church had got things so wrong. The "grace of the Spirit" had finally helped change those traditions, and the church was far better for it.

As the spirituality course neared its end, Bishop Kallistos gave me a copy of his book *The Orthodox Way*. One passage in it remains, to this day, one of the most beautiful summaries of faith I have ever encountered: "It is not the task of Christianity to provide easy answers to every question, but to make us progressively aware of a mystery. God is not so much the object of our knowledge as the cause of our wonder."[5]

This concept stayed with me throughout the rest of my theology degree—it seemed to sum up everything I had learned. I'd gone to Oxford to get answers, but I was learning that faith was less of a mathematical problem to calculate and more about surrendering to the vastness of God. We can love him wholeheartedly and follow him unswervingly, but we can never fully comprehend the Being who created us out of the dust and gave us breath. Honest faith begins with surrender and matures into wonder.

13

A heavy bell chimed from a tall spire, and a sea of undergraduates walked across a black-and-white-checkered marble floor. It was time for *finals*, the exams that would determine whether we passed or failed the degree. We were all a bundle of nerves. The pressure was immense, and students all around me had been swallowing caffeine tablets and all manner of other substances to pull revision all-nighters.

We made our way up a huge stone staircase to the examination hall. It was university regulation that we had to wear subfusc—the white shirt and black gown with tails and the flat mortarboard hat. Usually in these outfits we'd all run around pretending to be superheroes, with the tails of the gowns flying behind us like Superman's cape. Today there was no joking around—every face was etched with anxiety.

As tradition demands, Oxford students wear a white carnation in their buttonhole for their first finals exam. For the following ones, they wear a pink carnation. Then for the last examination, they wear a red one. This communicates to everyone around them where they are in their finals slog—just starting, in the middle, or at the end.

I couldn't wait for the afternoon to arrive when I could switch my pink carnation for a red one and walk up the stone staircase to my last exam. When the bell rang to signal the end of those three hours, a wave of relief washed over me. Somehow I'd made it through finals in one piece.

Staggering out into the bright light of the June afternoon, I'd forgotten that people would be there to congratulate us. By tradition, students from the years below wait outside the exam building for the emerging "finalists." If they see someone with a red carnation, they shower them with champagne and confetti.

When I saw those students running toward us, popping the cork of a bottle and spraying champagne in our direction, I burst out laughing. We all got doused in the expensive alcohol (slightly wasted on me, a teetotaler) and had boxes of confetti shaken over our heads. The result left us a sticky, colorful, grinning mess. Cheering loudly, they hoisted a couple of us onto their shoulders, spinning us around.

We headed off to the Turf Tavern, Oxford's oldest pub, dating back to 1381. I bought a coke and joined the noisy celebrations. "After this, how about we go punting?" one student shouted. An hour later, exhausted but happily willing, a gang of us headed down High Street toward Magdalen Bridge and the river.

"Punting," found in both Oxford and Cambridge, involves a long gondola-style boat that you propel along by pushing a long metal pole against the riverbed. Oxford's main river was filled with students attempting to master this skill, usually with a great deal of splashing and screaming and the occasional person falling dramatically overboard to the sounds of yet more laughter. We unmoored a college punt from the side of the river and all climbed in. It felt amazing to lie back in the reclining seat, stretch my legs out, and watch as we wound our way lazily around the bends of the River Cherwell, passing libraries, spires, and turrets on either side.

I breathed a long sigh of relief knowing that my exams were done. Whatever lay ahead, I was now twenty-one and had survived the pressures of Oxford without failing my course, without losing my faith, and without kissing any girls. All in all, that seemed like success to me. Lying back in the punt, blinking in the sunlight, and seeing my fellow students splashing one another with river water, I felt the tension leave my shoulders, and I smiled.

A few weeks later, the narrow streets were crammed with cars collecting students. Parents and siblings helped lug bags and belongings out of dorm rooms and into waiting vehicles. The college quads buzzed with smiling but solemn faces. There was much hugging and snapping of photos, as we unwillingly bid each other good-bye after our three memorable years together. It was bittersweet—the relief of exams done mixed with the melancholy of letting go of this chapter of our lives.

We were going our separate ways, to new jobs scattered across the country and the globe. Personally, I wasn't going far. Keen to stay in Oxford a little longer, I'd signed up for an internship at the Vineyard church, where I could be mentored in songwriting and continue to sing at national conferences. This was still the career I wanted to pursue—worship was the heartbeat of my existence, and I couldn't imagine doing anything else.

The internship kept me extremely busy. It also plunged me into full-time church work and a community where everyone held deeply traditional beliefs about marriage and sexuality. Away from the Oxford tutors and books, I let the big questions I'd begun to ponder about LGBTQ+ theology dwindle away. Loneliness was a daily battle, and all my friends were dating, or getting engaged. I shelved my pain, gritted my teeth, and told myself I could manage to stay single and just focus on my faith and my ministry instead.

Career-wise, things were moving fast. Before the year was out, I was sitting opposite a UK record-label representative with a recording contract in her hand, being offered the chance to go into a professional studio for the first time. I recorded my first album at ICC Studios, near Brighton, a hallowed place in the Christian world. It would be mixed and mastered at a truly legendary music venue—Abbey Road in London, where the Beatles recorded almost all their records.

Outside Abbey Road Studios stands the famous road crossing immortalized on the cover of the Beatles' 1969 album. I walked across it, feeling nostalgic about all the musicians who had trodden that ground before me.

The chief mastering engineer, Chris Blair, welcomed me into his audio suite, decked out with vast speakers and a mixing desk containing more knobs, sliders, and dials than a plane's cockpit. Chris had begun his career there back in 1969, starting as a basic tape operator. The first summer he worked there in this junior role, the Beatles had come in and recorded. He'd gone on to become a world-renowned mastering engineer, and on the walls were the album covers of famous artists he'd worked with: Radiohead, Paul McCartney, Ringo Starr, the Commodores, Olivia Newton-John, Marvin Gaye, Diana Ross, Stevie Wonder, Genesis, Kate Bush, Morrissey, Andrew Lloyd Webber, Sting, the Cure. He'd even mastered Queen's "Bohemian Rhapsody."

When my CD was done and copies arrived in the mail, it was amazing to hold it in my hands. Having my own album ramped up the pace of my career—before long I was going back and forth regularly to the States and Canada as well as playing across the UK and Europe. Music was proving a viable job, so I gave it all the energy I had; I was doing what I had always dreamed of—leading worship and writing songs for the church. At least one part of my life now felt fulfilling and exciting, and I poured everything I had into it. Very soon I would find that even more doors were about to open.

Not long after the launch of my album, I was in California playing at a Christian conference in San Diego with three thousand people in attendance. After I sang, a man in an expensive-looking black suit approached me backstage.

"Hey! I wanted to catch you . . ." he said, extending a handshake. He was from a Christian label owned by EMI Records. Giving me his business card, he said he and his wife would love to take me to dinner and talk. They drove me to the Hotel del Coronado, located on Coronado Island just off the San Diego coast, a stunning place that had been a favorite haunt of American presidents as well as Charlie Chaplin, Katharine Hepburn, and Clark Gable.

I wasn't used to being schmoozed like this and felt rather overwhelmed as I took in the beautiful chandeliers, dark wood ceilings, and luxurious red carpets. Outside, we sat at a dining table overlooking the ocean and watched the sun go down. It was a wonderful evening, and they couldn't have been kinder to me.

As our evening came to a close, he asked if I would be open to the idea of moving to the US full-time. If I was, he said, EMI would be interested in signing me to its Christian label. This was a lot to process: a move across the pond and a totally new life in a new country would be a huge step. I told him I'd give it serious thought.

Nervous but excited, I emailed a few weeks later, saying I was genuinely open to the move if they were able to make me a formal offer. He said the next step was to play in front of their staff team in Nashville, where their Christian music HQ was located. They invited me to sing at a megachurch in Franklin, just outside Nashville, so within a couple of months I was flying to Tennessee for a weeklong visit.

A long line of men and women, some in black suits, some in leather jackets, stood at the back of the venue. Peering around the backstage curtain, I'd seen them all arrive and take their places. As I began to sing, it was intimidating to see the record label staff watching, as they scribbled into notebooks, exchanged looks among themselves, and whispered into each other's ears.

After I played my final song, I walked into the backstage area, whispering a prayer of thanks and relief. The friendly man who'd treated me to dinner at the swanky Hotel del Coronado appeared, saying, "Everyone loved you. Come to the label building tomorrow. Let's all get around a table and talk."

Visiting the EMI office was an intimidating experience. From the large lobby a gold elevator took me up to the top floor and the label head's suite, complete with a panoramic view across the city. I was nervous, but the record executives put me at ease and even managed to find a cup of Earl Grey tea for me, which made me smile.

As well as saying positive things about my singing and songwriting, they helped me understand how the Christian music industry worked in the States and how vastly different it was from in the UK, where church music only occupied a tiny niche. If I was moving to start a new life there, I'd need to know how this genre of music worked.

In the US, they explained, Christian music was sold in all the main supermarkets, on the same shelves as the Top 40 pop and mainstream rock albums. I knew England had a small churchgoing population of around 2 percent in weekly attendance, but the US had vastly more, especially in the South, where there was a church on every corner. Ever a geek, I was interested in statistics, so with a few hits on Google I found that 89 percent of Americans believed in God, 55 percent prayed daily, and 50 percent attended a church service at least once a month.

Catering to that huge chunk of the population were megachurches, where literally thousands of worshippers attended every Sunday. Big Christian festivals were held every summer rivaling the scale of the UK's Glastonbury. Christian music in the US was a billion-dollar industry, with radio stations, merchandise, and vast bookstore chains. It was gargantuan in scale. I'd known about megachurches already, from my Anaheim trip, but understanding how the whole religious music industry worked was like staring into a supersized world; it was a little overwhelming.

I finished my Earl Grey tea, and our meeting drew to a close. The EMI executives were keen to have me on board; they just needed to speak to their wider team and make sure they could formally offer me a contract. "We want you here," one of them said, "but it can't be a definite yes until we get the green light about an official deal. Give us a few weeks to talk with our contract department," they said.

I flew back to the UK and, as the weeks passed, I wished the phone would hurry up and ring so I'd know whether they would offer me a firm contract. Not wanting to seem pushy, I left the ball in their court. Eventually, six weeks had passed since the Nashville meeting, and I still hadn't received a call. Christmas was approaching, so everyone around me was getting into the festive spirit, but I was struggling to relax without knowing the answers about where my future lay.

14

Driving up the steep winding hill into my parents' village, I was look-ing forward to spending Christmas there. It was always nice to visit the place I grew up. I drove past the beautiful thirteenth-century parish church where I'd gone every Sunday since I was twelve. This year, as we did every year, my parents and I would attend the Christmas Eve Nativity service.

When I was younger, I'd been in the Nativity play myself. Mary, the angel Gabriel, a shepherd—I'd played most roles through the years and loved it. It was an all-age affair too; my dad was always one of the three wise men. Each year he'd wear a robe made of old curtains and a golden crown that always seemed a little too big. It usually slipped down over his eyes by the time he delivered his key line, "I bring gold," laying his gift near the manger.

This Christmas Eve, I wasn't in the play—although my long-suffering father was donning the golden crown and playing a wise man with his usual good humor. So my mum and I were keen to get a good seat to witness it all. I was especially looking forward to my favorite moment—every year, near the end of the service, we turned off the lights and sang "Silent Night" by candlelight, which felt truly magical. To this day it remains one of my most treasured moments each Christmas.

The pews were packed, and the only seats left were right at the front, so we sat down there. I felt cheerful, but also distracted, as the record label in Nashville still hadn't been in touch. My life felt up in the air. Would I soon be packing everything and moving to the States? It was incredibly hard not to have clarity and be able to plan.

I looked at my watch, mentally calculating the time-zone difference: five o'clock in England was about eleven in the morning in Nashville. My heart sank, because I was sure there was little chance anyone would be in the office the day before Christmas. I had to let it go and assume they'd be in touch in January.

My thoughts snapped back to the present as the organ blasted out the opening chords of the first carol. Small children dressed as shepherds, with dishcloths wrapped around their heads, delivered their lines with heart-melting cuteness. Kids in angel costumes declared, "Glory to God in the highest," in their loudest voices, adjusting their lopsided halos made from wire clothes hangers.

Adults played their roles with great gusto—the innkeeper, the chief shepherd, the narrator—everyone was fully in the spirit of the evening. My dad, with his signature booming voice, did an excellent job as a wise man, and for once his gold crown seemed to stay in place.

My favorite part of the night was approaching. Candles were handed out to everyone, and the lights were switched off. The organ began to play "Silent Night," and in the glow of the flickering candles we sang, "How silently, how silently, the wondrous gift is given." I looked around, cherishing the faces of my childhood school friends and my parents in the thirteenth-century village church, and sensed that God was close by. Everyone was smiling, enjoying the atmosphere of reverence and magical wonder as we shared the warm candlelit moment. It was absolutely beautiful.

Right then, a horrendously loud clanging noise interrupted us all. It was the loud ringtone of a mobile phone. And, worse still, I instantly realized it was mine. Horrified, I reached into my jacket pocket and silenced it. All eyes swung toward me, and I wanted the thirteenth-century wooden floor to swallow me up.

I now faced a dilemma. Even worse than my phone ringing intrusively would be actually taking the call. The rows were full, and the aisles were packed with extra chairs—getting over to the door and outside would take a feat of Olympic magnitude. But I knew if I didn't take this call, I'd be stuck all Christmas break without clarity about my future. It might be weeks before people fully reengaged with work in January. Gritting my teeth, I shuffled down the packed pew, past everyone clutching their service bulletins, still midsong. Finally reaching the eight-foot-tall oak door with its huge bronze handle, I closed it behind me with a heavy thud. Despite my best effort, I couldn't have made a less subtle exit.

It was utterly freezing outside. I hadn't worn a coat, assuming I'd be inside in the warm building all evening. Our village was also pitch-dark; we had no streetlights. So I stood in the inky blackness, listening to the voice on the other end of my phone. A cow in the field opposite the church watched me, its eyes glowing in the night, as it lazily chewed a mouthful of frosty grass.

The EMI exec said they'd made a decision. I held my breath in anticipation. Even the cow stopped chewing, sensing my tense posture.

"We've decided," he continued, "it's a go from everyone here—we're saying yes." A huge grin spread across my face.

I was elated, but also freezing. I couldn't feel my fingers or toes, but I continued to stand in the dark village lane, telling the exec that I wanted to accept the offer and move to Nashville.

He said I'd need to get a US work permit, so he'd give me the phone number of Nashville's best immigration lawyer. "Do you have a pen and paper, so I can give that to you now?" he asked. Not wanting to admit that I was standing in a pitch-dark country road, surrounded only by a field of cows, I said, "Absolutely."

I scanned the street for something to write on, or with. My only option was the village notice board—but that December night it was covered in thick ice. As he read out the phone number, I licked my finger and wrote it into the layer of frost. I planned to grab a pen later from my parents' house and return to the notice board to copy it down.

The phone meeting ended, and he told me I was his very last call of the year before he headed off to Christmas with his family. As the closing hymn rang out—"O come let us adore him, Christ the Lord"—I snuck back into the service.

Debriefing with my parents over a cup of tea later, I told them I'd got the green light from the record label. My dad, an accountant, was understandably cautious. Would I be able to make ends meet? They weren't offering me much money as a signing bonus—how would I survive? Mum was worried about my emotional well-being. How would I cope alone in a new country? I'd be so far from family and friends. They were both happy at my news, but understandably concerned at the idea of me disappearing off to the other side of the world.

The next morning, I remembered I'd scribbled the immigration attorney's name and number on the ice-covered notice board on the street. But the sun had come up and a warmer day had unfolded. When I went to check, I found the numbers had melted and completely disappeared. I still smile about that every time I walk past that notice board in my parents' village. Note to self: never write crucial messages in ice.

PART III

America

15

As the news that I was moving to the States sank in, I began the process of applying for an American work permit. Eventually the voluminous paperwork was done, and I boarded a plane to Nashville. The first thing on my calendar was a signing meeting, where, on the top floor of the EMI building, I would put my signature on the long and detailed recording contract.

My lawyer had already gone over it, so I knew I was getting a fair deal and had his approval. But I was worried about something else—the "morals clause." Common in acting, athletics, and music deals, a morals clause allows the contract to be legally terminated if the person engages in behavior that brings disrepute to the employer. What "disrepute" meant in mainstream contracts was open to interpretation, but in the Christian music industry it had faith-based overtones and would be judged by evangelical standards of behavior. I knew that meant being openly gay or in a same-sex relationship would likely result in a one-way ticket out the door and the crashing and burning of my livelihood.

As Jennifer Knapp, another recording artist, wrote about her own

journey in American Christian music: "It's not unusual to have morality clauses woven into recording contracts. . . . The principal obligation
for every artist is to endorse and maintain that same evangelical stan-
dard, or look for another job."[1]

Nervously, I signed the contract knowing I was walking an emotional tightrope. I was excited to serve God with my music and looking
forward to a new chapter of life in a new country, but I was also terrified of what it meant for me emotionally and psychologically. Were
my feelings for women ever going away, and could I face a life of lonely
singleness forever?

My days at Oxford had led me to consider that being gay might not
be sinful, but I'd shelved those questions as my music career gathered
pace. Because of my career, my beliefs needed to remain traditional, so
at heart I continued to see myself as broken and shameful.

Other than the exorcism and the Catholic confession in my teens,
I'd still never told a single soul. I'd never acted on any of my feelings
for women, not even the briefest of kisses, and work had become my
sole focus. My emotional life was increasingly shut down and I was well
on my way to becoming a workaholic. I busied myself with the endless
logistics that come with moving to a new country. Alongside this, my
hectic touring schedule began.

The different internal time zones across the US were tough on my
body. I'd play a concert in California, then board a plane for five hours
to reach New York to sing there the next day. I felt the three-hour time
difference painfully; if I boarded a flight at nine o'clock at night in Los
Angeles, when I arrived in New York, it was five o'clock in the morning.
Relentlessly ping-ponging back and forth across the huge country, plus
regular flights farther afield to Europe, left me with constant jet lag.

One evening, one of the music-industry guys who'd clocked decades of living this way reached into his bag and pulled out a small bottle of pills. They were Tylenol PM, over-the-counter sleeping tablets.
"You won't manage this way of life without these—or a much stronger

version," he said. Handing me the bottle, he added, "Take one twenty minutes before you go to bed."

I nodded, anxious for something to help me beat jet lag. I took one that evening and sank into slumber more speedily than usual. Wary of becoming dependent on any form of medication, I thought, *I'll only take these when I'm exhausted.* But from that day forward, I found myself needing Tylenol PM nightly. Even in the first few weeks of my American music career, I was already entering survival mode.

The signing advance the label had given me was spent, almost entirely, on my immigration lawyer's costs in getting me the US work permit. The rest went to my management—as music managers typically take 15 percent of the artist's income. So I began my American life with zero in the bank.

The months rolled by, and the lifestyle was far more intense than I'd imagined. Days off didn't really exist, and every week looked the same. I was either at the label writing songs, in the studio recording them, or out on the road singing and doing promotional work.

Touring meant boarding the next plane, rehearsing the next band, playing my heart out, and collapsing into yet another cheap hotel bed, then getting up at the crack of dawn to catch another flight and do it all again. I was on the road in a foreign country, with hired musicians who were strangers to me, and it was nonstop without weekends or evenings to recover and rest.

Of course, there were bright spots too. I was doing what I'd dreamed of: a full-time career in Christian music. I was lucky, and I knew it. The adventure of living in the States was a lot of fun and a cultural learning experience. Although we speak the same language, the US and the UK are very different places.

First, I had to master the different terminology. Petrol was now "gas." What we Brits called the loo was now the "restroom." A flat was an "apartment" or "condo." Crisps were "chips," and chips were "fries." I made plenty of linguistic slipups during those early days.

One embarrassing error happened in a sermon I preached at a traditional church. I spoke about erasing fear and shame from our lives. In the UK, the word we use for an eraser is "rubber." I said from stage: "To make my point about removing shame and fear from our lives, I've brought packs of rubbers to hand out to you all, so you can take them home and remember this sermon every time you use them." There was a very awkward silence, and I had no idea why. Only after the service did a church member explain to me that in America erasers are just called "erasers." "Rubbers" refers to only one thing: condoms. As you can imagine, I never made that embarrassing mistake again.

As well as slipping up on words, another issue was my British accent. Occasionally, my pronunciation meant I'd get badly misunderstood in the simplest conversations. This happened the day I met the CEO of the biggest Christian radio network in America.

I was nervous to spend time with him; EMI told me he literally could make or break artists' careers by deciding who got radio play and who didn't. A lot rode on this visit—my new single had just come out and we needed to get it in heavy radio rotation on his vast network of 440 stations with 12 million weekly listeners.

The CEO's wife picked me up from the airport and drove me back to their house. She was wonderfully welcoming, chatting away about their latest project—remodeling their home and building a huge patio deck on the back, so they could sit outside and enjoy the view over the nearby trees.

When we got to the front door, he opened it. I decided to instantly strike up conversation based on what his wife had been telling me in the car. "Hi. It's lovely to meet you," I said as he shook my hand. Thinking their new wooden patio would be a great conversation topic, I added, "Your wife tells me you have an enormous deck."

Unfortunately, my clipped British accent made the last word sound like a different word altogether. He looked shocked. I realized what had happened and melted into a pool of bright-red embarrassment.

"The patio!" I blurted out. "She said you have a huge new patio on the back of your house that you're both really enjoying."

"Oh, the *deck*," he said, trying to suppress a massive smile. "Yes, we just had it built. Come on in. Let's sit out there and have some supper."

Nashville is a major hub for songwriters and is the epicenter of country music as well as Christian music. I quickly discovered a professional songwriter's workweek consists of scheduling back-to-back co-writing sessions, in the same way that businesspeople fill their appointment calendars with corporate meetings.

EMI had a suite of purpose-built writing rooms, each furnished with armchairs, guitars, a piano, and a coffee table. The walls were decorated with framed gold records, albums by EMI artists who'd sold millions of copies. Songwriters would book the rooms in two-hour blocks, often getting together with someone they'd never met before and attempting to craft a hit song from start to finish. This was new to me. I'd tried co-writing with a few other worship leaders in the UK, but we'd just gone to each other's houses and drunk tea, rarely actually finishing a song.

Nashville was a whole new world for me: writing with strangers, with the clock ticking and the pressure mounting to come up with a finished hit in just a couple of hours. This was not my style—songwriting had always been a very personal and introverted thing, rooted in times of worship. I wasn't sure I could do it on demand and with others I didn't even know. But I had to. Label staff told me that, from their research into Christian music sales, songs with multiple writers were performing better than those written by one person. So I needed to learn to get on with it.

Professional songwriters definitely have their quirks. One man always brought a potted cactus and his lucky pen. One woman couldn't write unless her dog was sitting under her chair. Whatever had worked for a previous Grammy-winning song (the cactus, the pen, the dog) had to be repeated at every session—just in case it had been the secret to that moment of inspiration. I suppose they were the musical equivalent of carrying a four-leaf clover.

Odd as they were, these rituals made me smile. I wondered if I'd develop my own eccentric habits, now that I was a professional song-writer. After all, I did like to bring my favorite mug to each session, so perhaps I was on a slippery slope toward owning a lucky cactus.

I took up residence in a writing room, as EMI needed at least ten songs for my first album. I was grateful whenever I heard my co-writer for the day was a worship leader too. Those sessions were a breath of fresh air, as we had much in common and worked the same way. We usually started our sessions with a time of prayer, played a few worship songs, then kept riffing around chords and phrases, experimenting until a song took shape. I experienced some amazing co-writing sessions like that, as the other writers had the same aim for their music as I did, but those days were the exception rather than the rule.

Songwriting is a tricky art. I was trying to write music that could be used in corporate worship meetings. This required a certain approach to lyrics, melody, and structure—the songs needed to be relatively simple and easy to sing and play. Pop writers preferred composing radio hits and loved elements of surprise and complexity in the chords and arrangements, and their phraseology just didn't resonate with me. The more pop writers I was paired up with, the more our collaborations sounded less and less like what I'd hoped for, and my personal connection to the music was minimal.

The label said my songs needed a commercial element; each album required radio play, and so a portion of the tunes had to be smooth, catchy, pop. Resigned to this, I didn't feel able to challenge the way my music was changing. My most popular songs, "Yesterday, Today and Forever," "Above All Else," "Captivated," and others, were written by me, alone, in times of prayer and worship. It confused me that they'd signed me based on songs like those, but wanted to take my writing in a different direction.

One of the A&R (artists and repertoire) guys the label assigned to manage me confessed he knew nothing about worship music or about the type of songs sung in churches. The resulting year was a series of car-crash moments where, at every turn, his lack of experience in worship music meant he made the wrong call on song choices, album artwork, marketing plans, and touring options. It was soul destroying.

As my music began to feel less and less like "me," the connection I had to my own songs diminished, the less impact I saw them having in churches, and the less I enjoyed playing them on tour. I'd made my career the sole focus of my life, having shelved all hopes of dating, marriage, and a family of my own. It was scary to sense my job was no longer filling the hole in my heart that it once had.

Behind all the busyness, my loneliness grew and grew. The moments in concerts when I sensed a connection with God and his people were dwindling as the songs took a more performance-based direction. Music had always been my outlet for faith and feelings, something that had brought me joy since I was fourteen, sitting in my room with my mum's guitar. Now it was increasingly about creating radio hits that would sell.

When I thought of my songwriting heroes, yes, I had huge respect for hallowed mainstream writers like Leonard Cohen, Bob Dylan, and Cole Porter, but my ultimate inspirations were the hymn writers from years gone by. I wanted to write for the church. One morning, working alone in a Nashville songwriting studio, I decided to pen my own modern-day hymn. My aim was to include some deep theology, as the hymn writers of old did, instead of producing a catchy radio hit. What I created that day would become the most requested song in my worship-leading career, "The Wonder of the Cross."

Every Easter Sunday, I received messages from churches that said it was their go-to song about the death and resurrection of Christ. Other churches told me they used the hymn every month, after they celebrated the Eucharist. I felt as though I'd finally written something that combined my love of theology with my love of music.

My most memorable live performance of that hymn was at the Crystal Cathedral, a vast building made almost entirely out of glass, in Orange County, California. Back in the 1980s when it was built, it cost $18 million and was said to be the largest glass building in the world. Although I didn't agree with the ethics of the high-budget building (surely that money could have been spent on better things) or other aspects of the church's theology, the experience of playing there was certainly unforgettable.

With a live orchestra behind me, I was blown away by how the hymn came to life. The church had one of the largest pipe organs in the world, and it resonated through every glass pane of that building. The performance wasn't just for the 2,500 people seated in the cathedral; it was also broadcast live for the TV program *Hour of Power*. I remember how amazed I was when I googled the viewing statistics: 1.3 million viewers watching from more than 150 countries. I was terribly nervous I'd get the words wrong or sing out of tune under the pressure, but thankfully the orchestra played so beautifully that the music swept me up and carried me along.

16

"Look down the lens! Give me some attitude!" one of the photographers called out to me. "Come on, *work it!*"

I stood awkwardly on the spot, unused to professional photo shoots and clueless about how to "work it" for the camera. We were in a big white warehouse the label had rented for the day, filled with racks of clothing, a stylist, a makeup artist, a hair team, and a group of EMI staff. Everyone had their eyes on me as two photographers and their assistants encouraged me to move around and try a few different poses.

For a relatively shy Christian girl, this was a lot to take in. I blushed and asked if we could take a quick break. Everyone was friendly and well-meaning; we needed photos for the album cover, so it was just part of the job. But it was a world away from my background and culture, and I was facing it alone, in a new world.

"Could we persuade you to wear this dress and these killer heels?" the stylist asked me. I explained that I wasn't a big fan of dresses and that I'd never gotten the hang of wearing high heels and keeping my balance. Thankfully, they dropped the idea of photographing me in a flowing dress standing in a waist-high swimming pool of water.

All of this felt like a different universe from singing in British churches. High-pressure situations had become a daily occurrence. If it wasn't a photo shoot with a roomful of label people staring at me, it was a radio interview going out internationally, or a live TV segment being broadcast to millions. Soaring adrenaline levels were now the norm, and my body was complaining. I was loving this new career, but it was taking a big toll on me. Other musicians pushed themselves hard too, but my workaholism had deeper roots: I was trying to outrun my own pain. If I could never be in a relationship or married, work needed to be everything, so I gave it every waking moment.

In the scarce free time I had, I tried to make friends in Tennessee. Being a British girl in Nashville was a constant source of amusement to the people I spent time with, and it made me smile too. These friends loved my accent and would copy it. Sometimes at dinner, they'd pretend we were all British, to see if they could convince the server. After a while they became excellent at disguising their Southern accents and perfecting the art of sounding British, fooling many into believing that we were "all here on vacation from England."

Some of it was fun socially, but the same old issues constantly resurfaced. A couple of guys I'd become close friends with told me they had feelings for me. When I said I didn't want to date them, they'd needed some space to get over it, and our friendship had ended. I was devastated to lose them, as they'd become a ray of sunshine in my lonely, busy life.

It was tricky with the girls I'd befriended too. They constantly chatted about which guy they wanted to date and constantly asked me which of the men I might be interested in. It felt isolating—a throwback to high school—as I couldn't join in these conversations or go on any of the double dates that formed a core part of the social scene.

Tennessee was very traditional when it came to gender roles. Compared to life in the UK, it was like turning back the clock. Men of all ages called me Miss Vicky or ma'am. Guys always opened doors for women. And Christians in the South were often married by nineteen or twenty.

This was, in part, lovely. The kindness and hospitality of American Southerners stood in stark contrast to the aloofness of most London-ers. In Tennessee, older women took me under their wing and baked me no end of casseroles and pot pies, all served with pitchers of sweet tea. There was always room for me at the table with these families, and I was grateful. But I feared that welcome would end in a heartbeat if they ever found out I was gay.

I was a tomboy and a feminist and had gentle but strongly held opinions. This didn't make for a good fit with the Southern men I was around. I believed women shouldn't have to stay home to cook and clean; they were entitled to their own career if they wanted one.

I was also uncomfortable with the way many Southern men took the lead in relationships and in home life. I knew I didn't want to wear dresses or have kids, and I didn't think the role of wives was to serve their husbands. I also wasn't willing to join in dinner conversations about how awful gay people were and how same-sex relationships were ruining so-ciety; I stayed noticeably quiet. Increasingly, I knew I wasn't fitting in.

The same wall I built to keep part of me in was also, emotionally, keeping everyone out. With the grueling work schedule I was keeping, my social life needed to be replenishing, but for the most part, it wasn't. Much of me existed behind an invisible wall, not able to talk about what I was really dealing with. Because of that, friendships brought their moments of joy, but overall felt fairly superficial.

As the months in the States gradually turned into years, I experi-enced the strange cultural shifts that others who'd moved to other countries had warned me about. Years earlier, an Australian friend who'd relocated to London had told me that after a while nowhere felt like home anymore.

She said it was like blending colors. Originally as an Australian, she'd been "yellow"; then she'd moved to the UK, which could be imagined as "blue." The two had merged, so now she was "green." When she went back to Australia she wasn't yellow anymore, as the UK culture and lifestyle had changed her—she'd been in London for years and felt part British. But when she was in the UK, she wasn't entirely blue either, as she would always be part Aussie and therefore different. She said being green meant nowhere was home. Wherever she was, she felt like an outsider to some degree.

At the time, I'd thought this sounded a bit bleak and dramatic. But after I experienced it myself, I started to wholeheartedly agree. If the UK was yellow and the US was blue, I was becoming green and feeling less and less as though I belonged anywhere.

If I went back to the UK to visit, I didn't quite fit; American culture had rubbed off on me. My accent had a bit of a twang now, and I found myself saying I was going to the "restroom" instead of the "loo." Americans saw me as quiet and reserved, but on trips home to England I'd got strange looks for being "too friendly," for striking up conversations with strangers on public transport or at grocery checkouts, which was the norm when I was stateside but never done in England.

My behaviors and my cultural outlook had changed. I was now "green"—and it felt lonely. When asked in casual conversations by unsuspecting strangers "So where's home?," it created a minor existential crisis and brought tears to my eyes. I didn't belong anywhere.

The one place I found solace and could finally exhale was in the air. On planes, I felt free. I was among strangers and had time to be alone with my thoughts. Planes were full of people in-between. They weren't home; they were between spaces. It was a green zone, neither yellow nor blue.

Up there, no one knew that I didn't belong anywhere. Up there, very few people were with their significant other or their family. Most people were in-between. And I liked that. Up there, I felt free. Beyond countries or cultures, I was floating in a neutral place.

I usually took overnight red-eye flights, as they were the cheapest. I'd swallow one of my trusted Tylenol PM sleeping tablets and let the tiredness sweep over me. It felt like a strange limbo, but up there, in the in-between, where no one quite belonged to the people around them, I experienced the closest thing to peace that I had.

Leading worship still brought me immense joy. I loved it as much as ever—looking out at a church full of people, teaching them my new songs, and experiencing God's presence together. It was deeply meaningful, and I felt lucky to do it as my full-time job.

But years were passing, and the relentless schedule was wearing my body down. Money was very tight, as the recording industry had been hit by the digital age, and downloads and streaming were killing the old business model. We all suffered as a result; gig budgets decreased, and record advances shrank. By chance, at the same time, airlines started to charge more for checked baggage, so it cost a fortune to take all the band equipment and cases of CDs and merchandise from state to state. Emotionally and physically, it was grueling, and now financially I wasn't making ends meet.

I often wondered if I should just move back to the UK, but this never seemed a viable option for me. A full-time career in church music was my dream, and that was virtually impossible in the UK; making a living relied on bookings from megachurches, airplay on huge Christian radio networks, and forty-city tours—all of which were unique to North America. Executives and managers in Nashville kept reminding me that "thousands of people would do anything for this opportunity," so the pressure to feel grateful weighed on me, and I tried to stifle my concerns.

Everyone around me told me I was living the dream, but in reality it looked like empty hotel rooms, heavy equipment, and endless pressure to smile, sing, say the right things, and keep quiet about my utter exhaustion, and my sexuality.

I was now in my late twenties, and most of my Christian friends were married or engaged. I had no clear answer to give to the guys who asked me out. Many of them were wonderful, and it was tough not to tell them the truth: I just wasn't attracted to men. Instead, I had to find excuses, none of which seemed to ring true. Usually they walked away feeling hurt and rejected.

One of those situations became extremely serious. I was out on tour and, due to budget constraints, didn't have a road manager with me, so I was in charge. It was just me and three session musicians, various players chosen from the industry who would rotate depending on who was available that week.

One of these musicians, Tyler (not his real name), told me he'd developed a major crush on me. Tyler believed that he and I were destined to be married and didn't seem able to take no for an answer. Because I couldn't talk honestly about my gay orientation, it created a weird vacuum. He knew I was single, and because we got on like a house on fire and had so much in common, he couldn't understand why I wouldn't give dating him a try.

As the months went on, his crush seemed to turn into an obsession. He was in a lot of emotional pain and became increasingly withdrawn, angry about my lack of romantic interest. I tried to believe it would get easier, not wanting to lose him from my band, as his musicianship was excellent and he could be a thoughtful, kind guy. But for now, that side of him seemed to have been swallowed up by pain.

After the closing night of a weeklong camp where we'd led thousands of young people in worship, I asked my band members where Tyler was. We needed to clear the stage and get ready to leave.

No one knew. I remembered he'd looked very strange during the final songs we'd played; his face had been blank and expressionless, rather than engaging with the rest of the band or the sea of people watching us. As soon as we'd finished the song, he'd walked offstage, and no one had seen him since. That had been at least forty-five minutes ago.

A few minutes later, looking as if he'd seen a ghost, one of the team ran up to me and said, "I don't know how to tell you this . . ." He explained that Tyler had tried to commit suicide in a backstage locker room. "We found him there a few minutes ago, struggling to breathe. We're figuring out what medical help he might need, and also trying to contact his parents."

It was awful. An unimaginable shock. I felt light-headed, dizzy, and sick. My heart ached for Tyler and the pain that had driven him to this.

One of the conference organizers had run over and joined us too. Looking frustrated, he chimed in, "You need to handle this extremely carefully. I don't want anyone on the premises who might be a danger to themselves; we have thousands of teenagers here, and we have our brand reputation to protect. Take care of this right away."

The weight of the situation hit me—I was in charge. I felt totally out of my depth, and my eyes swam as I scrolled through the numbers on my phone, trying to figure out who would even be awake at such a late hour.

The event organizer added a final comment: "This may be uncomfortable to hear, but I think it's important to pass on all that we know. When we asked Tyler why he tried to kill himself, he said it was because of you—because you broke his heart by rejecting him."

I went pale. This was another layer to the story I hadn't been ready for.

Pausing to catch my breath, I dialed my manager's number. Because money was so tight, we'd been traveling on tour without him, knowing he was just a phone call away. But in that moment, I felt utterly panicked by the pressure of being in charge. Tearfully, I told him all that had happened and asked for help with the logistics of getting Tyler help and the rest of us home.

The next few days went by in slow motion. Tyler was picked up by his parents and would stay with them for a few weeks. Meanwhile in Nashville, my manager, my other bandmates, and I tried to debrief what had happened and the ways it had affected our team.

One thing was clear: there was no way he could continue to play in my band. So my manager agreed to make the call and tell him that news. I assumed this would be the outcome expected by everyone, including Tyler himself.

In the days that followed, I discovered this was not the case. Tyler reacted badly to the news. He was hurt and outraged and began making threats.

My manager, and other band members, were the ones keeping in touch with him and handling the sensitive phone calls. They decided not to tell me what type of threats he was making, hoping things would cool down. I had to leave Nashville again for another gig, as the tour needed to continue despite the shock we all felt from the suicide attempt. With a new musician filling Tyler's old spot, we headed to the next venue, an arena in Canada where eight thousand people were expecting us.

I'd taken a later flight than the rest of the band, as I had a radio interview to do that afternoon; this happened more often than not—flying alone was pretty much my norm. As I stood in the airport on a layover, my phone rang, and the voice on the other end sounded panicked. It was one of my bandmates saying he'd heard from Tyler again: "He's furious not to be on tour with us. And he's still threatening stuff . . ."

The airline announcements blared out loudly, and for a moment I couldn't hear the voice on the other end. "Sorry, what?" I asked.

"Are you somewhere private?" he asked me. Not waiting to hear back, he carried on: "Look, Tyler is threatening to . . . rape you."

The words echoed inside my head, and the room grew blurry. He continued, "He told me he's really serious. He knows where you live, and where you're traveling to. He said he's coming after you, to make you pay for rejecting him."

I couldn't speak. I just listened, taking it in.

"It doesn't seem like a joke or a throwaway comment, Vicky," he went on. "Tyler has phoned me incessantly for the past forty-eight hours, raging and saying he's going to come back to Nashville and rape you as punishment for rejecting him romantically and for taking him out of the band. I didn't want to tell you, but I feel like I have no choice . . ."

My knees became weak and unsteady. I went into shock, and the phone slipped out of my hand and onto the floor. Shaking, I knelt down on the airport carpet to find it and scrambled to reach behind an airport trash bin where it had landed.

But once I was down on my knees, the shock of those words paralyzed me. I was already exhausted and stunned from his suicide attempt a few days earlier, and now . . . this. I totally lost it. In front of an airport full of passersby, I sobbed into my hands like a baby. I rarely ever cry, but at that moment I broke down on a monumental scale.

Looking back at it now, my self-controlled British personality is horrified at the thought of all those strangers witnessing such a tremendous outpouring of grief. But in that moment I was too broken to even think about it.

Somehow, I got up from the floor, put on sunglasses to hide my puffy red face, and found a quiet corner to sit and focus on my breathing. I called my manager to ask his advice, and he confirmed he'd heard the same threats too. We agreed that—if I possibly could—I'd continue to Canada and play the arena event, as eight thousand people had bought tickets. Then I'd fly home to Nashville, where my manager would accompany me to the police station, and we'd ask them what we should do.

"The show must go on," as they say in the touring business, and I'd come to believe it. The fact that I managed to go and do the Canadian show was proof of how adept I'd become at hiding what was really going on inside. Looking out at that sea of faces, I lost myself in an evening of worship, but emotionally I felt numb from shock and totally shut down; I was running on autopilot in an attempt to cope.

The next morning, I boarded the flight back to Nashville, fighting tears all the way home. My manager came to meet me and was incredibly supportive, saying he'd do anything it took to protect my well-being. We went to the police station together to file a report. It all felt surreal.

The police said that if Tyler knew where I lived, I should consider moving out of my apartment immediately. I lived alone and it seemed dangerous to put myself in such a vulnerable position. So my manager took me to my place to get a few things. I walked in nervously, asking him to check that the place was secure. Then, trying to force my brain to think clearly, I figured out what essentials I'd need for the next few weeks. I placed the items into a suitcase and got out of the apartment as quickly as I could.

Getting into my own car, I saw a police car driving slowly along the street. The officer nodded at me, rolled down the window, and said, "We'll be driving past to keep an eye on this place a few times a day while you're gone, just to make sure the guy doesn't show up or attempt to break in." I felt comforted by his calming Southern accent.

A couple of friends said I could stay with them short-term before I began the work of finding a new apartment. One of them had a porch swing, a common feature of Tennessee homes. Unable to sleep much, as I kept waking up with nightmares about Tyler, I would get out of bed, slip out of the front door, and sit on the swing. Out there, I could hear two of the most recognizably American sounds for me: crickets chirping loudly and the horns of distant freight trains.

The porch swing was a good place to breathe and to think. I knew there had been various factors involved in Tyler's situation. It was complex. But as I reflected on it all, I couldn't shake the feeling that my gay orientation had contributed significantly. If I'd been able to be honest about why I hadn't been attracted to him, perhaps he would have understood it wasn't a personal rejection. Even if he had been the most incredible man on the planet, I still wouldn't have wanted to date him because I was gay; surely his sense of rejection would've been less painful if he'd known that. Hiding that part of my identity was creating pain and complications for all of us. It was devastating to see it damage the people I cared about and worked with.

My mind flashed back to my moment of total breakdown on the airport floor. All I'd wanted in that moment of utter isolation was a girlfriend or a wife to hold me while I sobbed, then help pick me up off the ground and take me home. Someone who would lie next to me while I fell asleep. A life partner to be strong when I was weak. Not having that person in my life was getting harder and harder as the years went by and the pressures of my career grew.

Lots of recording artists traveled with their spouses, often having them work as musicians, road managers, or backup singers. It gave them strong emotional support on tour, and they had someone special to share the positive memories with. They had a partner to help them deal with demanding and exhausting schedules, and a soul mate to turn to for support when unforeseeable events hit.

Because I was gay, that was never an option. Friends and bandmates could try and help carry the load, but it wasn't the same. What I needed, and wanted, was a life partner and a lifelong commitment. And that person needed to be female. I felt isolated and alone.

As the weeks passed, things gradually calmed down. Thankfully, Tyler got the help he needed, never acted on his threats, and moved to another state to start over. I decided to get some therapy myself, to process the shock and fear the situation had created, as I was struggling to recover from the anxiety it had triggered in me. Being in a foreign country and carrying the weight of difficult work situations along with all my private pain were taking a huge toll. I knew I was breaking. Something had to change—and soon.

17

In stark contrast to all this inner turmoil, on the outside my life looked fantastic. *Billboard* magazine had dubbed me a "hit-bound riser" and "one to watch," and Christian radio stations were giving positive feedback about putting my singles into higher rotation. I was headed out on tour with two of the biggest acts in my genre: Delirious?, the most successful Christian band ever to come out of the UK, and Rebecca St. James, one of Christian music's biggest female artists, who I'd heard of back in my late teens because of her prominent role in the True Love Waits movement. I knew Delirious? and Rebecca personally, as we'd played at many of the same events and megachurches, and I was looking forward to spending time with them all during the forty-city tour.

A fleet of tour buses would be our mode of transportation—a huge improvement from my usual travels on budget airlines or fifteen-seater minivans. This time, I'd get to sleep in a tour-bus bunk, a brand-new experience. The sleek buses each had a lounge at the front with a fold-down table, a fridge, a coffee machine, and leather sofas. A sliding door separated the lounge area from the middle of the bus, which held all the bunks. These were stacked three deep: top, middle, and floor level, with twelve total.

Bunks were assigned on a first-come, first-served basis. We met at the start of the tour in a Walmart parking lot on the edge of Nashville, and I quickly hopped on board to choose a bed. Sleeping on the lowest bunk meant easy access; you sat on the floor and rolled into bed. But you also felt every bump on the road beneath you, far more than those sleeping higher up, and risked getting kicked by anyone shuffling to the bathroom in the middle of the night.

Those in the top bunk were farthest away from the feet of passersby and from the bumpy road. But those bunks were tough to get into, as they were so close to the ceiling. Plus there was the risk of falling out. One night on that tour, with a crash and a squeal, one of the merchandise sales girls fell out of the top bunk and onto the floor. The bus had turned a sharp corner and, still fast asleep, she'd rolled out of bed and crashed to the ground. Thankfully, she didn't break any bones and escaped with a few bruises.

Middle bunks were the most desirable, so on this tour I grabbed one of those. But even the best bunks took some getting used to. They feel a bit like a coffin—six and a half feet long and so close to the bunk above that you can't fully sit up. If you do, you whack your head on the bottom of the top bunk and wake up its occupant too. It only took one nasty head bang for me to learn that lesson.

Tour buses were certainly an adventure. As I chatted with the musicians each evening, after the concert was over, I found that many of them did forty-city tours all the time. Several of them didn't pay rent anywhere. "Why have an apartment," they said, "when you perpetually sleep on a tour bus? Might as well save the cash."

Life on tour was fun, but it also felt like living in a bubble. Each night we did the same show: I sang first, then Rebecca, then Delirious?. Each evening we'd return to the buses, eat pizza, watch reruns of *The Office*, and then crash into our bunks. While we slept, the bus rumbled along miles of freeways through the night, and we'd wake up in a new city and do it all over again.

R ebecca and I bonded over our non-American backgrounds (she's Australian) and enjoyed drinking endless cups of tea and discussing the latest books we'd read. We became fast friends; she's a wonderful person and I have great respect for her to this day.

Her hit song about sexual purity, called "Wait for Me," which I'd heard years earlier, was one that she sang most nights on that tour. On stage, Rebecca would share a few words, saying sex was only meant to take place within the confines of marriage, between a husband and wife. So Christians should wait until their God-given spouse appeared and remain abstinent until their wedding night.

After we'd toured together for a while, Rebecca's team asked if I'd like to introduce this theme into my future concerts too and talk about my belief in abstinence before marriage. There were a growing number of Christian artists doing this, as it was such an important value in the evangelical churches we all attended.

A popular band called BarlowGirl (three sisters with the last name Barlow) had made this one of their key messages. The slogan they'd shout from stage was "No more dating, I'm just waiting . . . my prince will come for me." When BarlowGirl and I played at the same events, I watched their show and was always taken aback when thousands of teenage girls joined in with them, shouting, "No more dating, I'm just waiting," over and over. Even though I agreed with them, the intensity of the shouting was a little unsettling; it felt militant and way over the top.

Rebecca and the three Barlow girls spoke confidently about their virginity, saying they wanted to be worthy women who were suitable for a godly husband. For them, this way of life had been helpful and life-giving, and they wanted others to benefit. From my knowledge of them, I believe their motives were nothing but good. But deep down, I couldn't shake the feeling that it all felt very extreme and I wondered if it might have unintended negative effects on people too.

I hadn't spoken about this theme from the stage yet, but I couldn't duck many more conversations about it. After that tour was over and I was doing solo shows again, I began to include the abstinence message in my music sets.

In between songs, I'd say to the crowd: "I'm saving sex until marriage. It's the best way—it's God's way. I'm a virgin, and I'm not embarrassed by that. Let's follow Jesus's teaching and believe that he knows best." All of this was true, and at that moment in time I believed it.

I still wore the purity ring I'd bought in my teens at one of the abstinence events, although deep down I had an increasing sense that this might not be the healthiest approach to life and love. It was almost impossible to question it, though; abstinence until marriage was a foundational belief in evangelical culture. So I promoted the purity movement publicly and yet questioned it in the recesses of my own mind all at the same time. It was a strange tension I knew couldn't last forever; I felt fragmented.

The fact that I, in my midtwenties, was still single and had never slept with anyone was seen as a badge of honor in that setting. People's assumption was never that I might be gay, but instead that I was waiting for the husband God would bring me. As a result, I found myself becoming perhaps the most unlikely spokesperson ever for the Christian abstinence movement—an ardent feminist and a closeted lesbian.

A few people in Tennessee were increasingly bothered that I still hadn't found Mr. Right. As we walked through the hallways of the record label one day, one of my agents made a joke, saying, "We'd better invent you a boyfriend, Vicky, in case any rumors start."

I was taken aback by this, wondering what he meant. No one had ever asked if I was gay or even insinuated that I might be. Here, for the first time ever, it seemed to have happened, albeit in a joking manner.

One of the song-publishing team, standing in the room with us, chimed in, "Yes, we've already had one 'girl with a guitar' in Nashville—on this Christian label in fact—who turned out to . . . umm . . . bat for the other team."

He nodded toward a large poster on the wall of Jennifer Knapp, who was a highly successful Grammy-nominated Christian artist who'd sold 1 million albums and had been signed to the same label as me. She'd decided to take a hiatus from music in 2002 and had disappeared from the scene. Nashville was rife with gossip that she was gay and in a relationship with her female tour manager.

They looked me up and down. I was a tomboy to the core, always in jeans and usually with an electric guitar slung over my shoulder. I didn't own a single dress. I was a geek too, obsessed by amplifiers, pedals, and recording technology. Not that any of that determines sexuality, of course, but it seemed to play into their expected stereotype.

"Yes," my agent replied, "maybe we could spread a few rumors that you're dating one of those handsome Australian guys from the band Hillsong?" They both laughed, and I forced a smile, hoping they couldn't see the embarrassment in my eyes.

I'd hoped I could outrun this, that no one would suspect, that the always-busy work schedule and the abstinence campaign would mean I could stay single and avoid questions. But the story about Jennifer Knapp had changed the tone of the debate; all of a sudden, everyone in the Christian music industry seemed to be talking about it. I'd never met Jennifer, but I fell asleep that night saying a prayer that she would be kept safe; I thought she was brave indeed and hoped she'd make it through in one piece.

The way the industry gossiped and hypothesized about Jennifer Knapp left me cold. Any vague hopes I'd had that the evangelical community would still accept me even if they knew about my sexuality were now gone.

If Jennifer wanted to keep playing and singing as an openly gay woman, it was clear she'd be doing it without a major Christian record label, locked out of the crucial network of Christian radio stations and megachurch venues. Making a living was tough enough, even with all of that machinery on your side; doing it as an indie artist or on a tiny label would turn it into more of a hobby than a career, as it wouldn't pay enough to keep a roof over your head.

Years later, in 2010, Knapp bravely told her story on the American talk show *Larry King Live*. She was gay and had needed to escape the Christian music scene, so with her female tour manager she'd moved to Australia and lived there anonymously for several years, recovering from the strain of living in the closet for so long.

That brief joke exchanged between my agent and one of the record label staff had totally thrown me. After that day, I went into high alert. I felt as if I was being watched.

A breathing space arrived. I would be singing at a conference in the UK called Spring Harvest. I'd see some familiar faces and get to escape the Nashville bubble for a little while.

Attracting around five thousand people, Spring Harvest was the flagship event for evangelicals in the UK and Europe. The director of the conference was a woman named Wendy Beech-Ward. Her husband, Simon, was one of the UK's top sound engineers, working with artists like Boy George.

That year at Spring Harvest, I sang every morning and evening in the large meetings and spoke at seminars in the afternoons. It was always a grueling schedule, but this year, thanks to all the emotional ups and downs in Nashville, I was running on absolute empty.

"Would you like to get coffee with us after the main meeting?" Wendy and Simon asked me one afternoon. I knew them reasonably well, but we'd never sat down for an in-depth chat. Aware that I needed to tell someone how much I was struggling, I wondered if this might be an opportunity to talk confidentially to safe people.

At the nearby Butlins café we ordered three giant hot chocolates, each topped with a mountain of whipped cream and chocolate sprinkles. After some small talk, Wendy asked, "How are things really going in America?"

I decided to trust them and say how hard things were: the incessant tour schedule, lack of sleep, lack of income, Tyler and the rape threats, feeling pressured to do what the music industry told me—it all came rushing out.

I also told them about several recent stalkers—another drama I'd been dealing with. A handful of men had written to me on social media (back then it was MySpace), saying, "God told me I'm going to marry you." I hadn't taken it too seriously and just ignored them. But, offended by my silence, a couple of them started threatening to show up at my local church or at a concert to find me. One actually flew across the country and worked hard to find my home address by asking my church members and posing as a friend of mine, but thankfully he never tracked me down. The authorities had been involved in that case. So the incident with Tyler was not the first time I'd dealt with threats or the police. As I told Wendy and Simon, I felt as though a weight had been lifted. It was good to be able to talk openly.

But despite trusting them with all that information, I said absolutely nothing about my sexuality. Deep down, I wanted to confide in them about the trauma I was dealing with as a closeted gay person in an industry that vehemently opposed LGBTQ+ equality. But I was far too afraid to tell anyone.

We finished our hot chocolates and walked back to the main venue so I could grab my guitar and do my prep for the evening meeting. I could see Simon and Wendy were visibly moved by all I'd shared, and by how tired and worn down America had left me. Both admitted that they'd had a hunch I was struggling and said they'd do anything they could to help. Wendy said she'd phone me once a week when I returned to the States.

True to her word, when the UK conference ended and I returned to the US, Wendy called me each week. I was highly stressed and reluctant to let anyone become a close friend, as the walls I'd built around myself were so well established, but her persistence and genuine concern won me over.

On one phone call, as we talked about the latest stalker the police were monitoring and the latest block of tour dates that would see me jump back and forth across the US for months without any breaks, she asked compassionately, "Is it *always* like this?!"

It was helpful to have a fresh pair of eyes seeing the relentless and stressful state my life was in.

"Yes, it's pretty much always like this," I replied, sounding more exhausted than ever. I wanted to explain to her the reasons for my extreme workaholism—that I was trying to drown my inner turmoil about being gay by distracting myself with constant momentum. Fear kept my mouth shut; I still couldn't bring myself to tell anyone this closely guarded secret yet.

Events like Spring Harvest were committed to women's equality, carefully balancing the number of male and female preachers who were on stage each year, something I loved and respected. But that commitment to gender equality was not shared by a large sector of more conservative churches—especially those in the Southern part of the States known as the Bible Belt.

I got invited to sing in lots of these Bible Belt churches. They didn't have a problem with me, as women were allowed to sing as long as they steered clear of preaching or teaching. In those settings, I was painfully aware that I was not considered equal to the men who stood next to me on the same stage.

One memorable day, I was invited to sing at a large church in Oklahoma that did not allow women to have the title of pastor or to preach sermons. On my way into the event, I ran into a friendly church member who asked, "Where are you headed?"

"Oh, I'm leading a few songs at the start of a meeting happening in the auditorium this morning," I replied.

"Really? They asked you?!" was his quizzical response.

His reaction seemed odd. I raised my eyebrows to signal I didn't understand.

"Hmm. You'll see . . ." he said, looking a bit worried, and walked away.

I'd arrived early, so I got my guitar out of its case and grabbed my Bible from my bag. I often read a short passage of scripture in between songs; it helped congregations to engage and added meaning to the song lyrics.

I tuned my guitar and went into the backstage greenroom to grab some water and make sure I had all my music ready. I could hear the auditorium filling up with people and the senior pastor of the church welcoming them. This was my cue to be ready in the stage wings, as singing always happened at the start of meetings.

Peering around the stage curtain, I noticed every person in the room was male. The leader greeted everyone, welcoming them to the statewide gathering of senior pastors for that denomination.

He introduced me, and on cue I walked out onto the stage. Picking up my guitar, I sang an opening song. After this, I took my Bible from the music stand and began reading out a few verses from the Old Testament and reflecting on what they meant for us today. As I did so, I noticed a few of the men raised their eyebrows. I continued speaking, and more of the men shifted in their seats and looked uncomfortable. It suddenly dawned on me exactly why: I was a woman and I was standing in front of them, in a church, teaching from the Bible. Embarrassed by their response, I stopped talking and sang my final song. They joined in, but less heartily than before.

As I left the stage, a local pastor took the microphone. He said they would be spending the next half hour praying for social-justice issues around the world—something I was keen to do. I put my guitar away and walked down into the auditorium. There were a couple of empty chairs left, so I sat down.

Then, to my surprise, I felt a tap on my shoulder. It was a senior leader from the church. Seeing me sit down and join the gathering of men, he'd rapidly made his way across the room. "I need to talk to you about something," he whispered.

I looked puzzled, responding, "Shall we talk later when there's a break? I can be around afterward if you need me—I'm keen to be part of this prayer meeting."

He shook his head. "It needs to be now. Can you come outside with me?"

I was mystified. As the men began praying, he led me out of the auditorium—noticeably past everyone else—and out into the hallway. Outside he stopped and leaned against the door, so my way back into the auditorium was blocked. Then he paused. I waited, wondering what could be so urgent that we had to walk out of a prayer meeting.

"What is it?" I asked politely.

He looked a bit flustered. "Umm . . . Well . . ." He tried to find an answer. Clearly there wasn't anything urgent at all.

"I just needed you to leave that room because . . . it's a senior pastors' gathering . . . and . . . as you know, women can't be pastors in this denomination . . . so that room needs to be men only."

It all began to make sense. The strange murmurings and frowns I'd seen when I'd read from the Bible and the awkwardness I'd felt from the men around me when I'd sat down after singing—it all became crystal clear.

"So you just walked me out of that prayer meeting because . . . I'm female?" I asked, with pain in my voice. He looked embarrassed and murmured something apologetic about it "just being the rules" and that they'd "always done things that way and it couldn't be changed."

At that moment, I saw two women walking past us into the auditorium. Noticing them too, the pastor said, "They are making the coffee for the refreshment break."

Great, I thought. *So women can't be pastors or teach the Bible, but they can be in the room if they're making coffee for the men.* I was crushed, and appalled, that my gender had barred me from being part of a prayer meeting and that it meant I could never be a pastor or church leader within a denomination like that one, even if I'd wanted to.

"Are you okay?" the pastor asked, as I stood there silent and visibly shaken.

"Not really," I said as I walked away. I'd gone there expecting a great time of worship and fellowship, but it had turned into a situation that felt painful and discriminatory; it was one I'd never forget.

The feeling of not belonging was one that frequently swept over me in those traditionalist churches. It often felt like a double dose; I was treated like a second-class citizen because of my gender, and underneath that I felt unseen pain about being gay. In those circles, to be qualified as a pastor you needed to be male, and to do anything in church leadership, you needed to be straight.

A few churches hired me to do regular Sundays. One of them, in the heart of Texas, wanted me to lead once a month and be considered one of its leadership team, a part-time staff member. The idea of belonging somewhere sounded good, so I said yes, but I discovered only too late that this church was even more traditional than I'd expected.

The man who'd had this part-time role before me was known as the Worship Pastor, but when I took the position, the title had to be changed to Worship Director (because, of course, women couldn't be pastors). I also discovered that in that denomination, male staff were paid, on average, double what women were for the exact same role. It was part of their theological ethos: men were the breadwinners of any family, they said, so a woman's salary would be smaller because she was the helper in the marriage, not the leader or the primary earner. I was shocked to find this out. I asked other women on staff about it and discovered a number of them had tried to challenge the practice but had failed.

If change were ever to come to these denominations, it would take years and years. I knew one thing: I didn't have the strength to stay in those environments much longer. After three decades of being in churches that saw women as second-class citizens and thought LGBTQ+ people were grievously sinful, this discrimination had worn me down, and I was reaching breaking point.

It had already damaged my mind and my emotions a great deal; I was anxious, lonely, full of shame, and constantly on edge. What I hadn't imagined was that it might also affect my body and my physical health. Sadly, I'd discover in the months ahead that it would.

18

Trying to stay positive, even when things are tough, has always been important to me. Amid all the struggles, I constantly tried to look for the best and to remind myself how grateful I was for the good stuff. Lighter moments did present themselves, especially when I was out on tour, and these were like oases. Anything that made me laugh was worth its weight in gold, as it helped me keep my sanity intact. Touring was certainly a very unusual work life, and as a result it brought with it its fair share of amusing incidents—things you couldn't invent, even if you tried.

One summer, my band and I were invited to play at a country fair. I'd never been booked for an event like that before, so I accepted out of curiosity. We arrived and were rehearsing when a voice came over the loudspeaker telling us to quickly finish our sound check. "The opening act has arrived—they need the stage," the voice said urgently. "Can you guys wrap up now?"

We obediently stopped, unplugged our guitars, and headed backstage. Whoever the opening act was, they had to be a big deal, as it was unusual to get hurried out of a sound check like that. Perhaps they had lots of complicated instruments to tune or some other special requirement.

A moment later, the strangest sounds echoed around us. I could have sworn it resembled barking—but I thought, surely, that was impossible. Walking toward the noise, I saw a large van parked right next to the stage. The vehicle had bright red lettering across its side, saying: THE ROCKET DOGS: THE PREMIUM CANINE CIRCUS ACT. The back door swung open, and a troupe of dogs, large and small, all poured out. Ushered up onto the stage, they began running in synchronized patterns and doing tricks, catching Frisbees out of the air.

The organizer of the country fair strolled over and slapped me on the back. "So here's our opening act—aren't they great! Have you ever seen such entertaining animals?!"

I walked backstage to my band and explained to them that, yes, before we led people in a worship service with our forty-minute music set, the opening act was a pack of circus dogs. An hour later, the event began. It was, most definitely, the strangest transition between artists I'd ever faced in my music career. The pack of barking animals did their tricks for twenty minutes, then exited the stage. I walked on, opened with a prayer, and played a hymn. You just couldn't invent a weirder mix.

I thought that was going to be the most awkward part of my performance at that country fair, but I was wrong. During one of my slower worship songs everyone sat down, so I'd closed my eyes and sung the whole thing with my eyes shut. When I finally opened them, I realized that there was a person standing at the front—and that he had, in fact, been standing there throughout the entire song. It was a six-foot-tall man in a chicken costume.

Perhaps he'd worn this outfit because it was a country fair. Who knows? But he had decided to dance and gyrate during my slow song, waggling his tail feathers suggestively in my direction. All the while my eyes had been closed, and I had been imagining the crowd engaged in a moment of prayerful worship. The whole audience had, however, been watching the giant gyrating chicken and wondering when I'd realize he was there. That experience with Mr. Chicken Suit combined with the opening act of the Rocket Dogs made it a truly unforgettable gig and a story that my bandmates told over and over again.

Another amusing, and embarrassing, standout moment from American touring was the night I played at Disney World Florida. Once a year, the entire park was taken over by a huge Christian music event. I'd been invited to play in one of their best venues, which had a hydraulic stage that rose up from about eighteen feet below ground. This was supposed to create a dynamic effect at the start of the concert—smoke would be pumped out, the stage would rise out of the floor through the fog, and my band and I would emerge, singing.

We had a run-through that afternoon, and all went smoothly. I was impressed by the technology, and we were excited by the novelty of it all. Unfortunately, when seven o'clock came around and the room was packed with people ready to hear us, it did not quite go as planned.

My band and I took the stairs down to the floor below, where the hydraulic stage was accessed before its epic rise. Taking our places, we heard the announcer upstairs say, "Welcome to Disney! Put your hands together for Vicky Beeching." That was our cue to start playing, so the drummer clicked us in and we began the song. The stage started to rise, and we rocked out to our loudest song. When we were about halfway up, suddenly there was a peculiar grinding sound. Without warning the hydraulics locked, and the stage stopped moving.

We were stuck with just our shoulders and heads protruding above the floor. We looked like half-visible meerkats peering out of a hole. We tried to carry on with the song, but looking around in panic, we stopped playing. Awkwardness reigned. We couldn't climb out or go back down. We just remained there in the silence, waiting for someone to rescue us.

Eventually, after the longest three minutes of my life, they managed to get the hydraulics fixed and pull the stage back down. My band and I hid in the greenroom for hours afterward, exploding in bursts of embarrassed laughter. We were horrified that thousands of people had seen our debacle. It was a choice of laughter or tears, so we opted to laugh. All those years of touring certainly gave me good stories to tell.

A year after my chat with Wendy and Simon over our hot chocolates, I was back at the Spring Harvest conference, singing and enjoying the event as much as ever. Scanning through the conference schedule, I was surprised to see two new names on the list of speakers: Andrew and Brenda Marin, an American couple who led an organization called the Marin Foundation in Chicago. The brochure said that the Marins worked to build bridges between the church and the LGBTQ+ community in Boystown, a well-known gay neighborhood in Chicago.

Though it was an evangelical conference and traditional in values, Spring Harvest had decided to take a bold step and invite them. This was, most likely, possible because Andrew did not publicly state whether he believed the Bible supported same-sex relationships or not. Instead, he saw his role as that of a neutral mediator, a human bridge between the gay community and the church, encouraging dialogue and urging both sides to listen. He was trying to break the taboo that prevented the church from talking about this huge issue.

Andrew was straight and described himself as formerly being "the biggest Bible-thumping homophobe" he knew. After his three best friends all came out to him as gay in the space of a few weeks, he became increasingly aware of the chasm between the church and the LGBTQ+ community. Andrew considered himself an unlikely candidate to help bring change, but he knew something needed to be done. As he was walking with his best friends through their journeys, he now had a foot in both worlds—LGBTQ+ and Christian—and wanted to help bridge the gap. So he and Brenda had moved to Boystown and started their organization.

Back then, it was extremely rare for evangelical churches on either side of the pond to openly discuss LGBTQ+ issues. Churches preached against homosexuality. But fostering discussion about how to improve relationships with LGBTQ+ people? Or considering whether they'd gotten their theology wrong? That had never happened. At least, not at any event I'd been a part of. I was very aware that Andrew and Brenda were breaking new ground.

Instantly, I hit it off with Andrew and Brenda, but I also felt nervous. What if, because they had spent so much time with gay people, they could tell this was my "issue" too? What if they had superpowered gaydar—radar for sensing who was gay—and figured me out? To my relief, they never did, and as the week went by, our new friendship grew.

Part of me wanted to attend Andrew and Brenda's seminar at Spring Harvest, but part of me was afraid that it would raise questions if I were seen there, as I was the mainstage singer and everyone would recognize me. Creeping in partway through, I stood at the back and listened, as though I were just drifting past the venue on my way to a band rehearsal.

Andrew had given the microphone to several people in the crowd who told stories about their own journeys, either as gay Christians or parents of gay children. I was amazed this was allowed. It was heartbreaking to hear how isolated they felt without Christian LGBTQ+ role models or safe places to discuss the issue with faith leaders.

I bought Andrew's book *Love Is an Orientation* and devoured it. I also gave copies to a few relatives and friends, to test the waters. Had any of those close to me softened in their views on LGBTQ+ issues? Several refused to read it, and the handful who did said they were worried about Andrew—that he wasn't clear enough that homosexuality was a sin, as he didn't openly condemn same-sex relationships. My experiment to see if people's minds were changing had proved they were not.

Although the Marins were hailed as brave voices raising important pastoral issues about how we should care for LGBTQ+ people, there was no sign of theological change in the air within UK evangelicalism. There were complaints that such open-minded discussions weren't suitable for Christian conferences, where the Bible was "taken seriously."

Politically, the UK was gradually moving toward the recognition of same-sex marriage in British law, and the traditional wing of the church was extremely unhappy with this. A campaign group, the Coalition for Marriage, had shared its message from the Spring Harvest stage, asking attendees to sign their nationwide petitions to block same-sex couples from tying the knot. I could tell the entire topic was gathering momentum in both the public and religious spheres. It was getting harder to ignore or outrun it, and my internal levels of stress and anxiety were getting higher.

B ack in the States, a similar political battle was unfolding. California's Proposition 8 had taken everything to a frenzied level. "Prop 8" was an attempt by those opposing same-sex marriage to overturn the 2008 California Supreme Court ruling that had made it legal. Its supporters argued that only marriage between a man and a woman should be valid or recognized in California, hoping to nullify the victory that gay and bisexual people had won in May 2008.

In churches across America, many pastors used their pulpits to speak about that political issue and tell their congregations what they should do. Most of those sermons described "God's intentional design for marriage," which could only ever be between one man and one woman. Californian churches booked me regularly, and I found myself hearing those sermons again and again.

One Sunday, I was singing at a traditional church south of Los Angeles. I led a few opening songs, and then the pastor stepped up and began to preach. He spoke about Prop 8 and said that "the devil planned to destroy humanity through homosexuality." Blushing at the mention of same-sex relationships, I squirmed in my seat, but there was no escape—I was the visiting singer, so I had pride of place, sitting right in the front row.

The pastor said that, by allowing gay marriage, California was "on a collision course with hell." As supporting evidence he casually mentioned: "The UK is already far further into this slide; after all it's basically a Muslim country now, and rampantly gay." I felt the eyes of the congregation turn to look at me, expecting me to nod in affirmation that his words were true. Instead, I stared awkwardly at the floor, thinking, "What a ridiculous statement."

He ramped up his rhetoric by saying that homosexuality was shameful—the worst of all sins; it was unnatural and sinister; no Christian following Jesus would ever have those desires or want to live that "lifestyle." My face was, by now, burning with shame. Tears began forming in my eyes.

I knew I couldn't go on like this. I was, most definitely, gay. I'd still never acted on it despite the fact that I was almost thirty. I'd prayed for twenty years to be different, to be free from this "shameful sin," but nothing had shifted.

The isolation I knew so well swept over me. *If the people in this church building knew I was gay right now, they'd march me out of here and tell me never to come back,* I thought.

My tearful moment of reflection was interrupted when I heard my name being called out, echoing from the loudspeaker. The pastor had finished the sermon with a flourish, shouting, "Brothers and sisters, hear it from me: the devil wants homosexuality to take over the world, but we will fight him in the powerful name of Jesus." He paused for a breath, then said, "And now the lovely Vicky Beeching will come and play a few of her songs as we finish. Please give her a warm welcome to the stage."

Everyone was applauding and looking at me. Brushing away the tears, I put on my "professional face" and walked to the stage. The lights shone in my eyes, and I went through the motions of singing the two closing songs. The service ended, and I was met by a flood of people walking toward the stage. They lined up around the room, several hundred of them, wanting hugs, photos, and autographs.

Out of the corner of my eye, I saw the pastor hugging and greeting the church members as they waited to speak to me. I thought, *How can churchgoers this warm and loving not realize how damaging and militant their views on LGBTQ+ people are?* They weren't even just preaching that *Christians* couldn't marry same-sex partners; they wanted to bar the *entire nation* from this human right. I tried to smile for hundreds of autographs and photos, but inside I was in pieces.

Evangelicalism was my home, and I wanted to belong. I wanted to let the kind, encouraging words people said about my music soak into my heart. But I felt an increasingly thick glass wall growing between myself and the faces I saw singing along to my songs. That Sunday at church was a prime example.

Faith-based organizations opposing same-sex marriage were gaining momentum, and more would spring up in the near future. The National Organization for Marriage in America, founded in 2007, played a pivotal role in promoting Prop 8. The UK's Coalition for Marriage, launched in 2012, would do its best to stop gay marriage from becoming legal in my homeland.

Because of this growing political push, I found myself singing in more and more settings where antigay messages were preached. Despite being right at the center—literally standing in the middle of the stage—I felt increasingly cut off from everyone in a culture that used to feel like family. "What if they found out my secret?" I wondered, terrified.

Everything in me wanted to interrupt those awful sermons and shout that LGBTQ+ people aren't just *out there*, but *in here* as well—within the church—and that I was one of them. Doing that would cost me everything: my entire livelihood, my record deal, my US work permit, which was tied to my work within the church, and perhaps all of my friends and family. It felt horrendous to hear these toxic sermons, not be able to say a word, and then have to stand and sing as though I endorsed it all.

Inside, I felt as though I was psychologically being ripped in two. My stress levels were skyrocketing, and I'd noticed I was feeling not only emotionally exhausted from it, but increasingly physically exhausted too. My body was signaling to me that I had to stop living this way; something had to give.

19

Saddleback is one of the biggest megachurches in the US, with a weekly attendance of over twenty thousand people. When I heard I'd been invited to sing at their big annual worship conference, I was delighted.

Blow-drying my hair in a hotel room, I was rushing around to get ready for the Saddleback event. I looked in the mirror and noticed something strange; a white mark had appeared on my forehead. The heat of the blow dryer had made the rest of my forehead bright pink, but one patch, about two inches wide and stretching from my hairline to my eyebrow, was white.

Baffled and worried, I looked again. I had no idea what it was or what I should think. It wasn't bleeding. It didn't hurt. But there it was: a stark white ridge running down my forehead, as though I'd covered that area with sunblock and then got the rest of my face sunburned. I grabbed a brush and began styling my hair so that my bangs (or "fringe," as we say in the UK) hid that part of my face.

A knock at the hotel room door interrupted my thoughts—it was time to go to rehearsal. I had no margin for error, as Saddleback's timing ran like clockwork, with state-of-the-art staging, lighting, sound, and visuals. Their volunteers were, by day, professionals who ran lights and sound for places like Disneyland. So it was high-tech, and I couldn't be even a minute late to my rehearsal slot.

A friendly woman in an SUV drove me onto the huge Saddleback campus, and as soon as we arrived, I was swept up in a blur of busyness. The white mark had been put entirely out of my mind, and it would stay that way for weeks, as the workaholism I'd developed over the years kept me moving forward to the next gig, the next plane ride, the next hotel, the next rehearsal. The lifestyle I'd created to drown out my inner sadness and loneliness had me on autopilot, and now it was preventing me from having a moment to investigate what might be wrong with my skin.

After a couple more months of intensive touring, I noticed a sudden drop in my already dwindling energy. I began to feel drowsy most of the time, and the musicians who traveled with me saw it too. A few nicknamed me Sleeping Beeching, as I'd fall asleep at the merchandise table after concerts, at the airport restaurant, or between sound check and the worship meetings.

One backup singer joked about starting a Twitter account called Sleeping Beeching, where she'd post pictures she snapped of me napping in weird places. It was nice to laugh about it; it helped. But more seriously, my band agreed that it was worrying. It made me think of the white mark again. "I must get that checked out sometime," I said, wondering when I'd be back in Nashville for more than a night, so I could visit a dermatologist. But that plan kept getting waylaid by the next tour date, and the next.

Later that year, the white mark on my forehead changed from white to pink. It was becoming inflamed and itchy. When a photo of my band playing outside at a music festival was posted on social media, my drummer saw it and asked, "What's wrong with your head?" Now that it showed more obviously, it had my attention again.

Life had been extra busy lately, as I'd signed with a new label, Integrity Music, which specialized in worship albums and had huge success getting songs into American megachurches. Integrity gave me lots of creative freedom, and the album we were recording was my favorite of any I'd made. It would be titled *Eternity Invades,* and we were recording it in a studio in San Diego, California.

Whenever I wasn't out on tour, we'd been working around the clock to get the vocals finished and everything ready to be mixed and mastered. I knew I had to deal with my forehead, so between vocal sessions I'd made a phone call and finally booked an appointment with a specialist at a medical facility in San Diego. Getting an opinion on what was wrong felt urgent.

We finished the last vocals on the album, and my producer danced around in celebration, high-fiving me. I joined in, but my mind was on the hospital appointment that I'd be heading to an hour later. I drove off toward downtown San Diego, hoping it would be a harmless diagnosis with a quick solution. *Maybe it's just eczema,* I thought. *They'll probably just hand me a tube of antihistamine cream, and I'll be good to go.*

The dermatologist welcomed me into his office and examined my head. He listened as I told him about my extreme fatigue, constant falling asleep, inability to sleep at night, and now this persistent skin condition. He looked serious as he took a piece of paper out of his drawer. He wrote something down and handed it to me. "You have something quite rare, I'm afraid—and it's serious," he said. "It's called localized scleroderma; the full name is 'en coup de sabre linear morphea.' The treatment you'll need is a form of chemotherapy."

He explained that localized scleroderma was an aggressive autoimmune condition in which the body was fighting against itself. This disease morphed healthy skin cells into scar tissue; it literally ate away at the fat, creating scarred areas wherever it took hold.

"If it's not treated, the results can be horrendous, and I don't say that lightly," he explained. "We need to use strong medication to stop this in its tracks, so your health—and your face—will be as unharmed as possible." Sensing I had a hundred questions, he added, "I'm afraid the only other advice I can give you is to google the condition at home, and you'll find out more. It's such a rare diagnosis that, in all honesty, I don't know much about it. Sorry I can't be of more help."

With that, I was outside, clutching the piece of paper and walking back to my car. The word "chemotherapy" echoed around in my head. It was getting dark as I unlocked my car and drove back to the place I was staying. Walking in, I felt so alone and badly in need of someone to talk to. As always, there was no significant other or spouse there for me, and I'd kept local friends at a distance behind the emotional walls I'd built. I was facing this diagnosis alone. I sat in the corner of the room and sobbed.

Later, I found the courage to turn on my laptop and type the name of the condition into Google. I stared at the results. Photos of people who'd been diagnosed with the same condition popped up, with plenty of worst-case scenarios. Several of their faces had been ravaged by the disease, the soft tissue of their foreheads eaten away. In some, the disease had spread downward below the eyebrow through the eye socket and left them blind. Some had lost the side of their mouth. In others, the scar had moved upward, through the hairline, leaving a two-inch hairless pathway up to the crown. I felt dizzy and short of breath as I realized how serious this all was, and I dissolved into sobs again.

It was evening in California. Looking at my watch, I calculated it was three in the morning in London. I couldn't disturb anyone at that hour. Crawling into bed, I lay there sleepless. As soon as the UK woke up, I called Wendy, then my sister, then my mum. Through tears I updated them about the diagnosis, the treatment plan, and how frightened I felt.

They could tell that everything I'd been through so far, plus this new blow, had brought me to a final breaking point. It was clear I needed support. Everyone was unanimous: the smartest idea was for me to go home to the UK, have this treatment through the National Health Service (NHS), and be close enough for friends and family to offer me the help and care I needed.

finished my album, and the tracks were sent off to get mixed and mastered. I should have been celebrating the year of hard work that had gone into it, but instead I was packing boxes, fielding calls from my label and booking agent, and doing everything necessary to organize my move back to the UK to begin the chemo treatment. Money had been tight lately as the entire music industry was struggling; pirated digital downloads and cheap streaming services meant albums just weren't selling like they used to. I gave most of my belongings to a thrift store and packed everything else into three huge suitcases.

I loved my new album, as did my record label, Integrity Music, so it was tough to have to walk away from the press-release events and marketing dates we'd planned for its launch. The fact that I couldn't tour in the coming year meant sales would be low and the songs I'd worked so hard on would barely be heard. The label staff were disappointed, but we knew my health had to come first. To stay in the US would mean vast health-care bills I couldn't afford and going through treatment without any family or friends on hand. There was no way I could tour—I was far too frail.

I landed at Heathrow, and London welcomed me back with its usual gray clouds and pouring rain. I wanted to be home, though; facing that illness in a foreign country sounded too hard to manage. I knew my body was signaling to me—waving a huge white flag—telling me I had to stop my workaholic lifestyle and address what was going on underneath. I knew the real reason I was running so fast through life—I was trying to escape the shame and heartbreak I felt about my orientation. I knew I must finally stop running.

PART IV

Returning Home

20

The British hospital was an endless maze of white hallways. Silence permeated every room and stairwell; it felt like a place where time stood still. After the incessant noise and pace of ten years on tour, this building was the polar opposite, and the abrupt stop was a shock to my system. Used to pushing myself relentlessly, with barely a moment to pause and think, suddenly here I was, lying totally still with nothing to stare at but a white ceiling, white walls, and white curtains.

An IV was running into my veins, pumping steroids into my bloodstream to try and stop the disease, scleroderma, before it caused any more damage to my cells. After the drip had transferred all the drugs, I took my chemo tablets and then was wheeled down for an ultrasound scan. The doctors wanted to see how deep the damage ran beneath the surface of my forehead and also to test me for epilepsy, which they said was a common comorbid condition with scleroderma.

Shuttling back and forth to appointments like this became the rhythm of my week. I'd leave my tiny studio apartment for yet more checkups, scans, and IVs, then return home, collapse into bed, and sleep. I was too sick to work, plus my career had been based in the

States for almost a decade now, so I had few work opportunities in the UK. I'd looked highly successful to the large crowds I played in front of, but really things had been financially tight for years. Living on my meager savings, I was in survival mode.

The number one priority was stopping the scarring from spreading, so all the appointments focused on getting drugs into me as fast as possible. One thing I hadn't really figured out, though, was *why* I had gotten this aggressive illness in the first place. I was lucky enough to be under the care of one of the UK's scleroderma specialists, and during one clinic visit I decided to ask him about the cause of the disease.

"Well . . . there's no proven genetic cause for morphea or scleroderma," he said. "It's pretty mysterious, as are many autoimmune diseases." He explained that the body was "fighting against itself," a phrase that the specialist in California had used too; it was destroying its own healthy cells.

Pausing and looking at me more intently, he continued, "Often, I find autoimmune conditions like scleroderma have psychological and emotional triggers. People may be genetically predisposed to having one of these diseases, but it may stay dormant for their entire lives—unless they go through something hugely traumatic or stressful, and then it triggers."

I squirmed in my seat. This was definitely not the direction I'd imagined the conversation going. He continued, "Is there something in your life that you'd consider highly stressful or traumatic? Something that weighs heavily on you psychologically, that creates major anxiety?"

One topic instantly, and obviously, sprang to mind. Seeing my awkward body language, he quickly added, "No need to tell me what it is—that's your private business. But if there is something . . . please get help and find a solution. It may well have triggered this in your body as a warning sign, like dashboard lights flashing when a car is breaking down. Please don't ignore anything that could be causing this."

I felt reflective and melancholy as I made my way out of the doctor's clinic and into the parking lot. His message rang in my ears: *If there is something causing you major strain and trauma, please get help and find a solution. It may well have triggered this in your body as a warning sign.*

There was only one thing that had caused vast emotional strain in my life for years. I'd known I was gay since I was twelve or thirteen. Keeping that hidden for two decades had been wrecking my heart and mind. Now, as I neared the age of thirty, it seemed to be wrecking my body too.

All these years, I'd prayed and fasted, submitted myself to an exorcism, confessed to a Catholic priest, believed that conversion therapy could change a person's orientation, read the Bible until my eyes were sore, and never acted on my attractions even once. I'd done anything and everything to try and become straight or to shut down any desires for a life partner. My immune system, my adrenals, and my sympathetic nervous system were all stretched to breaking point from years of living in fight-or-flight mode, constantly terrified someone would find out my closely guarded secret.

Extreme stress, the doctor had told me, was worse than chain-smoking cigarettes all day, every day. I'd never touched a cigarette, and I was a teetotaler, but the impact of a lifetime of psychological trauma was proving how damaging stress could be. He'd also added that loneliness and isolation had similar physiological effects. It was a lot to process.

Out in the parking lot, it was a gray, rainy afternoon, so I put my umbrella up. I touched the red, inflamed patch of scar tissue on my forehead and felt sick with worry about how this disease might damage me further. Needing chemo drugs was awful enough. I just hoped I wouldn't also lose part of my face, like the patients I'd seen on Google.

Standing in the rain, holding my umbrella, I felt tears run down my cheeks. Touching my forehead again, I made a decision: I had to face my gay orientation and decide what to do. I couldn't sweep it under the carpet anymore. Finally, I'd found something even more frightening than losing the evangelical world I knew and loved—and that was this disease, which was spreading aggressively through my cells. As well as taking my medication, I knew I had to stop the underlying stress and trauma that had contributed to it.

I needed to face the unsettling question: What did the Bible *really* say about same-sex relationships? I had to give myself the freedom to read, study, think, and pray. My mind wandered back to the pro-gay interpretations of scripture I'd read about years earlier at Oxford. I remembered standing in the library on that memorable day of the snowball fight, awkwardly hanging around the Sexual Ethics shelf. Many times since, I'd wondered if those authors were right, but breaking step with my evangelical Christian community was not something I'd been willing to contemplate, and I'd shelved the thought every time.

Scleroderma had brought with it a sense of urgency. Life could not go on as it had before. I needed to dig into theology books again and try and unravel the answers to my questions. Could I finally make peace with this aspect of my identity? Could I be gay and Christian? These questions terrified me because I knew answering them would cost so much.

The chemo and steroid treatments increased in regularity and dose. Between hospital visits, I was stuck at home, alone, with a headful of questions about facing up to my sexuality. I could think of nothing else. The drugs alone would have been plenty to deal with and created their own emotional fallout, but I was dealing with so much more.

As I began to process this painful issue, all the sadness, loss, and pain about my sexuality seemed to hit me like a tidal wave. The disease had forced me to stop in my tracks, and now that I had, I was face-to-face with my damaged inner world. Everything I'd shelved since I was thirteen crashed down on me; every moment of feeling shamed and guilty about my orientation rushed back with startling clarity and potency. Fear of revisiting what the Bible actually said, and perhaps then having to leave my livelihood and face vilification from Christians around the world, felt debilitating. All I could do was cry.

I had always been so strong and independent, but this had reduced me to nothing. I struggled to do basic tasks at home. I couldn't face seeing anyone. If I wasn't at the clinic, I was in bed, curled in a ball, sobbing. Worse still, I didn't feel able to tell anyone exactly *why*, because I still feared telling anyone I was gay, even those closest to me. All they knew was that I was a wreck.

The sobbing and fragility went on for weeks. After encouragement from Wendy and from my sister, Jo, I found a therapist. Christopher, my new therapist, helped me understand why I was such a lifeless, sobbing wreck. After two hours of asking in-depth questions and assessing my symptoms, he said, "Vicky, you've had a nervous breakdown. There's no other way to describe it." Looking me in the eye, he added, "It's going to be okay, though. I can help you navigate this and get you back on your feet again."

In our sessions, I found the courage to tell Christopher about my orientation and my lifetime of pain around it. The fact that he was bound by professional confidentiality gave me the security I needed. It felt so strange to finally voice the words "I am gay" out loud. After the Catholic confession and the exorcism years ago, I'd vowed I would never tell another soul. But now I finally had.

We also discussed unhelpful teachings about mental health I'd been exposed to in the church. In charismatic, evangelical, and Pentecostal circles, many had taught that depression, anxiety, or a nervous breakdown was a sign that you were not living in the power of the Holy Spirit, but were somehow living in sin and in need of prayer ministry to expel the dark forces attacking your life. Anyone in a position of leadership in the church should not be consistently dealing with those things, they'd said.

For many Pentecostals, prayer was held up as the primary way to be "healed," and taking medication showed a lack of faith. This led to a lot of fear, and a sense of taboo, around mental health in many churches. It sounded bizarre explaining it to Christopher, as he had grown up nonreligious, but these ideas were considered normal in many of the congregations I had visited and sung at.

We also talked about anger, because I *was* angry. I was confused about what I believed or didn't believe about same-sex relationships and why I'd had to live such a sad and isolated existence. I was angry that my life had crashed and burned and left me in a hospital with IVs in my arm. Angry that I'd had a teenage exorcism. Angry that I'd had to sing in churches where pastors preached that homosexuality was, "in God's eyes, on a par with pedophilia." Angry that I'd finally been reduced to a nervous breakdown.

The straight male worship leaders and Christian recording artists in the evangelical sector hadn't faced this cruel choice: having a spouse, or a music ministry, but not both. Most of them were married to loving wives and raising beautiful children. They had families to go home to *and* a job that they loved in the church. Whatever my theology would or wouldn't turn out to be in future, I had a lot of unprocessed anger and grief about how unfair and destructive it all seemed.

Evangelical theology didn't have much room for anger or grief; it mainly promoted forgiveness and gratitude and being gentle and gracious to everyone. Anger was an unattractive emotion in those circles. I found solace in the Psalms where David shouted at God and railed against injustice.

"It's okay to be angry," my therapist, Chris, would say. "It's a healthy emotion, signaling that you've been in situations that are not safe or good. You've been through so much, and you're still not out the other side. It's no wonder you feel grief and anger about what you've been through and what you are still facing." It took a lot of therapy sessions to begin to unpack all of this mess.

I knew things needed to change in my life, so I told Christopher that, as soon as I felt stronger, I wanted to revisit what the Bible actually said about same-sex relationships. He agreed that it sounded like a good plan.

"All this shame and fear about being gay has knocked the life out of you completely," he said. "Only you know what's right for you, but I think doing that Bible reading and research sounds like a very good idea. You can't keep running away from this issue. It's crushed you to the ground."

It had, indeed, crushed me, and it took time for me to begin to heal. After six months of therapy, I slowly began to regain my strength. It had been a bleak experience, both the nervous breakdown and the chemo drugs. I still hadn't told anyone besides Chris that I was gay. Therapy had helped, and I was determined to finally face my fears. I would revisit the Bible's teachings on sexuality, and I would figure out, once and for all, what to do about the issue that had led to my breakdown and my autoimmune disease.

Everyone was awaiting my return to Nashville, full-time Christian music, and my touring career. My health was improving, but I knew I couldn't go back to life as usual. I had a list of megachurches keen to book me in the US and Canada. I'd also been offered the chance to sing at a few UK worship events later that year, and I said yes to a few local British ones, hoping I could stall a return to America. Something had to change, and everything was hanging in the balance.

The Brompton Oratory, built in the 1880s, stands majestically in South Kensington, next to London's Victoria and Albert Museum. It is London's second-largest Catholic church; only Westminster Cathedral is bigger. I'd visited the oratory a handful of times before, as it stands next door to one of the UK's most popular evangelical churches, Holy Trinity Brompton.

I remember the first time I walked inside on a dark wintery evening years earlier: the architecture took my breath away. Vaulted ceilings

drew my eyes upward. The roof was decorated with mosaics and fres-
cos, all embellished with gold. Black marble pillars stood underneath
stone arches. It was an inspiring and yet also immensely calming place.
Barely lit, with only a few candles illuminating the shadowy walls, it felt
like stepping into another world.

When I'd considered a good place to go and read theology books
about faith and sexuality, the Brompton Oratory instantly came to
mind. I didn't want a library; I wanted a place of prayer and worship
as my venue. At the oratory, prayers had soaked into the stones for decades. The building was always open, and there was rarely anyone in
there between the lunchtime Mass and the evening service. It seemed
ideal.

I arrived for my first afternoon of reading with a backpack of books.
It felt good to be out in London and around other people after so much
time at home during my breakdown. A couple of hours passed quickly
as I pored over books and took notes. Heavy, sonorous bells chimed,
and the whole building echoed. Hearing them, I paused and prayed.
Faith was still the heartbeat of my life; God was still the center of
everything—as he had been since I was four, when I walked around the
schoolyard telling him about my thoughts and feelings.

Day after day, I returned to the oratory to read. A jumble of emotions
surfaced as I studied and took notes: fear of what I'd do if I concluded
God did *not* approve of gay relationships, and also fear of what I'd do if I
concluded that he *did*. Both pathways sounded immensely challenging
in different ways. At the end of each day of studying, I attended evening
Mass, then sat in quiet for half an hour of silent prayer. I invited God
to speak in the quiet, to direct my conscience, to help me understand
what I'd been reading, and to guide me toward the right conclusion,
whatever it might be. Therapy had shown me that I was hurt and angry,
but, despite that, I was still totally committed to my faith. Thankfully,
I felt able to process these theological questions *with* God, not without
him, asking for answers and listening for his voice.

A month had passed, and I'd made my way through a pile of books. There were six or seven Bible passages thought to relate to same-sex relationships, and I'd looked at what scholars had to say about each as well as studying the wider themes in scripture of creation and marriage. I'd also dusted off my Oxford notes about the desert fathers and the Christian mystics from my studies with Sister Benedicta and Bishop Kallistos. I'd revisited the topics of slavery and of women's equality too, as they were a relevant reminder that the church's official views had been seriously wrong before.

I reread all the books I'd nervously skimmed through at Oxford, when I'd hidden myself in the library's Sexual Ethics aisle. They seemed far more balanced and God-centered than I'd remembered. The authors weren't the sly, cunning liberals I'd formerly considered them—leading people down a slippery slope. Instead, they had a deep love of the Bible and a vast understanding of the historical cultures in which the texts had been written. My studies in the oratory were bringing some clarity; it felt as though my eyes were being opened.

Eventually, I neared the end of the couple of months I'd put aside to think about these issues. On the last day I planned to spend at the oratory, I decided to keep it simple. All I packed was one book—my Bible. It was the one I'd been given by my parents on my sixteenth birthday, and I'd used it daily ever since. It was marked with coffee, fingerprints, and a few teenage stickers and had countless notes scribbled in the margins. It had been with me for over fifteen years and felt like a familiar friend.

I didn't really know what I should read that day. I'd done exhaustive study on all the passages in the Old and New Testaments thought to relate to same-sex relationships. So today I was open to whatever would unfold, hoping for a sense of God's leading. I flicked through the Bible and stopped at the New Testament book of Acts. It struck me that in the early days of the church, Christians were dealing with lots of complex questions about who could belong. So it seemed a good section of the Bible to look at again today.*

I leafed through the pages of Acts, waiting for something to catch my eye. Suddenly, the silence was broken by the sound of the organist beginning his practice for the evening service. Chords filled the cavernous ceiling space and reverberated off the stone walls. Young voices joined in as the oratory boys choir began rehearsing the evening's hymns. As the organ played and the voices soared, something in the pages of the book of Acts jumped out at me.

The tenth chapter of Acts wasn't a part of the New Testament I'd especially connected with in the past, but reading it that day, I felt the hairs on the back of my neck stand up. I sensed I'd found the right passage for my final afternoon of study. The words jumped off the page, as though they'd been written just for me. My months of study had been rigorously academic. When I studied, I was naturally led by my mind, not by emotions, so this was far from my typical approach to Bible reading. It was an experience I couldn't ignore, though; it felt like an answered prayer, as it was so out of character for me. Something significant seemed to be happening, and I wanted to fully take it all in.

Acts 10 describes how St. Peter wanted a quiet place to pray. Houses in his culture often had flat rooftops, so he went onto the roof and started his devotions. Acts says that this happened in the middle of the day, around noon. Suddenly Peter had a vision. He saw a huge white sheet being lowered down from heaven. On the sheet were "all kinds of four-footed creatures and reptiles and birds." As he looked at this bizarre sight, he heard a voice saying, "Get up, Peter; kill and eat" (10:12–13).

Peter was shocked, because the animals and birds on the sheet were ones prohibited by Jewish law—they were unclean food. Peter prided

---

* If you're not someone who has interest in the details of what the Bible says about same-sex relationships, feel free to skip to chapter 22.

himself on keeping that law fastidiously, so he replied, "Surely not, Lord! I have never eaten anything impure or unclean." The voice came back with an authoritative reply: "Do not call anything impure that God has made clean" (10:14–15, NIV).

This conversation happened three times. Each time Peter heard: "Get up, Peter; kill and eat" (or paraphrased: "It's okay, Peter; this food is clean and permitted"). Each time he was indignant, saying it would be wrong because it was against Jewish law. Each time the voice replied, "Do not call anything impure that God has made clean."

If you're not familiar with this story, you may be wondering what on earth it's all about. Why would visions of animals on a giant sheet be in the pages of the Bible? Its meaning was highly important. So important, in fact, that it changed the trajectory of the Christian faith forever. The meaning of the story was this: God was announcing that the Gentiles (non-Jews) were now welcome into his kingdom; they could become followers of Jesus too.

Previously, Jewish followers of Jesus believed only Jews were God's chosen people and Gentiles were outsiders. To challenge this was unthinkable for Jewish Christians. Nowadays, most Christians are non-Jews. It's easy to forget how shocking and radical this idea sounded to Peter and the rest of the early church. It was so unexpected that they could hardly take it in.

Right after the vision, three people arrived at the house where Peter was praying. They'd been sent by a Gentile, a military commander named Cornelius, who was hoping Peter would visit him and explain how he could follow the teachings of Jesus. In that era, Jewish law considered it shameful for Jews to enter the homes of non-Jews. If they did so, they became ritually unclean. Peter was nervous—surely going to Cornelius's house was not okay. But the voice from the vision told him, "Go with them without hesitation; for I have sent them" (10:20). God was showing him that Gentiles were clean, despite what Jewish law said. He was being asked to follow heaven's inclusive agenda.

Obediently, Peter went to the home of the Gentile centurion, Cornelius, and preached the gospel there, saying, "I understand now that God is not one to show partiality [as though Gentiles were excluded from God's blessing], but in every nation the person who fears God and does what is right [by seeking Him] is acceptable and welcomed by him" (10:34–35, AMP).

As Peter preached, Acts says, "the Holy Spirit fell upon all [the Gentiles] who heard the word" (10:44). This same baptism—experienced by the Jewish disciples earlier in the book of Acts at Pentecost—was not something they ever imagined God could give to non-Jews. Shock waves went through the crowd: "The circumcised believers who had come with Peter were astounded that the gift of the Holy Spirit had been poured out even on the Gentiles, for they heard them speaking in tongues and extolling God" (10:45–46). How could God extend his welcome and the gift of his Spirit to these outsiders, people they'd been raised to see as unholy?

But Peter took charge, inspired by the powerful vision of the white sheet, and said, "Surely no one can stand in the way of their being baptized with water. They have received the Holy Spirit just as we have." Then he said the Gentiles present could be baptized in the name of Christ (10:47–48, NIV).

It seems so normal now—*of course* non-Jews can be Christians. But back then it was jaw-dropping. God had done the unthinkable. Many Jewish Christians were offended to their core. "We've always done it this way," they said. But God had opened a new door.

As I read all of this, sitting in the Brompton Oratory, the chords of the organ music continued to rise and fall, rebounding from every inch of the ancient stone walls. The floor seemed to shake with the lowest notes. It was as if the entire building were singing its own song.

The tenth chapter of Acts had really stirred me. Yes, it related to Gentiles being welcomed as Christians all those centuries ago. But the story felt as though it had wider relevance too, that it was about other "outsiders" hearing God's voice saying they were welcome, saying that they were "clean."

As I read about Peter's vision, I felt as though I were there myself, looking at the sheet falling from the sky. For me, the "unclean things" on that sheet represented my gay orientation. And, like Peter, I was arguing with God, saying, "Lord, I've never so much as touched a person of the same sex romantically. I've kept your law and commandments. I would never disobey your word."

And what God had said to Peter, I felt he said to me too: "Do not call unclean what I have made clean."

The main thing stopping Peter from taking in the news was his spiritual pride. "I've kept your laws perfectly!" was his instant, knee-jerk reaction. I realized my pride had also made me unable to hear this message before. I believed I was honoring God by shelving my gay orientation—by rejecting what I believed to be unclean—despite having known about it since I was thirteen. It was hard for me to accept a new perspective. I was offended at the idea of losing the badge of righteousness I had earned by holding to traditional Christian views.

But only one voice ultimately matters in time and eternity—God's voice. Peter realized that, and as I sat reflecting on it all, it felt as though it was sinking in for me as well.

God was letting me in on a new perspective, one of radical acceptance and inclusion. "Do not call unclean what I have made clean" echoed around my head and heart. The person I'd always been—a gay person—was not something to be ashamed of. God accepted me and loved me, and my orientation was part of his grand design.

There was nothing unclean about it, and nothing to run away from. Just as the Gentiles could fully join God's family, now LGBTQ+ people could too. They were on an equal footing with straight people, so there was no reason why they couldn't love and be loved, marry and raise families, and enjoy full membership in church and society. If there was nothing unclean about gay relationships, there was nothing to condemn. God had spoken.

I closed the Bible and sat in silence for a long time. It was a lot to process. All the material I'd read over the previous two months was finally settling into a coherent whole. Acts 10 had brought it all together for me.

It was now early evening, and people were arriving at the oratory for the final Mass of the day. I put my Bible into my bag and stepped out into the crisp air to walk to the Tube station. The sun was low in the sky as the day neared its end, but for me it felt as though dawn was finally breaking.

21

The French-born novelist Anaïs Nin once said: "We don't see things as *they* are; we see them as *we* are." That quote kept coming back to me as I tried to process my weeks of study and the way the tenth chapter of the book of Acts had impacted me so significantly.

I was realizing more than ever that we all see the world through our own lens, shaped by our background, culture, and values. Because of this, it's very difficult to see anything objectively. Our bias can keep us from adopting alternative viewpoints, even if we consider ourselves to be open to different ideas.

This seemed particularly relevant to the way we read the Bible. When people argue that "the Bible clearly says . . . ," it is primarily an individual interpretation based on their own values and life experience. It seemed to me that a huge dose of humility was needed in all discussions of theology; everyone had to be open to the possibility they needed to see things from a different angle.

Yesterday, studying Acts 10 had been such a powerful experience. Today, I decided I would read more of Acts and see how the story progressed in the chapters that followed. I felt there was more for me to learn from Peter's vision of the white sheet and the message for the Gentiles and deeper layers of meaning that related to LGBTQ+ people and the church.

Where should I go to do that? I'd been to the oratory so much; perhaps a different venue might be called for. Over breakfast, I thought, *If I had to sum up the last eight weeks in one word, it would be "perspective."* I'd seen firsthand that a change in understanding could lead to a total change of view. *Going somewhere to read where I can also physically do something related to "perspective" would be fun,* I decided, trying to figure out where that might be.

After another mug of Earl Grey tea, I decided St. Paul's Cathedral would be a great choice; it had a staircase that led all the way to the top of the dome, where you could look out across the entire city. In hindsight it probably wasn't the wisest thing for anyone to do after a drug treatment and a nervous breakdown; my body was still fairly fragile. But it seemed a good way to explore the idea of "perspective," and I wanted to mark my new paradigm—the tangible, visual memory it would give me would be worth braving the hundreds of steps.

Arriving at St. Paul's, I walked through a crowd of pigeons as they pecked around at crumbs on the pavement. They scattered, taking to the air as I stepped past. The steps of the cathedral rose in front of me, flanked by giant pillars and heavy wooden doors. Inside, I walked past a statue of two angels—they stood at least seven feet tall—both carrying swords. Tourists lined the aisles as they too stared around at this masterpiece of a building. I made my way to the back of the sanctuary and turned toward a small doorway, the way up to the highest tower. A mind-spinning, narrow staircase led upward and upward, 528 steps and almost 365 feet in height.

Everything was worth it the moment I ended the climb and stepped out into daylight. When I walked out onto the balcony, London was laid out below in a stunning panorama: Parliament and Big Ben, the Shard tower, the London Eye, the River Thames. It was glorious in the morning light. This gorgeous view and the theme of "perspective" injected energy into me for my reading that day, and I descended the hundreds of stairs, found a quiet pew, and opened my Bible to the book of Acts.

In chapter 11, I read that Peter found himself in hot water, thanks to his new perspective on welcoming Gentiles into the Christian faith. In Jerusalem he was accosted by "certain Jewish believers who followed the Law" (11:2, AMP) who were shocked that he'd preached in the homes of non-Jews and allowed them to be baptized. Tensions were at boiling point. As theologian Jane Williams explains, the New Testament provides "a glimpse of how difficult and bitter the move to include non-Jews was in the early days of Christian mission."[1]

Peter defended his views, explaining all that had happened: the vision of the sheet, the Holy Spirit telling him to go without hesitation to visit Cornelius, the amazement he'd felt when he saw God's presence show up in the Gentile household. Impassioned, he told them: "When I began to speak, the Holy Spirit fell on them just as He did on us at the beginning [at Pentecost]" (11:15, AMP).

His closing argument was this: "If then God gave them the same gift he gave us who believed in the Lord Jesus Christ, who was I that I could hinder God?" Thankfully, this helped his critics see things more clearly.

As a result, "When they heard this, they were silenced. And they praised God, saying, 'Then God has given even to the Gentiles the repentance that leads to life'" (11:17–18).

Outrage had given way to surprise, then amazement, and finally joy, as they realized former outsiders were now insiders. God had done something so powerful, and all they could do was marvel and try to catch up with his divine plan. His kingdom was bigger, wider, and more welcoming than they'd ever imagined.

Not everyone was able to accept this new theological shift, though. Concerns bubbled under the surface about exactly how Gentiles should be integrated into the church. Some Jewish Christians decided that if

Gentiles were allowed in, the least they could do was keep Jewish traditions: they should eat kosher, the men should be circumcised, and they should observe Sabbath day restrictions. A campaign to enforce these rules among the Gentile Christians was growing in momentum.

To deal with these heated tensions, Acts 15 says, a council meeting was called in Jerusalem. By now, the apostle Paul was also fully in favor of including Gentiles, having seen in his own missionary work that the Holy Spirit was active in their lives (14:27). At the Jerusalem meeting, Paul defended the freedom of the Gentiles and the way God was at work in their lives. Peter was also present, and he reminded the council about his powerful vision and the way God had declared the Gentiles "clean." Loading them with responsibilities God had not requested was not appropriate.

Peter urged them to accept this, saying: "God, who knows the heart, bore witness to [the Gentiles], by giving them the Holy Spirit just as he did to us, and he made *no distinction* between us and them, having cleansed their hearts by faith. Now, therefore, why are you putting God to the test by placing a yoke on the neck of [these] disciples?" (15:8–10, ESV). The apostle James added a powerful plea: "It is my judgment, therefore, that we should not make it difficult for the Gentiles who are turning to God" (15:19, NIV).

After thought and prayer, the council reached a decision—the Gentiles would *not* need to keep the law of Moses. They would *not* have to keep kosher. They would *not* have to be circumcised. All that was asked of them was that they abstain from food that had been sacrificed to idols or meat that had been killed in a way that Jewish law prohibited, and that they remain faithful in sexual conduct and in marriage—not engaging in lust-driven pleasure where other people are used and abused, but honoring sex within faithful, lifelong monogamy. No other requirements were placed on them that would weigh them down or cause them harm. The Jewish Christians now understood that the Gentiles' welcome was total: God had said they were clean just as they were.

From my newfound point of view, believing that a person *could* be gay and Christian, these chapters in Acts seemed to have multiple layers of meaning. I couldn't help thinking it had overlap with the place of LGBTQ+ people in the church today.

Many congregations had struggled to accept LGBTQ+ Christians at all. When some finally did, they argued that anyone identifying as gay or lesbian must take on the additional requirement of staying unmarried and celibate. The buzzword increasingly used in evangelical circles was SSA, which stands for "same-sex attraction." Traditional churches and various organizations were teaching that you should call yourself "same-sex attracted" rather than "gay" and consider your feelings deeply sinful and never to be acted upon. The only chance you would have for a life partner would be if you could change your orientation by becoming "ex-gay" or "post-gay" and marry someone of the opposite sex. Otherwise, you should never date or marry.

The term "same-sex attraction" stems from "Same Sex Attraction Disorder" (SSAD), a psychological classification indicating that homosexuality was historically treated as a disorder, although SSAD has been removed from the diagnostic manual now for forty-five years. Whenever the term "SSA" is used today, it echoes back to SSAD and the days when homosexuality was seen as a psychological disorder. "You're not actually 'gay,'" traditional Christian leaders now often say, "you're dealing with SSA and disordered desires; you just need to obey Christ by living a life of celibacy."

This approach was gathering momentum among evangelicals, and it seemed like a neat, tidy answer to the "issue" of homosexuality and what to do with LGBTQ+ Christians. "You can be SSA and stay inside our community," churches said, "but here are the restrictions you need to follow in order for us to let you belong." Gay and lesbian Christians' desire for a spouse was seen as dirty, sinful, and broken. This teaching on SSA was even being taught at UK Christian youth camps.

I'd been around these views all my life. It was given different names:

conversion therapy, reparative therapy, or even just prayer ministry for people with SSA. The goal was the same, though; either to change someone's orientation or to reinforce their need to reject their attractions and stay single for life. I'd undergone my exorcism as a teenager based on that idea. I'd also been part of several churches in the States that publicly offered "healing courses" for anyone gay or bisexual; they blamed it on emotional damage from childhood, like a lack of sufficient bonding with your parents, or someone abusing you, and believed prayer could "heal" a person back to their original "ideal state" of being heterosexual. Back in the UK, more and more organizations were promoting this.

Some of the Christians teaching about SSA were people I'd known for years, people I care about today. They said they simply wanted to honor God and be faithful to what they believed the Bible said. They argued that "the church has always done it this way" or "the Bible clearly says . . ." I understood their desire to honor God, and knew many of them had good intentions, but with the help of my new perspective, I could see that the mantras "we've always done it this way" and "the Bible clearly says" were both reminiscent of the arguments about slavery and women's rights, and I recalled how painfully wrong the church had been before.

Of course, I respected anyone's right to choose celibacy or singleness for themselves, regardless of their orientation; it's an individual decision, and plenty of straight people have chosen celibacy throughout church history and were happy, whole, and thoroughly fulfilled. The problem was when this choice was rooted in the belief that same-sex relationships were sinful and when this view was enforced on others, teaching that the *only* option for gay people is celibacy or opposite-sex marriage. That's when I had seen it become extremely damaging to myself and many others.

In Acts 15, when the early church tried to load Gentiles with extra requirements, Paul and Peter told them this was *not* God's way. In this, I saw a possible precedent for LGBTQ+ Christians. We could be accepted as we were—equal—and without extra legalism that would prevent us from having the blessings enjoyed by straight Christians: loving and serving a spouse, creating a home, and raising children together. Yes, staying away from the worship of "idols" was required of all Christ's followers, as was a commitment to sexual faithfulness. These were the same standards set for all, without discrimination.

In all of this, I sensed God speaking to me again. If he said my sexual orientation was "clean," then I needed to accept that and believe that having a same-sex spouse someday was not only possible, but something God would bless. Being forced to remain single, simply because I was gay, would be the equivalent of the red tape loaded on the early Gentiles—above and beyond what God required and leading to loneliness and isolation rather than abundant life.

In that moment, it felt like a huge weight fell off my shoulders. I had clarity, and I felt peace for the first time in ages. Instead of feeling broken under the shame of having same-sex attraction, a teaching that had almost driven me to suicide, now I knew I was loved and affirmed right to the core of my being. I was free to reflect God's love in the way I would love and serve a future female spouse.

As with the Gentile and Jewish Christians, I was on an equal footing with straight people in the church; I was not a second-class citizen, barred from some of the sacraments. Healing flooded into me as I accepted that my future could be one filled with love and warmth rather than isolation and shame. I was not disordered; I was whole.

St. Paul's cathedral towered around me as I sat in a pew, taking all of this in. It was inspiring to have read about what the apostle Paul himself had said and done, while sitting in this vast cathedral named after him. Wiping tears from my face, I packed up my Bible. I walked through the majestic nave, past the statues of the seven-foot-tall angels with their swords, with a huge sense of peace and God's protection filling my heart.

As I went to leave, someone called my name. "Vicky Beeching?" I heard a voice say. I turned and met a family who were visiting from overseas and had come to the cathedral as tourists. "We thought it was you," the mother said with a smile. "We sing your songs in our church in Australia; we've all benefited so much from the 'good fruit' of your life. The Holy Spirit is on display in your music and your songwriting. Thank you for all you do."

I was touched by her words of encouragement. We all hugged and took a quick photo together, and they headed off to see the rest of the cathedral. As I left, the woman's words echoed in my mind: "good fruit." These words referred to one of Jesus's teachings. He'd said that Christians were like trees and that their actions were like fruit. His argument was that a good tree would produce good fruit, and a bad tree would produce bad fruit. Jesus used this teaching to specifically warn against "false prophets" (a title thrown at me by traditionalists since my coming out). Christ said that false prophets could be identified by the "bad fruit" their life would naturally produce. The point was that people's faith was seen to be true or false based on what their lives produced; that evidence was what proved whether they were true followers of Jesus or not.

Christians from around the world had told me for years that my music and songs were helping them connect with God—that they were good fruit. I'd done all my music ministry as a gay person. Sure, I wasn't in relationships, but I was still wired the same way. How could I have produced this good fruit if being gay was so sinful? Surely that would make me a "bad tree" and I should've been producing bad fruit. It reminded me of what Peter and Paul had said to the council in Acts: *Look at these Gentile Christians—God is powerfully alive in their lives. How can anyone deny that the Holy Spirit is with them? They are genuine followers of Christ and on equal footing with everyone else in the church.*

It also made me think about SSA and the kind of fruit I'd seen in the lives of many people who embraced the idea that their gay orientation was sinful and disordered. Many were isolated, depressed, fearful, and even engaging in self-harm because of their feelings of shame and loneliness. People contacted me regularly through my website telling me this was what they were dealing with, many of them Christian teenagers.

This wasn't good fruit; this was just heartbreakingly sad. Many put on a brave face, but behind closed doors were honest about the vast toll this shame and crushing legalism took on them and their well-being.

I could totally imagine a church committee like the council of Acts 15 happening in Christian circles today with regard to LGBTQ+ people. "Yes, maybe these people can belong to the church, but let's talk about the boundaries, the rules, the paperwork . . ." It's human nature to put our own limits, or rules, on anything new in order to retain a sense of control. It's easier to stick to habit. However, as Jesus said in Matthew 9:17, new wine requires new wineskins—sometimes our model has to grow and flex, just as it did when the Gentiles were welcomed into the formerly Jewish-only church.

It had been a long afternoon of reading and reflection. I finished by spending time in prayer, offering it all to God. I packed up my bag of books and walked out of St. Paul's Cathedral, staring up at the majestic ceiling as I left.

What an intense couple of months it's been, I thought as I headed home. My mind kept running over all the things I'd encountered in my studies, especially in the book of Acts. Finally, I had come to terms with who I was and that God had created me this way. Finally, I'd begun to find some clarity on the complex issues of celibacy and same-sex marriage too.

My stomach lurched as I thought what all of this would mean for my life. These were not conclusions I'd arrived at willingly—I'd fought them mentally and emotionally all my life, trying to hold on to traditional theology. Accepting I was gay and endorsing same-sex marriage would mean huge things for me; speaking publicly about them would cause my entire life and career to implode.

I was still on a partial hiatus from touring and recording, but this had only ever been temporary while I had the chemo and regained my health. Anytime now, I was expected back in the States, and the machinery of my Christian music career would whirr back to full speed. Having been through a nervous breakdown and seen the damage that living in the closet had caused, I knew it was not an option to return to that way of life. I needed to step out and be my authentic self, and I needed to do that publicly. But the prospect was terrifying.

One thing steadied me: I knew God's voice was the one I must follow. I'd sensed his guidance in all the research, study, and prayer of the past few months. I remembered Peter, and how unsettled he was by the vision of the sheet, and the struggle he went through to help the church become inclusive. I also remembered Galileo, Martin Luther King Jr., Wilberforce, and the suffragettes; they were a good reminder that sometimes you have to take the road less traveled and that love always wins in the end. I needed to trust that God would give me the courage to walk the road ahead.

22

As the train rushed through the British countryside, fields, forests, and houses sped past in a beautiful blur. I was on my way to visit Wendy for an important conversation. Finally, I was going to tell someone, other than my therapist, that I was gay. I wanted to tell Wendy my secret, and also about all I'd learned from studying what the Bible actually said about sexuality. Wendy was the safest person I knew to go to with this; she'd showed me such care and support throughout my drug treatment.

Wendy, Simon, and their two daughters live on the south coast in a peaceful beach town, so I made the journey down from London. She had no idea that I wanted to talk about something so serious, but I hoped there'd be an opportunity during the day.

A big sign saying "Welcome to the Sunshine Coast" hung over the railway station as I arrived. We jumped into her car and drove along the road beside the sea, with a Coldplay CD playing at full volume. It was great to be well again, healthy and energized.

The Eastbourne Pier stood, white and ornamental, stretching out into the water. It looked so beautiful that day, sparkling in the summer weather, so we decided to park the car and walk along it. The pier was full of tourists buying cotton candy, playing arcade games, and eating ice-cream cones. With the sun warming our faces, we walked all the way to the end. The water stretched as far as the eye could see toward the horizon, which was almost indecipherable as the blue of the waves melted seamlessly into the turquoise of the sky.

Leaning against the railing, I found the courage to clear my throat and bring up the topic. Somehow, stumbling over my words, I managed to tell Wendy that I was gay—and about all that had happened during my study at the Brompton Oratory and St. Paul's. I told her I believed the Bible didn't condemn same-sex relationships, and that I was going to find the courage to come out and hopefully try and make a difference in the church.

It helped that I'd spoken to Chris, my therapist, about it, but telling a friend felt very different. I didn't know what words to use, and I was trembling with nerves. At the end of my rambling sentences, Wendy was tearful. She could sense the pain I'd been in and how hard it was to finally get it off my chest.

"I'm really honored that you're trusting me with something so private," she said. "I'm so, so sorry you've had to carry this on your own for so many years." She handed me a tissue, adding, "I still think you're just as brilliant as I always have, and this changes nothing in our friendship. I'm not going anywhere. I'll be here for you. So will all of my family, as you journey forward with it all."

Relief washed over me. I exhaled a long breath as my nervousness was replaced by gratitude that our friendship would remain strong. I knew not all Christians would have had the same response.

Why did I wait all these years? was my next thought, aware that I had made it past the age of thirty before telling any of my friends about my sexuality. It was a lot to process—the relief, the sudden regrets about the past, the happiness of being accepted unconditionally. My brain felt overloaded by this sudden wave of emotions, and I burst into tears. Leaning against the railings, with my head in my hands, I sobbed it all out.

"It's okay," Wendy said. "Let it all out. It's no wonder there's a lot of pain in there."

Once my tears had subsided, we walked back along the pier talking. She asked whether this had been something I'd ever expressed in my music. I told her about writing "Above All Else" in the Wycliffe chapel. And I told her about another of my songs, "Undivided Heart," which had been a prayer that God would change me from gay to straight. I googled the lyrics, and she looked at them to refresh her memory.

UNDIVIDED HEART

Brokenness has brought me to my knees.
Face to face with all that's dark in me,
I can barely see you through my shame.
Jesus, come and wash me white again.

Flood me with your healing light,
Help me choose what's true and right.

Give me an undivided heart,
I want to love you with every part.
Give me an undivided soul,
I want to be yours alone, yours alone.

At the cross I find your open arms,
Reminding me there's grace for all I've done.
With your blood you wipe away my past,
Taking on yourself my sin and scars.

By your power help me change,
Break off every single chain.

Give me an undivided heart,
I want to love you with every part.
Give me an undivided soul,
I want to be yours alone, yours alone.

You make all things new,
So take my ashes and make them something beautiful.
Do what only you can do,
Take my ashes and make them something beautiful.

We both stood looking at the words on the screen of my smartphone. It was interesting to consider what they'd meant to me in the past, and what they could mean now. Back then, I'd thought being undivided meant rejecting my orientation, seeing it as sinful and shameful, so I could be wholly committed to God. But now, in the light of all my biblical study, it meant something different. Being undivided meant accepting both my faith and my sexuality. God had never required this sense of fragmentation in me. He simply wanted me to be the person he'd created.

Looking at that song reminded me that I would no longer get to sing it in American megachurches or UK evangelical conferences if I took the step of going public with my sexuality. Wendy knew, as I did, that my well-known platform in that part of the church would crumble. It felt like such a cruel choice, but one I had to make.

We chatted about how and when I was thinking of speaking out publicly. I told her I hadn't figured out the timing yet, but that I'd probably find a safe journalist and trust that person to interview me and tell my story. I knew it couldn't be within the evangelical Christian press, as anyone interviewing me from that sector would likely skew the article based on vehement disagreement with me.

As we walked along the seafront, watching seagulls soaring in the sunshine, I knew I'd taken a monumental step in finally telling a friend that I was gay. Wendy dropped me back at the train station, saying, "You're not alone in this anymore—and there will be plenty of others like me who'll stand with you as you take this brave step."

On the journey back, I felt glad, but also a little shocked, as it sank in that I'd finally said the words to someone outside the walls of a therapist's office. And if I could tell Wendy and have it go well, maybe I could find the courage to talk to others too.

knew coming out was going to mean the loss of my Christian music career and my place in the evangelical faith community. It was a devastating prospect. I had to start thinking about how on earth I would make a living when that happened. Otherwise, I'd be left without a roof over my head.

I had built my church-music career for the past fifteen years into something I'd imagined I would do for the rest of my life. The questions felt overwhelming: Should I retrain for a different type of work altogether? What else could I do besides music? What did I even enjoy?

For now, I needed something I could develop, alongside the worship leading I was doing at UK events. My delay in returning full-time to Nashville could be justified by the fact that I'd started taking worship conference bookings again in the UK, and strengthening my platform in the UK benefited album sales. All of this would give me a little more room before everyone expected me to return to American megachurches full-time and start work on a new album.

So what other career could I start to train in that would survive my coming out? The recurring answer coming to mind was my love of academic study and of writing. I thought back with fondness to my years at Oxford, reading in the libraries for hours and writing papers. Reading at the Brompton Oratory and at St. Paul's Cathedral had reawakened all of that. Maybe returning to academia could be an alternative career for me? I began pondering the possibility of starting a part-time

PhD. I also loved journalism and had been writing for American magazines, and on my own blog, for years about theology and current affairs. Maybe I could transition into a mixture of academia and journalism, as I faced the loss of my full-time livelihood in music.

Grateful that my health was now back to normal and that the scleroderma, although it had left a significant scar on my forehead, was now benign, I whirred into action. I submitted applications for PhD programs, went for interviews, and as a new academic year approached, I got the letter I'd been hoping for. I'd been accepted into the PhD program at Durham University.

Durham is a beautiful, historic city in the northeast of England, and its university ranked close to Oxford and Cambridge in league tables—so I was delighted to get in. Juggling this study plus continuing to lead worship at UK Christian conferences was a lot to handle and required constant train rides up and down the country, but it felt like I finally had a piece of my life that didn't hinge on my appearing to be straight.

My area of research was an interesting one—the way technology, social media, and artificial intelligence (AI) are changing our behavior as a society. I was exploring the ethical implications that these new developments in human history brought with them. I had an academic background in ethics, plus a geeky interest in technology—I lived my life surrounded by guitar pedals, recording gear, and the latest gadgets—so this topic felt like a natural fit for me.

I read voraciously, absorbing every piece of research I could find in Durham's libraries. I began writing blogs on what I was learning and also pitched articles to national newspapers like *The Guardian* and the *Huffington Post* commenting on current affairs in both the tech sector and the religious sector.

To my surprise, these articles gained traction. As I progressed through the PhD, my cell phone started to ring with calls from TV and radio stations. They were looking for young academic researchers with journalistic talent to appear on programs and discuss stories. They'd heard about my experience of speaking and singing to large audiences and felt I'd be comfortable on air. "We don't always want professors on our shows, because they can get so lost within the confines of academia that they can't explain things in a simple sound bite. We need people who are doing academic research—PhD or post-doc is fine—who are skilled at making complex things understandable to the public and who have their own opinions." Grateful for their interest, I said yes.

As the months passed, these calls increased. Appearing on one show seemed to lead to another and another. I found myself going to the BBC or Sky News studios and radio stations at least once a week; it had quickly become a big part of my life, alongside singing and studying. We debated fascinating topics like cyberbullying and online abuse, how kids could safely engage with the internet, and the place of robots and artificial intelligence in the generations to come. In view of my theology background at Oxford, they also asked me to comment on religious affairs like the resignation of Pope Benedict XVI and the announcement of his successor, Pope Francis. I was also invited to do "Thought for the Day" regularly on BBC Radio 4's *Today* program, a show reaching around 7 million listeners a week.

One Saturday morning, I sat in the Sky News greenroom, waiting to meet the man I'd been paired up with for a news program. He walked in, impeccably dressed in a blue velvet suit jacket, and said his name was Patrick Strudwick. I discovered that he was openly gay and frequently published groundbreaking articles on LGBTQ+ issues in national papers.

Patrick greeted me warmly, and we drank coffee while exchanging small talk. He was genuinely interested in who I was, the work I did, and my background. But I didn't tell him about my sexuality—that remained something very private to me. After Patrick and I did the broadcast, he gave me his card and said I should stay in touch. I realized, as I drove away in an awaiting taxi, that I'd found a journalist who was himself gay and was someone I could trust.

Soon I'd be ready to publicly come out as gay. Through academia and the broadcasting work, I'd started building a different career alongside my music—one that would hopefully be there as a safety net, when leading worship and my place within evangelicalism imploded. Patrick had made a huge impression on me. I had a strong hunch that when I came out, I would go to him with the story; he seemed the perfect person to write the piece. This filled me with a sense of hope, but also with dread. I knew how much vitriol going public would create, and that losing my music career and my community would be the price I'd have to pay.

23

Big Ben chimed as I walked past, its magnificent stone tower rising into a pale-blue sky. I was headed into Parliament, to a gathering of female journalists held in the House of Commons. I felt humbled to be included, and excited to visit such a historic venue.

After airport-style security, I was inside the House of Commons and taken to a small wood-paneled room with oil paintings on the walls and a direct view of the River Thames. It was great to feel energized and healthy, and to know I was growing my professional network beyond church circles. Inside, about forty women mingled around, swapping business cards. I found myself chatting with some of the most fascinating people I'd ever encountered.

"Now, who haven't you met yet?" one of the organizers said, wanting to ensure everyone made good connections. "Have you been introduced to Jane Czyzselska? She's the editor of a magazine for LGBTQ women. She's openly gay herself and highly respected for her work championing diversity and equality."

Those words unnerved me—I hadn't expected anyone to bring up the topic of sexuality that day. I was still very much in the closet, and even the mention of "LGBTQ" was enough to make me anxious.

"Umm . . . no, I haven't," I replied, trying not to look awkward.

She waved Jane over and left the two of us to chat. I panicked internally, thinking, "Jane's a lesbian—so does that mean she's got a flawless gaydar? What if she can tell . . . ? What if she looks into my eyes and just . . . *knows*?"

I shook her hand and tried to make small talk. She was delightful, and we had a great chat. Finding out that I was a Christian, she said she hoped the church would progress on LGBTQ+ equality issues. I nodded, thinking, *Goodness, so do I, for my own sake as well as for others'.*

· We swapped business cards and said we'd keep in touch. Walking away, I felt relieved—her gaydar hadn't figured me out. As Jane strolled off to meet others in the room, I watched her networking with the other women. As far as I knew, she was the only openly gay woman at that gathering. I noticed that she carried herself with a huge amount of confidence and dignity.

Everyone there was wearing tight-fitting dresses and dainty high heels with pointed toes. I hated dresses, but had started wearing them for TV work, as most women on screen seemed to. That day in Parliament, I'd walked uncomfortably around the room in my restrictive dress and pointed heels. Jane was wearing loose-fitting suit trousers and a pair of beautiful honey-brown, round-toed brogue lace-up boots. She looked professional and stylish, but in a way that was different from the other women there; she seemed authentically herself, effortlessly comfortable in her own skin.

I'd lacked LGBTQ+ role models all my life and had never been around openly gay people in my church settings. Meeting Patrick Strudwick had been really significant for me. Now, Jane was the first openly lesbian woman I'd been around in a professional context. As I watched her, it struck me how fearful and ashamed I was about being gay. Years of homophobic Christian teachings and sermons had left their mark. I was nervous about how I'd carry myself publicly after coming out.

But here was Jane, a woman who had absolutely no qualms about her identity or fear of what others thought. She was in Parliament, networking with some of the most powerful women in the UK, dressed in her own unique style and openly proud of being a lesbian.

A voice inside my head piped up: *If she can do that, maybe you can too.* Perhaps I could become that confident in my identity. Perhaps I could walk with my head held high rather than being fearful about what others would think and living under a cloud of worries and old shame. Maybe I could dress in the tomboy style that I'd always wanted to. I felt as though she'd given me a glimpse of a whole different reality.

Visiting the House of Commons had increased my interest in politics. Later that year, when an organization working to combine faith and political activism invited me to meet them, I jumped at the chance and found myself walking past Big Ben again and into Westminster.

As I entered the lobby in the Commons, a TV screen showed what was being debated that day in the chamber. To my surprise it said "Marriage (Same Sex Couples) Bill." I knew that an MP named Maria Miller had championed this within Parliament, as the Conservative Party was considering trying to legalize same-sex marriage in the UK. Today, it turned out, was one of the readings of that bill.

"I'd love to see if we could poke our heads into the Commons debating chamber before we sit and meet?" I said to the man from the faith and politics organization as he greeted me in the lobby. "I'm still new to this place, so I guess I still feel a bit like a tourist, wanting to see all the sights," I added, keen to stress that it wasn't the particular debate that interested me, just the chamber itself.

He disappeared to have a word with the relevant people. Coming back brandishing a piece of paper, he said we were in luck. We walked along winding hallways decorated with oil paintings and up narrow stairs to the Commons viewing gallery. "We can stay for three or four minutes," he said in a whisper as we pushed open the wooden door and walked onto the balcony.

When I looked down, there was Maria Miller standing at the dispatch box, speaking about the bill and how she believed it was time for the UK to embrace same-sex marriage. I watched, my heart pounding, grateful that I was able to witness such a special moment in LGBTQ+ history; the UK was slowly changing for the better.

Sitting there watching her, I felt so many emotions. I wished I could voice my support for LGBTQ+ equality in society, even if I didn't say it was about me. Now that I was certain of my own theology, it was increasingly hard not to speak up for social justice. I'd wanted to talk to Patrick Strudwick about my new views, and to Jane Czyzselska too, but I'd been too afraid. I felt like a traitor, not doing my part. Plenty of straight people were adding their voices to the campaign for same-sex marriage, so perhaps it was something I could do *before* taking the bigger leap of telling the world I was gay.

The TV shows I often appeared on covered stories about LGBTQ+ rights from time to time. Sometimes I was asked for my opinion. In the past, I'd tried to deflect this topic, but now, I decided, I had to start expressing my new views. I knew this would create a lot of fallout for me, because the vast majority of evangelicals would consider me a traitor. One straight pastor, Steve Chalke, had stuck his neck out for this cause and been kicked out of the Evangelical Alliance, branded a heretic. I knew I was likely to get the same treatment.

It felt important, though. Inspired by that day in Parliament, I knew I couldn't wait any longer to add my voice to the same-sex marriage campaign. Maybe it could be a way of tackling the coming-out process in stages: first I would come out in support of LGBTQ+ equality, and then, second, I would say that I myself am gay. I was nauseous at the prospect of both, but splitting the journey into two stages seemed like a slightly softer approach.

I led worship at several large Christian events around that time, and each seemed to happen in slow motion. I looked out from the stages at the sea of faces, listening to them singing my songs. I knew that this vast and precious piece of my life and identity was soon going to end. The crowds had no knowledge of my changed views on LGBTQ+ equality, and they assumed I was as traditional as they were. Once I voiced my support for same-sex marriage, I knew invitations to play at conferences would slow down. Then when I came out, I knew the doors would all slam in my face.

As I stood on those stages, I looked across at my UK bandmates and tears filled my eyes at the knowledge that I would no longer get to play with them at the large evangelical conferences that had become such a big part of our lives. The prospect of losing so much was heartbreaking.

When the right moment presented itself, I spoke out. It happened organically when the topic came up in a TV show. I said I'd come to the conclusion that the church *should* offer marriage to same-sex couples, and that I believed there was *nothing* in the Bible to condemn it. That same week, I published a series of blogs about it.

I wasn't ready for the wave of criticism from fellow Christians. I knew my words would be negatively received, but I hadn't expected such a tsunami. Comments poured in from evangelicals and Pentecostals in the UK, the US, Canada, and beyond. People said they were utterly shocked and disappointed in me, that I had clearly lost my faith, and that I would never be welcome to sing in churches again. Staff from the agencies and labels I was working with on both sides of the pond suggested that I should be very cautious; I knew I was on dangerous ground. My music career wasn't totally over, but it would be irreparably damaged as a result of this step.

It was crushing. I couldn't believe how two-faced people could be. Only days earlier, many of them had been posting on Facebook and Twitter how much they loved my songs and enjoyed seeing me on tour.

But as soon as I made my pro-gay theology public, they called me every name under the sun. Doors were already slamming in my face.

Expressing these views before actually coming out, I had hoped, would show me people were *more* open-minded than I'd expected. But it proved the opposite. At moments, I wondered if I should abandon the next stage of my plan, to personally come out as gay. The wave of criticism and abuse was alarming, showing me that the Christians I worked with around the world were still staunchly against same-sex marriage. Many of my relatives were horrified that I was expressing these pro-gay views, suggesting I stop talking about it and reexamine my theology. No one had any idea it was about me and my orientation, though; simply holding the views themselves was a one-way ticket out of evangelicalism. Coming out as gay would be a thousand times worse.

Needing some support, I headed to Kent to visit my sister, Jo. I loved being around her and her kids. They were still young, and it was fun to read them stories, watch Disney movies together, and be Auntie Vicky. One evening, when the kids were all tucked in bed, Jo and I sat having a quiet cup of tea.

Breaking the silence, she said, "You know, if you ever brought a special someone home one day, to meet the wider family, it wouldn't matter to me if it was a guy or . . . a girl."

I was really surprised and had no idea where her comment had come from. I'd never talked to her about my orientation. She knew that recently I'd been saying supportive things about same-sex marriage online and on TV, but no one had connected the dots and imagined that it related to me. People didn't seem able to conceive that an evangelical poster girl might be dealing with something like that. Gay people were seen as *out there*, located far away, not inside the walls of churches or standing on stage leading worship for thousands of evangelical conference-goers.

Somehow my sister had a hunch. Perhaps it was a sibling thing, a special connection.

Oddly enough, I'd been sitting on her sofa that evening feeling immensely sad that I never got to bring a partner home to meet my relatives. "Do you have a boyfriend, Auntie Vicky?" one of my nieces had asked earlier. I wished I could have said, "Actually I don't like boys. I like girls. And maybe one day I'll have someone special you can meet." But all I could reply to my niece was, "No, I don't have a boyfriend," as I felt my cheeks burning with awkwardness.

Jo was, it seemed, the one person in my life who'd had a vague hunch about my orientation. And I was totally knocked off balance as I tried to figure out how to reply to her. Though we were both raised in the same Christian home, my sister isn't someone who identifies as religious anymore, so she didn't have any faith-based reasons to oppose same-sex relationships. I probably could have told her long ago, but I hadn't wanted her to have to carry such a big secret when my wider family didn't know.

That night, I still wasn't ready to talk about it, perhaps just because the moment had come so unexpectedly. Turning pink, I just laughed it off and said, "It's great to know how open-minded you are about things like that." In true British style, I said, "Would you like another cup of tea?" and hurried awkwardly into the kitchen to put the kettle on. I said nothing further about it all evening.

When I went to bed, I lay awake for hours. I was taken aback that she'd mentioned my orientation out of the blue, but it was a weight off my shoulders to know she would accept me unconditionally when I finally confirmed her suspicions. *If only everyone was as understanding and unconditionally kind as my sister,* I thought. I knew most of my friends, relatives, and church colleagues would have totally different views. Faith can be a wonderful thing, but it can also build huge walls between people—even blood relatives—and I knew most of mine held lifelong beliefs that homosexuality was wrong and sinful.

Jo's comment was a good reminder that I did need to tell my family *before* I came out publicly. It was only fair; I didn't want them to hear it from a newspaper interview. I knew my parents would need time to process it before everyone else found out and was asking them questions about it. But likewise, I needed them to keep it confidential, and I didn't want them to feel alone with that heavy information for longer than a couple of months.

This played on my mind in the weeks ahead. After a lot of thought, I concluded that I would talk to my parents and sister in the spring of 2014, then do the interview with Patrick in the summer. Finally having a timeline made me feel sick with nerves. But I also sensed I was, at last, glimpsing light at the end of the tunnel.

24

April 2014 brought with it some unexpected and devastating news. My grandmother was very ill and had been taken to hospital. It looked as though she was close to death, so we were asked to visit as soon as possible.

Walking into the Queen Elizabeth Hospital in Margate, Kent, and following a nurse to the ward, I saw my grandmother—or Nanny, as we always called her—lying on a hospital bed. She was a frail shadow of the person she'd been, so weak and pale. The nurse said she'd been slipping in and out of consciousness all day.

My mum and dad had been to visit a lot that week and said that Nanny had been awake and talkative the previous day. But during my time there, she didn't stir much and barely opened her eyes. At one point when I was talking to her, it seemed as though she smiled a little and squeezed my hand, but I couldn't be sure.

It was heartbreaking not to be able to chat like we usually did. I already missed her warm, mischievous smile and the way she'd hug me and want to hear every detail of my life. We knew she was beginning to slip away from us, and the hole she was leaving in our hearts was going to be vast.

As I stood at her bedside, grief hit me, and tears ran down my cheeks. Mum noticed I was crying, and this started her off too. We stood, hugging, as we watched Nanny fighting for her life and struggling for breath. She'd be leaving us soon—and I knew this might be the last time I ever saw her. It was, as she would die a few days later.

Being in the Queen Elizabeth Hospital in Margate reminded me of my own entrance into the world. It was the hospital where I'd been born. It seemed so strange to think of the full-circle nature of life. I'd come into the world in that building in 1979, and my grandmother had visited me in the maternity ward. Now full circle, in 2014, here we both were in the same building again, and I was saying good-bye to her. It made life feel so brief and fragile. My mind sped forward. Would this be the same hospital that I would lie in, someday in the future, when I breathed my final breath? Our time on earth suddenly felt so limited; many things that seemed to matter faded away in the light of this.

Mum, Dad, and I wiped our tears and said good-bye to Nanny as we headed out of the ward. These thoughts of life and death had created an urgency for me. I needed to talk to my parents about my gay orientation. In our grief and sadness that day, it felt as though our hearts were open to each other in a deeper way than usual.

In the car I fixed my makeup, as I was going to be part of a radio program in Canterbury that same afternoon. My parents were driving me there and dropping me off. The program was a BBC Radio 2 special about Easter on the theme of pilgrimage. Clare Balding, one of the UK's most well-known broadcasters and a national treasure, would be the presenter interviewing me. She's the most famous openly gay woman in British media, the UK's equivalent of America's Ellen DeGeneres.

When we arrived in Canterbury, Dad found a parking spot and waited with the car, while my mum walked me over to the hotel where I'd meet Claire Balding and the BBC producer who would be recording the program. We had a few minutes, so Mum and I stood outside the venue, the Falstaff Hotel, a fifteenth-century building with beautiful wooden beams and leaded windows decorating its white frontage. As we made small talk in the spring sunshine, it felt like the right moment to get vulnerable and tell her what I'd needed to say for so long.

Through tears, I told her I'd known I was gay since I was twelve or thirteen and that I finally needed to come out. I knew the news would be hard for both her and Dad—a real shock. I was also aware it would put them in a difficult position with their own evangelical Christian community. Previously I'd been loved by churches around the world, but now I would be seen as a heretic; my parents would constantly be asked for their views on it all and put in difficult situations. All of this raced around in my head as I told her about my orientation.

Mum was shocked and surprised by my news. Despite being taken aback, she remained her gentle and thoughtful self, reassuring me: "This is a lot to process, but we still love you unconditionally, of course." It was a bombshell; I knew it would take a long time for her and Dad to come to terms with it.

In a stroke of amusing unlikelihood, in the middle of this intense conversation, someone walked up behind me and tapped me on the shoulder. "Vicky, it's Clare. It's great to see you."

It was Clare Balding, arriving at the hotel for the BBC recording. "I'm really looking forward to recording the show with you today," she said with a smile.

I introduced Clare to my mother, enjoying the moment of light relief in the middle of such a serious conversation. Clare had no knowledge of what we'd been talking about, but her timing couldn't have been more ideal. Smiling, I thought, *How many people can say that halfway through coming out to their mother, the best-known lesbian in the UK popped up and gave a cameo appearance, like an advertisement for the fact you can be gay, out and proud, and have a happy successful life?* I laughed at the timing of it all.

Clare excused herself, saying she was heading inside. "See you in a few minutes in the lobby," she called back. Mum and I continued our chat, and she was tearful as the news continued to sink in. As well as impacting our family, she knew it would also change my career, irreversibly.

"I'll talk to Dad about it," she said gently as we parted ways. I had no idea what she was going to say to my father or how they would deal with it together, but I was glad she would tell him instead of me needing to have a second "coming out" conversation that day. Mum assured me they wouldn't tell anyone else until I went public, which I really appreciated. I knew that secret would be a lot for them to carry, but she said they'd be grateful for the privacy and space to process it together before it hit the news.

Walking into the Falstaff Hotel, I felt dazed. I'd just come out to my mother after all these years of holding that secret inside. My sister, Jo, needed to know too, and I wanted her to hear it from me, so I dialed her number and told her. As expected, she didn't have a problem with it and just said she wished I had been able to talk about it back when I was in my early teens. She was pleased I'd finally taken the step.

Just as I finished chatting with my sister, Clare Balding and her producer appeared in the lobby. I finished the call, grateful for Jo's unconditional acceptance. Trying to switch my brain into broadcasting mode, we headed off to begin the BBC recording. I said nothing to Clare or her producer about all that had just happened to me; I still wanted to keep the information within my close family for now.

As the BBC show was a discussion about the theme of Easter and of pilgrimage, we were recording it outside, walking a path that led to Canterbury Cathedral. As we walked and talked, I couldn't help thinking how relevant that theme of pilgrimage felt to me—in my own journey as a pilgrim of faith, I'd just taken a very significant step toward greater authenticity as I trusted God's leading and moved forward in obedience.

My taxi pulled up at the Old Palace, a tenth-century stone building nestled in the shadow of Canterbury Cathedral. The Old Palace has been the official Kent residence of the archbishop of Canterbury since those distant, ancient times.

The BBC recording had gone well, and I was looking forward to spending the rest of the Easter weekend with the family of Justin Welby, the archbishop of Canterbury. The Welbys had become friends of mine, especially their eldest daughter, Katharine, and I loved their company.

I had never spoken to them about my orientation—nor would I during that stay. I hoped it wouldn't affect our friendship when they finally found out. (Thankfully, when I did tell Katharine later that spring, her response was overwhelmingly kind. She was deeply saddened that I'd had to carry such a weighty secret for so many years and assured me it didn't change anything in our friendship.)

That Easter weekend, I just wanted to enjoy their company. I would stay with the Welbys on Saturday evening, and then on Sunday I would join them at the cathedral for the annual Easter service, at which Archbishop Justin would preach. That night, after a lovely dinner together, I headed to bed. My room had a direct view of Canterbury Cathedral; towering into the sky, it was illuminated by lights that switched on at sunset. It looked majestic. Gazing at it through the leaded windows, I reflected on what an intense day it had been.

Finally, my parents and sister knew I was gay. And, quite coincidentally, I was spending the night in one of the oldest and most inspiring church buildings in the country. It felt like a comfort after such a scary step. Somehow it felt symbolic too. Having followed God's lead and spoken out about my orientation to my family, I was sleeping in the shadow of Canterbury Cathedral itself—the heart of Anglican geography. Rather than driving me away from God or the church, my coming-out journey was taking place in the shelter of God's love and mercy.

Today's date in the church calendar felt relevant too: Easter Saturday, the day when Christians remembered Christ in the tomb, silent in the darkness. It's known as a day of waiting, a day of mystery, a day of experiencing the pain of Jesus's death and the tension of not yet knowing he would rise. I've always had a deep connection with Easter Saturday, as it felt so much like my spiritual journey: the mystery of not knowing what to do about my orientation and the "dark night of the soul" that I'd experienced so potently over the decades as a result of it.

As I thought back through years of sadness and struggle—the day on the London Underground when I'd nearly jumped, the unending isolation and heartbreak, the weight of the shame and fear I'd had to carry—it felt like I'd been a "dead person walking" for as long as I could remember. It was as though I was partly wrapped in "grave clothes"; so much of who I was could never be fully alive.

Yet today, on this sacred date on the Christian calendar, I had finally said what I needed to say to my family. And tomorrow was Easter Sunday, the day Christians celebrated the resurrection of Christ. It was known as the day everything had changed, the moment the world had been made new.

A surge of emotion filled me as I realized my Easter Saturday was almost over—both literally and figuratively. The journey of being able to live authentically was beginning and tomorrow, Easter Sunday, marked "resurrection day." I would be able to attend the cathedral service and celebrate the Easter message with an added sense of joy. In that tenth-century room, with the cathedral bells ringing out the hours, I fell asleep exhausted but smiling.

The Easter morning service at Canterbury Cathedral, led by the archbishop, was powerful. I shed a few tears as the choir sang its anthems and the organ echoed through the cavernous building. As we recited the liturgy, "Christ has risen—he is risen indeed," it held even more significance for me than usual. Part of me had come back from the dead. It was a new beginning.

Returning from that trip to Canterbury, I felt a kaleidoscope of emotions: relief that my family knew; inspiration from the Easter service; gratitude for the friendship of the Welbys; but also fear that relationships like those, and my entire ministry, might soon hang in the balance when I came out publicly.

25

Rainbow flags fluttered in the breeze as I walked through Soho, the bustling LGBTQ+ district of London. It was an area of the city I'd always felt nervous to visit; it raised so many emotions—seeing others openly walking around hand in hand with their same-sex partners. It was a place I'd longed to go, yet had never felt I could.

Today it felt like the right location for the meeting I was about to have. I'd given my parents a couple of months to process the news about my orientation, while no one else knew. Then when spring became summer, I'd emailed the gay journalist I'd met at Sky News, Patrick Strudwick. Not telling him exactly what I wanted to meet about, I'd simply said, "I have a story that might be of interest to you."

We'd agreed to meet at a café on a Soho street corner and, grabbing a seat in the window, I watched as people walked by. Soon the annual Pride march would take place here, and the streets would be full of thousands of people walking, and dancing, through London campaigning for equality and respect.

Patrick arrived, and although it was lovely to see him again, I was on edge with nerves. Knowing I would struggle to tell him my story without crying or dissolving into anxiety, I'd decided to type it up and print it out. So after we ordered coffees and exchanged small talk, I reached into my bag and pulled out the pages.

"So about the story . . ." I began. "I've got some information printed out for you to read."

His eyebrows rose; it must have seemed strange that I couldn't just tell him. But, being his usual easygoing self, Patrick just smiled, took the pages, and began to read.

It felt like an eternity as I clutched my coffee mug, watching him scan through all that I'd written. I knew when he'd reached the part about me being gay, because he took an audible breath. He'd had no idea, and aware of my successful Christian music career, he knew what an internationally controversial and life-changing step coming out would be for me.

Finishing the last sentences, he looked up, tearful. "I'd love to be the one who helps you tell this story," he said. "And I'll do my absolute best to get it out to as many people as possible. I believe you're going to help thousands of LGBT people of faith find their own courage and freedom."

We sat in silence for a while, then chatted about the practicalities: when he would do the interview, which newspaper he would pitch the article to, which date we should aim to have it printed by. We decided to shoot for publication in mid-August.

A few days later, I took a taxi to Patrick's house. Greeted at the front door by his cat, Liza, I walked into the lounge, and we got ready for the interview. Turning on his audio recorder, he placed it on the arm of the sofa, and we began. We talked and talked, much of the conversation heavy and emotional.

One lighter moment made us erupt into laughter. Liza the cat, clearly feeling she wasn't getting as much attention as she required, launched herself from the floor, leaped onto the arm of sofa, and sent the recorder flying. Both the cat and recorder fell to the floor in a comedic heap. It was good to have something to make us smile.

Leaving Patrick's home, I was relieved and nervous in equal measure. My story was told. It would now be written and printed, and there was no going back. I had no regrets, but it was tangibly real. Only a few weeks remained of life as I knew it. Patrick would keep me updated on his writing process and on which newspaper had accepted it. All I could do was sit tight and wait.

PART V

Into the Unknown

26

"I'm heading off on my summer vacation," Patrick told me. "The story's written, and a national newspaper has accepted it. They're really enthusiastic about having the exclusive interview—and it'll be published within the next few weeks, depending on which day it fits best with their other stories."

I hadn't seen the piece yet, but I knew Patrick's journalism was always excellent. Working with him had been such a positive, healing experience, and I knew I was in safe hands. He gave me the email address of the newspaper editor who would be publishing it, and I told him I hoped he had a great holiday.

Meanwhile, to calm my nerves, I decided to reach out to a few LGBTQ+ leaders. I would need allies around me when everything hit the fan. I emailed Jane Czyzselska, the magazine editor I'd met in Parliament, and she said she'd love to meet and talk. I also contacted the CEO of Stonewall, Ruth Hunt, and she was happy to get together too. I told both of them about my career in the American Bible Belt, that I was gay, and how frightened I was about how the church would respond and what my future would be. Both were incredibly kind and supportive. Being around them sent a shot of courage flowing into my veins.

They made a few calls to others, for which I was really grateful. As a result, Clare Balding and her partner, Alice Arnold, invited me over for tea. It helped a great deal to sit in their kitchen, come out to them, and then hear their encouraging words (and to eat cake, which frankly helps with any life crisis). Another well-known lesbian, BBC news anchor Jane Hill, also invited me for coffee and an empowering chat. I was so grateful for their kindness and their confidentiality. It was wonderful to have this growing group of women around me who had navigated their own public coming-out journeys and were there to steady me.

Patrick sent me a text from his vacation saying the publication of the article would be in the next couple of days. The newspaper editor confirmed this, and I gritted my teeth, ready for the moment to arrive. As is normal for newspapers, due to a few last-minute changes the publication day was moved later, and then earlier. My heart missed a beat as I read an email telling me the interview would be published online *tonight*. It would also be printed in the following morning's paper.

I was a bundle of nerves. It was all happening, and I only had a few hours to go. Home alone, all I could do was pace up and down in my tiny studio flat. I called Wendy. Then I called my sister, Jo. Their support was keeping me sane.

I put on my pajamas and climbed into bed with my laptop. I knew that as soon as the piece went live, all my social media accounts would blow up with messages, and my former career within the evangelical church would be over. I just sat there, hitting "refresh" on the newspaper website over and over as ten o'clock approached.

And suddenly, there it was.

I knew the piece would be significant in Christian media, but I hadn't expected it to explode in mainstream media to the degree that it did. The topic of LGBTQ+ equality and the church had been in the news a lot recently, and my story was carried by that momentum. As social media buzzed, the piece began to go viral in the UK, the US, and beyond—all of that before the newspaper article had even appeared in the next day's print edition.

I switched on the late-night news. Journalists were discussing the front pages of tomorrow's papers, as they'd just arrived hot off the press. Shocked, I saw that the newspaper carrying my coming-out story had advertised it on its front page. Its "sister" newspaper, produced by the same company, did too. I'd never imagined my story would get that kind of placement, with my face on the cover. As a result, it was discussed on air that night as commentators reviewed the front pages.

I got little sleep that night, watching messages fly into my inboxes. America was wide awake, as it was the middle of the day there. Responses flooded into my social media channels and through my website's contact page from Christians who said how appalled they were. They told me how sinful I was to "give in to the lie that I was gay" and that I should be utterly ashamed of myself and never darken the doors of a church again. Others said I was a danger to the church, leading people into sin, and that I'd be better off dead. Some even went as far as to hurl death threats at me.

Along with these were messages from pro-gay Christians who did their best to make themselves heard amid the shouts of damnation. Their encouragement meant the world to me. They were from more liberal parts of the church, and although their words helped, it was my evangelical community that I longed to be affirmed by. Sadly, evangelicals were the loudest in telling me that I was wrong and was now destined for hellfire and damnation.

Waves of love came in from the LGBTQ+ community, telling me how welcome I was and how excited they were to have me as one of the family.

Reading these messages felt like being in an emotional tumble dryer—I felt joy, pain, gratitude, and heartbreak as I read so much hate and so much love.

Early next morning, my phone rang and rang with interview requests. People had seen the print edition of the paper and wanted to discuss it. Grabbing a notebook, I could tell that my calendar was going to be very full for the next week. I was also trying to stay on top of social media, but every time I hit "refresh," the amount of new comments, shares, and mentions was too fast moving to keep up with. It actually felt a little frightening, like riding a roller coaster and hanging on for dear life. Channel 4, a UK prime-time news channel, invited me onto the six o'clock evening broadcast to debate a Christian who believed that being gay was a grievous sin.

A nd we're live," the studio manager shouted, as we all took our places on set. The intro music played, and the show began. I was on after several other guests, so I paced around the greenroom nervously. I still hadn't heard exactly who I would be debating that night, and I was curious to know.

"Okay, Vicky. We need you now," a friendly floor manager said, beckoning me into the hallway. We walked toward the studio, and during a prerecorded segment they fitted me with a lapel microphone. "You'll be debating a man called Scott Lively," one of the producers told me. "He's coming to us live from the US on Skype."

I had a few seconds to grab my phone and google Scott Lively's name. It sounded familiar. My eyebrows rose as I read about him. He was a pastor who, according to the *New York Times*, met with the Ugandan government in 2009, right before they introduced the Anti-Homosexuality Bill, under which anyone found guilty of a homosexual act could receive life imprisonment or, for serial offenders, even the death penalty. Lively denied any involvement whatsoever with the Ugandan Anti-Homosexuality Act and denied allegations that he supported the harshness of the penalties it carried.

In 1995, he'd written a book called *The Pink Swastika: Homosexual-*

ity in the Nazi Party, which argued that gay Nazis were the driving force behind Hitler's movement. Rather than leaving these ideas behind him or softening them as the years went by, Lively continued to develop the book, defending its thesis with more and more research. Today, I discovered, *The Pink Swastika* existed in its fifth edition and contained views more firmly expressed than in the initial printing.

Lively was featured in a documentary called *Sodom*, which aired on a Russian TV channel funded by Vladimir Putin's government. In 2013, he wrote an open letter to Putin, congratulating him for taking "a firm stance against this scourge by banning homosexual propaganda in Russia" and praising him for "setting an example of moral leadership" against this "destructive and degrading sexual agenda." In 2014, Lively was sued in US federal court for crimes against humanity for allegedly conspiring to persecute the Ugandan LGBTQ+ community. The case was later dismissed in 2017 on jurisdictional grounds.

This was a lot to take in, as I scanned my phone's internet browser during the couple of minutes before we went on air. He was far more extreme than I'd imagined—I had no idea what he would say to me or what line of argument he'd take.

The anchor interviewed me first, putting me at ease and showing sensitivity. They played a short film we'd recorded earlier, and then the large studio screen was filled with the face of Pastor Scott Lively. Lively was asked for his response to my interview, which he'd been watching by live link. I felt sick as I waited to hear what he'd say.

"I have a lot of sympathy toward Vicky herself. My sister was a lesbian, and, in fact, I was the person that she came out to as a teenager, and I was the person she turned to later when lesbianism had almost destroyed her. And she became a Christian and overcame lesbianism. So I have a lot of sympathy for people who struggle with the challenge that Vicky is facing. I'm very sorry to hear that she has given in to the lie that she is a homosexual instead of continuing to try to overcome this challenge that is in her life."

"So you're living a lie, according to Pastor Lively," said the anchor, turning his head toward me. "Vicky, what's your response to that?"

It was difficult to hear a Christian pastor promoting the same painful teachings I'd been exposed to my entire life, but I remained as composed as I could, determined I would not get tearful on TV.

"That's what I've been raised to believe," I responded, "but psychologically it's very damaging to people—it makes you feel as though you're fighting against yourself. Many conservative Christians, maybe Scott too, would agree that it's actually a kind of demonic thing, so you begin to look within yourself, thinking actually these feelings are not only bad, but I'm being controlled by the devil." My mind spun back to the exorcism experience in my teens. "I think, actually, it's about coming to terms with who you are and realizing we need to accept our sexual orientations as a God-given gift rather than making it sound like it's a battle between who you're meant to be and who you are," I added.

Scott Lively responded, "All of us struggle with various temptations. . . . But we are called to rise above the temptations and follow the guidance of God. He gave very, very clear, explicit instructions about sexuality—he established the one flesh paradigm in Genesis 1:27 and 2:24 that 'therefore shall a man leave his family and cleave unto his wife and they should become one flesh.' And all sexual activity outside of that covenant that he's established for us to have between one man and one woman is illicit and wrong. Just because you have temptations, strong temptations, to go outside of that bond doesn't legitimize them."

He added: "I'm a married man, I've been married for thirty-three years, but, being a man, I'm attracted to women other than my wife, but I've never given in to those temptations, and I'm just asking Vicky to do the same."

I bristled. Many evangelicals over the years had told me being gay was comparable to the way heterosexuals also had to "control their lustful impulses," and now Lively was saying the same. The parallel was illogical: for me, and countless other gay people, it wasn't about controlling lust—it was about wanting a spouse and a soul mate for life, just like any straight person might hope for.

"It's a very different situation," I responded to Pastor Lively. "If you're a straight person and you say . . . it's wrong . . . as a Christian to have sex outside of marriage, so [you're] going to commit to one person of the [opposite] sex, that actually gives you the hope of having a life partner, of finding one person and committing to them. But if you're saying that a Christian gay person . . . can't have sex [or marry] outside of that heterosexual paradigm, there is *no hope* for them to have a life partner."

I wanted to say, *Check your privilege! You're straight; you have the church community cheering you on as you date, get engaged, marry, and raise a family. Sure, you can't just sleep around once you've committed to someone, but how is that small restriction in any way comparable to being barred from marriage entirely, for life?* I knew how isolating it felt, never being able to enjoy a relationship, get married, or create a home with someone special. It was in no way comparable to straight Christians "controlling their lusts." The parallel was nonsense.

Lively chimed in with his next argument: "It's a false premise. There's no such thing as a gay person—it's just an identity that you adopt."

"So you do not think that people are born gay?" I replied. He'd made a statement that was even more controversial than I was expecting.

"Absolutely not," he responded emphatically. He did not believe in gay people.

"So how come I can't change the way I feel?" I asked, struggling not to show pain in my voice. "I believe that God has made me the way that he has made me. It's taken me thirty-five years to come to terms with that, and I believe it's actually part of my God-wired identity."

"Vicky," he said, "God has the power to help you to overcome your homosexual inclinations. First Corinthians 6:9–11 . . ."

Interrupting, I answered, "That kind of teaching has been so damaging to me, and it damages so many people. . . . It's one of those things that can really psychologically scar people."

"Vicky," he replied, sounding frustrated, "you keep referring to psychology rather than spirituality. I think that's your problem. You have adopted the thinking of the world, including the idea that being criticized damages you."

"Like science, you mean?" I responded. "So science is not God-ordained—God didn't give us a brain, or an intellect—psychology for you does not reflect God's intellect in us as humans? Because I would say . . . God gave us that ability, so . . . the studies into sexuality are very much important." It seemed absurd to me: he was denying the value of psychology and putting it at odds with faith.

"True science and biblical theology are perfectly consistent," he replied. "Don't you care what God thinks?" He later continued: "My position is the biblical one."

I'd heard so many times that the evangelical view on sexuality was "the biblical one" and that it trumped all others; it left no room for asking questions or considering other ways of interpreting the text.

"There are many biblical perspectives though—and I think that has to be acknowledged," I said. "I'm doing a PhD in theology . . . and I love the Bible." It mattered to me that he knew I was academic and that I took the Bible seriously. It was my love of the Bible that had kept me in the closet until the age of thirty-five. It was equally my love of the Bible that convinced me, during my studies in the Brompton Oratory and at St. Paul's Cathedral, that we had misunderstood those texts and that being in a same-sex relationship *was* something God could bless.

The anchor checked the time, knowing our segment was almost up. "One final question for you, Reverend Lively," he said. "Have you ever had any homosexual thoughts yourself?"

After a pause, Lively said, "Fortunately for me, I have never experienced same-sex attraction. But I understand. I was an alcoholic and a drug addict—that was my challenge. I had temptations to indulge in substances of various kinds, and by the grace of God I surrendered my life to Jesus Christ and I was healed and delivered from that—just as many of my friends have been whose temptation was homosexuality . . ."

I raised my eyebrows—he had just compared being gay to alcoholism and drug addiction. In fact, that was the way it had been spoken about my entire Christian life. Same-sex relationships were not a viable Christian way of life; they were something to try and escape from, something damaging that held you in a grip of addiction and brokenness, like drink or drugs. I'd heard far worse over the years, though. Plenty of traditionalist Christians had said the sin of gay sex was on a par with bestiality and pedophilia. It was crushing; I wanted to please God with my life, yet I was being compared to people who had sex with animals or abused children.

Lively snapped me out of my thoughts. "Vicky, you do not need to succumb to the flesh, you can overcome that . . ." Even in the closing seconds of the show, he was raising his voice, urging me to embrace the teachings of the Bible and walk away from sin.

And that was it. The big screen with Lively's face on it went blank. The show moved on to its next segment, and I was led back to the greenroom. The runner helped untangle my microphone, removed it, and thanked me for being part of the broadcast.

Stepping into the awaiting taxi and heading home, I was utterly exhausted. I knew I didn't need to take Scott Lively's vitriol to heart, because I was secure in my decision and in my faith. But he represented the demographic of Christians I had been part of for years, and I knew that just as he condemned me, most of them would too. My email inbox, sadly, was proof of that. I exhaled, watching the lights and sights of London rush past through the taxi window. My first full day as an openly gay person had been a roller coaster.

27

Over the next two weeks, interviews continued at a steady pace. Now that I could finally speak up about LGBTQ+ equality, I wanted to take every opportunity I could. I hoped I might change hearts and minds within the church and also reassure other LGBTQ+ people that they were not alone. I began to lose track of how many interviews I'd done, shuttling back and forth from BBC studios, to Sky News, to the offices of magazines. Some of the international broadcasts were done in other languages using translators, and I did my best to stay on top of it all.

Sitting in a tall building overlooking London's Leicester Square, I prepared to go on air at LBC. It's one of the UK's most popular talk-radio stations with a current listenership of over two million people. They were doing a phone-in where listeners could ask questions or make comments about my story and the situation of LGBTQ+ equality in the church. Several callers were antagonistic, saying I wasn't a Christian anymore and should be ashamed of myself. Little did they know how ashamed I *had always been* of myself, until the moment I came out. I refused to let their hurtful words sink into my heart and remained courteous but firm in my responses.

Next, Jacob (not his real name) phoned in, saying he was a Christian too: "I read Vicky's story," he began. "I'd sung her songs . . . and to see someone like that come out as gay and as Christian . . . Well, I thought, why can't I do the same?"

I listened intently as he continued to tell his story. "I've been struggling with my sexuality and my Christian faith for years. I'm twenty-one," he said. "I felt I *could* tell my non-Christian friends and be accepted, so that was okay, and a big step in itself. But the teaching in church felt so condemnatory . . ."

How sad, I thought, that he could easily tell his non-Christian friends about being gay, but that he had to keep it a secret from his church community. I could relate to his sense of fear and trepidation and was delighted he'd finally taken the leap. Hearing him say that I'd helped him make that life-changing decision was so meaningful that it moved me to tears.

"Do you want to say anything to Vicky?" the radio host asked. Jacob took a breath and talked directly to me—it was an emotional moment for us both.

"Yes. Hello, Vicky," he began.

"Hi, Jacob," I replied.

"Vicky, I just want to say a massive thank-you for your example, for taking such a bold step and helping so many people, including myself, because without you we wouldn't have stepped out." I felt tears welling up in my eyes. "I hope your step helps speed up change—it has already," he added.

Deeply touched, I replied, "Wow, thank you so much . . . You encapsulate my hopes for having spoken out, that it can have a domino effect, that we can break the taboo within the church, that God loves us exactly for who we are."

As the phone-in ended and we neared the end of my interview segment, the radio host asked why I was still choosing to remain a Christian. "You went through some massive traumas at the hands of the church, didn't you?" she questioned.

"Yes," I replied. "But I love the church, and I consider it my family. It's extremely painful when families inflict damage on one another, but I'm choosing not to walk away. I want to stay in the church and have open and honest dialogue. Hopefully, someday, we'll see LGBT equality become the norm, although that seems a distant dream right now."

Jacob's call had a big impact on me. Among all my fears about coming out, I'd had one hope: that it would encourage other LGBTQ+ people of faith to take the same step, leading to change in the church. I was only a tiny drop in the ocean, but hopefully I could make a difference. Hearing my coming out had helped Jacob showed me that this was starting to happen, and that meant the world.

Opening my laptop that night, I caught up with the mountain of messages coming in through my website and from Facebook. I read one email after another:

"I'm a Christian and never felt able to tell anyone I was gay—but I read your story and tonight I came out to my family."

"I'm bisexual and Muslim. I was scared, but I spoke to my parents and to my imam after reading your interview, and as of today I'm openly bisexual."

"I never thought I'd be able to find the words to tell my church-going mum and dad that I like girls, not boys. But I cut your interview out of the newspaper and left it on my mum's bed with a Post-it note that said, 'This is my story too.' It was the only way I could think of coming out to them, and it worked. Thanks for helping me to be brave."

Emails and social-media messages like these continued to arrive. LGBTQ+ people, young and old, from the UK, the US, Africa, India,

South America, and Europe wrote in, and I was touched and taken aback by the number of them.

My post-office box was full too. Handwritten letters told the same story: people of faith who'd been in the closet all their lives had felt encouraged by my step and had come out. I thumbed through the letters, treasuring each one for the individual life it represented.

In the mayhem of that "media month" I attempted to reply to as many of these messages as I could. I tried to link up those living in far-flung places with LGBTQ+ organizations in their own country or city, so they could find support. The most heartbreaking letters and emails came from young people in countries where it remains illegal to be gay—and my heart still aches for them today as they continue to try and navigate their journeys.

The sympathetic interviews, emails, and letters were an encouraging aspect of coming out. But alongside them, painful, negative responses also poured in. My evangelical community in the US and UK had, for the most part, slammed the door in my face. Every time I saw a damning assessment of me in an article or on social media, it felt like another punch, knocking the air out of me.

Some justified their anger and judgment toward me as a reflection of God's own character, quoting Old Testament passages where God punished those who worshipped idols or chose a life of sin. Hearing this theology brought back the feelings I'd had as a child, when I'd read picture books about Noah and the flood, or Sodom and Gomorrah. It left me with much to think about.

They *did* have biblical evidence that God had condoned violence and destruction in the past and quoted the book of Revelation, which says that he will deliver judgment again in the future. They also referenced the crucifixion and "penal substitution," saying that God "did violently punish to pay the debt of sin, even in the case of his own son." I couldn't escape the fact that they had vast amounts of scripture to support this attitude; the wrath and judgment of God were woven throughout the Bible, and they saw it as license to justify their aggression. It didn't sound like the God I'd always known and followed, but it was hard to rebuff as they quoted verse after verse from the Bible about him doling out violence, murder, and punishment. It was hard to process.

My face-to-face interactions with Christian friends and former ministry colleagues were also extremely difficult. The way they looked at me had changed. Their eyes used to communicate love, welcome, and easy friendship, but now there was an element of distance and distrust. It was subtle, but it was there. I was suddenly a stranger to them.

Around these evangelicals, I felt like an awkward relative at a party, the person everyone tries to avoid. People made small talk and then excused themselves. "Got to dash—I'm so busy today," they'd say, looking uncomfortable. They only seemed to see one label on me now: gay.

Op-eds, blogs, and videos continued to appear online criticizing me. Seeing familiar names of people I'd known well and considered friends in the bylines of these articles was heartbreaking. Churches I'd played at, that had felt like second families to me, made public announcements on social media distancing themselves. They told their congregations I'd never be welcome to sing or speak there again. Tour promoters said they were closing their circuits of megachurches and Christian festivals to me. Religious bookstores said they were pulling my products from the shelves.

I'd hoped pastors and leaders I'd worked alongside for years might pick up the phone and say, "Wow, what a big step you've taken. I might not agree with you, but I'm concerned. How are you coping? Are you okay?" Instead, most just published Facebook posts or media articles saying I was wrong and that I was promoting sin.

Belonging is such a basic need for humans. We all require a tribe, and losing mine felt like the ground had given way beneath my feet. Yes, I had lots of love coming in from more liberally minded people, but the judgment from my former world was crushing. My social and professional network was still predominantly evangelical, and they'd left me out in the cold.

I felt stuck between worlds. I knew that in the future I'd get to know some liberal Christians and that I'd start hanging out in the LGBTQ+ community as my friendships with people like Jane and Ruth grew, but at that moment I was in limbo, dumped by evangelicalism and not yet integrated into a pro-LGBTQ+ social network. I was somewhere in the great divide, walking through no-man's-land.

'm ordering a set of CDs for you," my grandfather told me. "There are forty CDs in the series; each is an hour long. It's a Christian preaching series about homosexuality, how the Bible teaches that same-sex relationships are sinful, and how you can be healed from it."

The visit to see my grandad—the first time we'd met up since I came out—was one I knew might be painful for us both. If there was one person in my life who represented faith to me more than any other, and had inspired me in my own Christian journey, it was him, so this visit felt huge.

Throughout the years he'd told me I was his pride and joy, and even his hero, as I had such a prominent role in the global church with my songs. He was my hero too; he was the missionary trailblazer I'd aspired to be like when I was little. I utterly adored this man.

My heart sank when he mentioned the set of theology CDs. I'd had so many Christians critique and reject me over the weeks since my interview had gone live, and I was reaching breaking point from it all.

He sat in his big recliner, keeping his legs elevated, as Parkinson's disease was causing him pain and tremors. As always, he was surrounded by his large-print Bible, a giant mug of Bovril, and several Christian books. His eyes had gotten worse lately, so he now had an MP3 player loaded with sermons he could listen to. Faith was everything to him, and, especially since my grandmother had passed away, he spent all his time reading and praying.

"So what do you think?" he asked, taking off his glasses and looking me in the eyes with a loving but concerned gaze. "I'll buy the forty CDs, and we can sit and listen to them together over the next few months when you visit."

I knew there was no way I could sit through those CDs. I simply could not handle any more of that rhetoric—even though I'd usually do absolutely anything for him because I loved him so much.

"Grandad, I understand where you're coming from," I said falteringly. "I know your beliefs on this . . . but I can't listen to those CDs with you." I was disappointing him, I knew, and I felt my chest tighten.

"It's extremely painful to be around that sort of teaching," I tried to explain, struggling to stay composed. "I've heard those views all my life, and I've finally found the freedom and peace to step into a new direction. So I am asking you—even if you can't agree with my theology—to respect my choice and know that I've based it on the views of well-respected Bible scholars."

He looked worried and tearful. I could hear the concern in his voice; he believed I was walking away from God's path. I didn't doubt for a second that he wanted the best for me, but it was difficult to hear that he wanted me to change. That strange tension was one I was having to navigate with many people from my Christian world.

I sensed Grandad needed to get things off his chest, so I let him talk. He shared his concern that I'd lost my faith, that I was not going to heaven anymore, that I was leading thousands of people astray as they followed my example. "If you have to accept you're gay," he said, as he brought his concerns to a close, "then at least commit to singleness and celibacy and serve God that way. Will you do that?" he asked.

My memory rushed back to all the wonderful times we'd shared over the years: visiting Zimbabwe, splashing each other in the spray from Victoria Falls, and holding baby crocodiles in the safari park.

I recalled the sermons I'd heard him give in our Pentecostal church when I was little, how proud I'd felt that the man in the pulpit was my grandad—and the mischievous smiles he'd flash at me as I sat watching in the front row. I remembered how delighted he and Nanny had been when I first played them "The Wonder of the Cross," the hymn I'd written for them. It was their favorite song, and we'd sung it at my grandma's funeral at her graveside. I thought of how many times Grandad had hugged me tightly and said, "You can do it, kiddo!" or "You're my inspiration."

Since my Oxford days, he'd often asked for my views on how to interpret the Bible. These conversations had been so much fun over the years. He'd ask, "Do you know what this Greek word means?" or "How do you think this psalm should be interpreted?" I could sense the days of our Bible-based conversations were over. I'd known everything would feel different after I came out, and it already did. We didn't love each other any less—it just placed a huge, awkward elephant in the room.

"You can choose a life of singleness and celibacy," he said again. "That's the only way to honor God in this difficult situation." I took a breath, aware this answer wasn't going to be easy either. I wish I could have said yes, that I could have made him proud of me, but I had to follow my conscience.

"Grandad, I believe the Bible says celibacy is always a choice, never a demand." I felt confident in that theology; St. Paul wrote clearly on it. Looking him in the eye, I continued: "Because I believe same-sex relationships are holy in God's eyes, I don't feel it's right to place restrictions on myself or any other gay Christians."

I pulled out my Bible and talked about everything I'd been reading in the Brompton Oratory—St. Peter's vision in the book of Acts and the Gentiles' hearing they were accepted into God's kingdom. "Why would anyone be barred from something that God has called 'clean' and 'holy'?" I asked him.

"You're just seeing what you want to see in the Bible, darling," he responded with gentleness. "You can argue anything from its pages if you want to make it fit your narrative." He respected my academic background and my personal faith, but this new way of understanding felt too different from what he'd always believed.

Nearing ninety years old, he was getting tired and needed his after-noon nap. I loved him as much as ever and didn't want to upset or stress him out. He was frail and needed to rest.

Before I got up to leave, I remembered a helpful quote I'd read recently—something Billy Graham had said. Graham was perhaps the most well-known evangelist in the Christian world and someone re-spected by the majority of Christians, so he seemed a good person to draw from.

"Grandad," I said, "Billy Graham has a quote that might help us here. It goes like this: 'It's God's job to judge, the Holy Spirit's job to convict, and my job to love.'" I read it twice.

"Can you leave it with God to judge me, if he needs to, and just focus on you and I loving each other? Our 'job description' as Christians is to love. God's job description is to judge. Sometimes we get our roles mixed up; judging other Christians isn't something that should be our focus. We have plenty to keep us busy—learning to love others the best we can."

This quote changed the atmosphere, and Grandad thought for a while. "I suppose we do get our job description muddled up some-times," he said with a smile in his eyes. "God is the one we're an-swerable to ultimately. And you're right, we are supposed to love unconditionally . . ."

We sat for another moment as he pondered it all. "Maybe that's the best way," he said. "I could leave the judging to God, putting that in his hands, and just love you as my granddaughter."

I stood up and gave him a big hug. Our theological differences hadn't changed, but it seemed like we'd found a bridge across them.

Hopefully, that could keep us connected. He would try to surrender his need to judge or correct me, trusting God would do that if necessary, and he would respect the ways I had come to understand the Bible. We could move ahead and not fall out, remaining part of each other's lives.

"I might not understand it all or agree with it, but I still love you so much," he said, squeezing me as hard as his frail body could manage. "You're so precious to me."

As I walked toward the door, he added, "If your grandmother was still here, she'd want you to know that she still loved you dearly too. She understood the Bible the same way I do, but despite that, I know she'd also say that our love for you is unconditional."

My eyes welled up, and I gave him a teary smile.

True to his word, since then he has never brought up anything judgmental or corrective; he just does his best to love me unconditionally. Grandad is a hero to me and always will be. In our relationship I've caught a glimpse of something wider too: it's given me hope for the parts of the church that don't theologically agree. Yes, that's a complex situation indeed, but perhaps there is a way for the church to remain united, and to see love triumph over judgment.

28

The plane touched down bumpily on the tarmac, shaking me out of sleep. Landing back on American soil for the first time since coming out as gay was a strange feeling. It was a country I'd lived in for almost a decade, so I was returning to a familiar place, but in an unfamiliar new season of life.

Walking through the airport brought back memories and the painful reminder that my Christian music career was over. I'd spent ten years carrying my guitar on flights around the world, but this time I was traveling with no musical instrument in my hand. I'd be speaking, not singing, from now on. My entertainment lawyer was liaising with the record label in the process of formally dissolving my contracts, and it was heartbreaking to let it all go.

The logical side of me understood the mechanics of why I couldn't be a full-time worship musician anymore; I knew how the system worked. Christian record labels couldn't invest money in artists who were considered morally controversial, and being gay placed me in that category. No one was directly admitting, "We're firing you because you're gay"; that would look like discrimination. It was all far more subtle. Health reasons were a useful scapegoat, despite the fact my scleroderma had been successfully treated and was now totally benign. Everyone was even-tempered and polite throughout the process, though, so at least there was no tangible animosity.

Christian contemporary music runs like a giant machine—unless your singles are played on the vast religious radio networks and unless megachurches and big Christian festivals book you, you won't sell enough albums to keep a major record label happy. Those doors all slammed shut as soon as you came out as gay.

I'd considered making an album with an indie Christian label on a tiny budget and playing to small rooms of liberally minded people, but that wouldn't keep a roof over my head. I'd also considered venturing into mainstream nonreligious music, but starting from the ground up with a totally different audience would be a vast undertaking. Plus, I was in my thirties, which felt too old to start an entirely new genre of artistry. My life had been poured into a specific musical niche, and my audience had now shut me out. On top of this, my American work visa was specific to that one form of employment in religious music and touring. The career was over; I had to accept that and let it go.

The new career paths I was exploring, the PhD and work in TV, radio, and journalism, were some comfort. But money was extremely tight as they paid so little, and big questions about the future remained. How would I make ends meet? Could all of this evolve into a sustainable career?

On top of that, a boycott of my songs was gathering momentum. Churches in the UK and the US were contacting me, saying, "We're so appalled that you've come out as gay—we'll never sing your songs again." This reduced me to tears countless times. It felt as if my songs had been thrown in the trash, even by churches where I'd regularly sung and shared a precious sense of community. They knew songwriters got paid a small amount each time a song was used in church (a copyright system known as CCLI), so they were also hitting my financial survival by championing the boycott.

Today, I felt lighter, though. I was landing back on American soil because I'd received a message from the Gay Christian Network, a US-based organization that supports LGBTQ+ Christians and their allies. They'd asked if I'd be a keynote speaker at their January conference. I could hardly imagine getting to stand in a room of two thousand LGBT-affirming Christians. I knew it would be a healing experience.

The event, in Portland, Oregon, was everything I'd hoped for. It felt like walking into a totally new world. Here, LGBTQ+ people were in the majority, which was amazing, as we were used to feeling like a minority everywhere we went.

The times of sung worship were just like the ones I knew so well, with drums, electric guitars, and contemporary songs. A few people waved rainbow flags as they stood and sang. We heard from inspiring speakers, spent time praying together, and got to know each other over coffee afterward. Several times I had to pinch myself. Was this real or was it just a dream? I felt as though I'd come home at last.

On the second night, during the worship time, the hairs on the back of my neck stood on end when a song began. *I recognize this song*, I thought. And then I realized why: it was one of mine.

I hadn't even picked up a guitar since my interview had been published. None of the churches or conferences I'd played at over the years had sent me their usual booking invitations as I was now far too controversial. "Sorry, we just don't agree with your new sinful lifestyle," they'd written to say. "You've made your choice, and we have to make ours too."

But as the worship band at the Gay Christian Network started playing my song, tears fell down my cheeks. It meant so much that they'd chosen my music. Hearing my lyrics and melody sung by other LGBTQ+ Christians and their supporters was deeply moving.

"Glory to God, glory to God, glory to God forever"—the crowd sang the chorus over and over. We reached the last part of the song: "Take my life and let it be all for you and for your glory, take my life and let it be yours." I sang those words, still struck by how different it felt to hear them in a gay-affirming venue. Worship music and LGBTQ+ equality merged in that brief moment, and my heart soared.

The final day of the event arrived, and I read through my script one more time as I downed a cup of tea. Suddenly my phone flashed with a text message: "Are you aware that Westboro Baptist is coming to picket?" I hadn't been, but I quickly googled their website to find out if it was true.

Based in Topeka, Kansas, Westboro Baptist is the most well-known antigay church in the world. Its members have been outspokenly protesting for the last twenty years. They travel around the country and are instantly recognizable with their GOD HATES FAGS banners. As British journalist Louis Theroux put it: "In the annals of strange religious groups, Westboro Baptist occupies a place of some distinction." Their website tells people where they'll be picketing that week, enabling local people to join in and swell their numbers.

As I pulled up the Westboro website, I was startled. It mentioned me by name. Westboro protesters knew I'd be speaking at the Gay Christian Network, so they would be flying from Kansas to Portland to picket specifically before my speech. This was more than I'd bargained for at my first appearance stateside since coming out.

Walking from my hotel to the conference venue, I heard them before I saw them. A man with a loudspeaker was preaching a damning message about homosexuals going to hell. As they came into view, I saw the GOD HATES FAGS signs waving. I was surprised to see how young many of them were; two girls who looked about eighteen were holding placards saying FAGS BURN IN HELL.

Stepping through the line of protestors, I felt nervous. Westboro church members were known as nonviolent, but I had no idea who else their website advert had encouraged to come along. They'd named me, so if anyone knew what I looked like, perhaps I was in danger. I decided friendliness might be a wise approach, so I smiled at the protesters and said hello to the two youngest ones. They looked at me awkwardly, brandishing their FAGS BURN IN HELL placards.

"I just wanted to say hi," I ventured. "I'm the keynote speaker tonight, the one you named on your website, but I'm really not the evil person you think I am."

They didn't say a single word. They just stared straight ahead.

"Well," I said with a smile, "I hope by meeting each other we can remember we're supposed to be Christian family, not enemies." Someone nearby snapped a picture of me standing in between the two girls, their offensive signs still held high.

I headed on toward the Oregon Convention Center. Seeing another line of people, my heart sank. *Surely not more Westboro people,* I thought. Getting closer, I saw the message on their placards was the exact opposite: GOD LOVES YOU JUST THE WAY YOU ARE and YOU ARE QUEERLY BELOVED. They were local Christians who'd heard Westboro was coming to picket and decided they would organize a counterprotest, sharing a message of love.

As delegates arrived for the conference, they had to walk through Westboro's picket line. But they also walked through the "wall of love"— Portland Christians shouting that God loved LGBTQ+ people unconditionally, offering free hugs, and handing out rainbow ribbons. It was beautiful and a stark contrast to the hatred.

Several online news sites, including the *Huffington Post*, picked up the photo of me standing between two Westboro protesters, with their signs waving; we were an unlikely threesome indeed. They also reported on the Portland Christians forming a wall of love as a counterprotest. The topic of faith and LGBTQ+ equality was getting a lot of coverage in mainstream media these days; it was an inflammatory issue right now.

As I gave my speech that night, I told my story. I also talked about theology, especially what I'd learned back in Oxford about the Christian mystics and their focus on mystery and wonder. I tried to lighten things with moments of humor too, and we all laughed as much as we cried. It was an emotional keynote speech for me and one I knew I'd never forget.

M y sister looked at me with a smile as I sat in her kitchen, back on the southeast coast of the UK, drinking tea. "So what about dating?" she said. "I mean, now you're 'out,' have you started to think about seeing anyone?"

"Well," I replied slowly, "there is an American girl I met through a mutual friend. She's been a huge support recently, and she's gay. I love chatting with her on the phone. She said she comes to the UK for work trips sometimes, so I'm hoping it might turn into something more."

My sister grinned. "Does she like you back?" she asked.

"Umm . . . I think she might," I said.

"I bet she does," my sister said with a wink.

I blushed and grinned. It was amazing to talk openly about the idea of dating a girl; I'd never been able to speak to anyone about this before. Most heterosexual people had been chatting about crushes or love interests since their teens, and now finally I could do the same.

The American girl I liked, Mackenzie (not her real name), came to London on a business trip, and we decided to meet up for dinner. When we decided that it would be an official date, I was terrified and delighted in equal measure.

It brought up so many questions for me, which showed the naïveté and sheltered nature of my past. What did gay people do on dates? What did lesbians wear? And what about the gender roles I'd been saturated with in the Bible Belt, where the man always paid the bill and opened the doors for the woman? Who paid on a lesbian date?! Did both people open doors?! It was hilarious and confusing in equal measure, and I found myself floundering, with no blueprint to follow.

She let me choose the restaurant, so I picked an Asian place. "I wonder if she'll think I'm strange for not drinking?" I worried. Alcohol was not approved of in Pentecostal circles, so it had never been part of my life. Wycliffe Hall had been one of the only Oxford colleges without a bar, and when I moved to Tennessee, the vast majority of Christians were strongly against drinking, so I'd fitted in well. In this new situation, I was worried she might think me weird.

Another topic concerned me too: my background in the abstinence movement. Would that come up over the meal? What did I think about all of that now? I hadn't had to think about it much until the prospect of dating loomed.

It would be ironic, I thought with a smile, *if I'm too gay to belong in the evangelical church, but I'm too traditional to fit in with the LGBTQ+ community.* Hoping that wouldn't be the case, I finally chose an outfit and got ready to leave.

Thankfully, the date was a great experience. Mackenzie wore an outfit a lot like mine—dark jeans and a shirt. Conversation flowed easily, the hours flew by, and from that first evening it was clear we were falling for each other. We spent every spare moment together during the week she was in town. She also met Wendy and they got on like a house on fire, and we Skyped my sister, Jo. It was great to see that Mackenzie got a thumbs-up of approval from them both.

We were slightly daunted by the prospect of a long-distance relationship with an ocean between us, but we committed to try and make it work. Often, I returned home to my London apartment to find she'd sent me flowers, and I looked forward to our evening phone call all day. It was such a life-giving experience. I'd spent so long figuring out the theology of being gay; now I was getting to experience it—I had a girlfriend, and it felt amazing.

Long-distance relationships are challenging, of course. Some days it was tough—I'd waited so long, and now the person I was falling in love with was in a different country and a different time zone. We couldn't go on dinner dates, watch movies, or attend events together. All we had were phone calls and Skype. But somehow the energy of it all carried us along.

I had several speaking invitations at American LGBTQ+ conferences in my calendar, so Mackenzie and I were able to see each other there. She flew into each city, and we spent our downtime hanging out. I loved speaking at those church gatherings, as ministry was still my passion, and it was the best feeling to finish my work and then have Mackenzie waiting to take me out for dinner.

It dawned on me that this was simply normal life for the straight worship leaders and pastors I knew. They got to do their vocational work in church *and* have the company and support of their significant other; they didn't have to choose between the two. Something so normal for most heterosexual Christians was brand new to me after a lifetime of being barred from it, and it was wonderfully healing. Finally, I was living the life I'd always longed for.

M um, would you like to meet my . . . girlfriend?" I asked nervously. Now that we'd been a couple for a while, it felt right to have my parents meet her.

"Of course," she said. "We may be on a journey with all this, and we might not see eye to eye about theology, but you're still our daughter and we love you dearly and want to be part of your life."

I told them when Mackenzie's next London visit would be, and we marked a date on the calendar to meet up. Dad was happy to come too, as were my sister, Jo, her husband, Tim, and my nephew and nieces.

Battersea Park was the place I'd chosen for this get-together, a leafy green oasis in the middle of London with direct views across the River

Thames. As we gathered at the park entrance, I said, "Mackenzie, meet my family," introducing each of them in turn. Everyone began chatting easily and naturally. I exhaled, relieved. It was going to be a good day.

It did feel surreal, though, walking around Battersea Park—seeing my parents chatting with her, and my little nieces and nephew asking her to join in their games. My youngest niece grabbed Mackenzie's hand and walked along, hand in hand with her. It was adorable. Years ago, I couldn't have imagined this scene would ever exist. We rented bikes and rode around, then hired boats on the park lake and splashed and laughed as we avoided the ducks and raced each other around the bends. It was perfect.

As time went by, dating long-distance began to take its toll. Eventually we reached a crunch point: her career was in New York, and she couldn't leave it, and I loved England, and being near friends and family, too much to move stateside. We knew long distance couldn't continue forever, and neither of us wanted to relocate, so we'd reached an impasse.

After hours of phone calls, considering all possible options, tearfully we decided it had to end. We chose to stay friends rather than allowing the experience to leave a bitter taste; I knew I'd been lucky to have had a great introduction to what a relationship could be like.

29

No breakup is easy, and despite how conciliatory it had been, the relationship left me with things I needed to process. The biggest one was this: although I now believed being gay was fine, I couldn't get rid of the "tapes" playing in my head telling me that I should still feel shame any time I was affectionate with a woman. Decades of being taught it was sinful to express romantic intimacy toward someone of the same sex had lodged deep in my psyche, creating a Pavlovian connection.

After a few months passed, Mackenzie and I both began going on dates with other people. I found the same thing happened to me, whoever I was seeing; affection and intimacy instantly triggered shame.

Most people start dating when they are in their teens, but, like a lot of Christian LGBTQ+ people, I hadn't had that opportunity. Many of us lived in the closet, desperately trying to get free from our so-called sinful attractions. Some had been brave enough to secretly date people of the same sex, but others, like me, had been too scared, because we remained within traditional church communities. It was weird to try and get the hang of dating in my thirties, when most people had been doing it since they were in high school. Harder still, though, was my inability to shake off the feelings of shame.

I had adored Mackenzie. A couple of other girls I dated in London grew to mean a lot to me too. Despite that, the physical aspect of all those relationships proved tough. Anytime I was close to a girl, what should have felt meaningful and affectionate was overshadowed by guilt. Whenever they touched me, I suddenly felt as though I was outside of myself, watching from a distance, dissociated.

The desire was all there, and I found these girls beautiful inside and out, but there was a disconnect between me and my body. Thinking back, I'd always viewed my body as the enemy. Since I was thirteen, life had been a battle against my sinful attractions, and I'd done all I could to shut my body down and feel them less and less. I'd imagined, when I came out as gay, that everything would be instantly fixed, but I was realizing it wasn't that simple.

Now in my thirties I felt little response, even with women I found incredibly attractive. I seemed frozen in time, having shut myself down years ago. Messages of shame filled my mind and left me distracted and stressed out. This was heartbreaking after waiting so long to be in relationships; I wondered if I'd ever be free to enjoy being affectionate and intimate, or whether the impact of my past was just too powerful to undo.

I knew I needed some help to talk this through, so I called Christopher, who'd counseled me previously, back when I had had my breakdown and the chemo treatment.

It was good, and yet painful, to be back in his office. "I hoped I was starting a brand-new, happier chapter of life when I came out," I said to him, "and that I wouldn't need to be sitting in your therapy chair anymore. But I'm finding the teachings I was raised with are still having an impact, creating shame that I just can't shake. And I feel so dissociated from my body."

Christopher was his usual sensitive self. He asked questions, but mostly just let me talk. As our sessions progressed, I realized that it wasn't surprising that three decades of indoctrination were difficult to undo. I also realized that it wasn't just shame about being gay that was affecting me; it was fear and anxiety connected with sexual attraction in general. The purity movement (True Love Waits) had impacted so many Christians my age, straight and gay, and thousands of us were left trying to recover from its influence.

As a nonreligious person, Christopher was intrigued by how staunch and severe the True Love Waits ethos had been. I brought in an old copy of *I Kissed Dating Goodbye*, the flagship book from the purity movement, and we chatted about its contents. We also watched a documentary made by Matt Barber, an American guy who'd grown up around those teachings and was processing his experiences. Barber's film was an interesting assessment of the American church culture that had crossed the pond and influenced me and others in the UK's Pentecostal and evangelical circles.

Christopher and I did a Google search on Joshua Harris, author of *I Kissed Dating Goodbye*, and found that Harris had received so many negative letters about the damage the book had done to people that he and a small team were creating a documentary to interview people who'd been affected by the book, and also to share his revised views. So many people wanted this exposé documentary to be made that they'd raised over $40,000 on Kickstarter to fund it.

All of this made one thing clear to me: thousands of other Christians were dealing with similar issues as they processed what the purity movement had programmed into them, whether they were straight or LGBTQ+. For so many of us, all forms of romantic affection were tinged with fear and shame.

Outside of therapy, I chatted about this topic over coffee with a straight friend, Emma, who'd been raised in a British evangelical church. Emma told me her marriage was on the verge of divorce and that she felt it was because of over-the-top teachings on sexual abstinence that had been drummed into her during her teens and twenties. Back then, various books and sermons left her feeling guilty whenever she felt sexually attracted to her Christian boyfriend. The couple gritted their teeth, pushed those feelings away, and managed to save sex for marriage.

On her wedding night, Emma couldn't switch off the guilt and shame she'd always associated with sex and found herself in floods of tears, on the verge of a panic attack. The couple couldn't consummate their marriage, and as the months went by it had created growing tensions for them. Sobbing as she told me this, Emma said the issue looked as if it would cause them to divorce. She desperately wished the connection between sex and shame had never been woven into her mind and body by the church. My heart ached for her.

Another friend, Kate, whom I knew from a Pentecostal conference I used to attend, confided in me that she had a similar situation. She was straight and married and had been diagnosed with a medical condition called vaginismus, an involuntary contraction of the vaginal muscles that disallows penetration.

Her doctor had asked her why she thought she'd developed this. Both Kate and her doctor concluded it was because she'd had such a deep-seated fear of sex before marriage; she was frightened that she'd "go too far." Her church had taught that sex outside of marriage was a grievous sin, so she'd disconnected herself as much as possible from all sexual feelings. As a result, her body had shut down. Now married to a man she loved, she couldn't undo the association. And it was breaking their marriage apart.

Kate pulled up an NHS article and let me read more about her diagnosis: "Having feelings of shame or guilt around sex could contribute to vaginismus. For example, you might feel uncomfortable with sex if you have had a very strict upbringing where it was never discussed, have been told that sexual desire is wrong, or are affected by cultural or religious taboos around sex." She also showed me a piece from *Psychol-*

ogy Today that reported vaginismus was frequently caused by "religious values that conflict" and "negative messages or beliefs about sex." She cried as she talked about it all and told me she was seeing a therapist as she tried to unpack the fear-based teachings she'd heard throughout her teens and twenties.

Daniel, a guy who'd grown up in a charismatic Anglican church, told me that every time he had sex, it left him with strong feelings of shame afterward, as if he'd disappointed God and committed a sin. No amount of therapy had been able to deprogram the association forged in his Christian youth-group days, when he'd read books like *I Kissed Dating Goodbye* and been told at UK youth conferences that masturbation was a sin and that his sex drive was something to fight against and suppress.

Daniel had been married, but was now divorced, and said the big reason he and his wife had rushed into walking down the aisle at twenty-one was because they were too scared they'd "slip up" and commit the sin of premarital sex. After hurrying into that commitment, they later realized that they weren't suited as life partners at all. A messy divorce had followed with pain on all sides.

A new friend, Alicia, told me that she'd been raised in a British church youth group that taught sex outside of marriage left you as "damaged goods" that no godly husband or wife would want. When she was sexually abused by an older man, she saw herself as "damaged goods" and her self-esteem plummeted. She believed her hope of finding a godly husband was over.

Alicia ended up in a string of abusive relationships because she believed she didn't deserve any better; she was "damaged," according to church teachings. Now in therapy, she was making progress, but it was devastating to hear what she'd been through.

All these stories broke my heart. I wondered what resources were out there to help us all find healing. Christopher, my therapist, was a lifesaver and helped me immensely as we talked each week. I also tried to read anything I could find on the topic—and discovered there was a lot. Dianna Anderson, a bisexual Christian, wrote an entire book on her journey as she tried to undo the influences of the purity movement. Her book, *Damaged Goods: New Perspectives on Christian Purity*, was extremely honest and left me with much to think about.

Sarah Bessey, a straight Canadian author, blogged bravely about the topic. She told of the shame she was made to feel by the church when she lost her virginity before she was married: "I was nineteen years old and crazy in love with Jesus when that preacher told an auditorium I was 'damaged goods' because of my sexual past. Over the years the messages melded together into the common refrain: 'Sarah, your virginity was a gift, and you gave it away. You've ruined everything. No one honorable or godly wants to marry you. You are damaged." Her conclusions today were that "virginity isn't a guarantee of healthy sexuality or marriage" and that "there's a lot of baggage from this whole purity movement."

Another great book I picked up was by Amber Cantorna, the lesbian daughter of a Focus on the Family executive. She grew up around an especially severe version of purity culture and shared her recovery process in the memoir *Refocusing My Family*. As I read these stories, they each helped at different points in my healing process. They were invaluable and a crucial reminder that I was not alone.

Many church youth groups still teach teenagers today that masturbation is a grievous sin, and that adult couples who are dating should avoid even heavy kissing, in case it "leads to more." These pressures create a lot of anxiety and guilt, especially in kids whose minds are still forming. Sex and sexuality are gifts from God, and the way that Christians talk about them needs revisiting.

I respect the choice of anyone who wants to date or not date, to save sex for marriage or not. But the manner in which these topics are addressed in churches needs far more care and consideration. Well-meaning theology about respecting sex can, if delivered badly, create indelible associations between intimacy and shame. I'm living proof of that, as are many others.

Thousands of Christians are dealing with the fallout from this today—gay and straight, married and unmarried—and it's a discussion the church needs to have. I don't know exactly what the answers are, nor am I pushing a particular agenda beyond LGBTQ+ equality. I just see the damage in myself and in many of my friends and hope Christian teachings about sex can be thought through with increasing levels of wisdom and sensitivity.

30

I'd lost so many friends when I came out, and I was grateful to be making new ones. Especially meaningful was getting to know gay couples who'd been together for years. I'd never seen what a civil partnership or long-term commitment between two men or two women could look like, because such a thing hadn't existed within my church circles. Same-sex marriage had become legal in the UK in 2014, so lots of couples were tying the knot. Finally, I had the role models I'd lacked my entire life, the quality of their relationships was evident, and these men and women were a joy to be around.

I was enjoying spending time with a married lesbian couple named Eliza and Sam. Eliza had grown up in a Christian family, the daughter of an Anglican priest, so sometimes we chatted about faith. One day over coffee she asked me, "Since coming out, have you found a good church where you feel welcome and supported?"

"In all honesty," I replied, "I haven't. I'm still looking; it's a bit of a work in progress." I felt in limbo about church, and it was something I felt awkward talking about.

The services I was used to in evangelicalism were a world away from the ones that more liberal LGBT-affirming churches held. I missed what places like Holy Trinity Brompton offered: big gatherings of people with lots of energy and enthusiasm, worship bands with drums and guitars, home groups that met during the week, and ministry times where people offered prayer. That was where I felt at home stylistically.

I'd visited several big evangelical churches in London since coming out, but each time I'd quietly exited, in tears, halfway through the service. It was immensely painful to see people I knew standing at the front, leading the songs I used to sing. I knew I'd never be welcome to do that in those churches now that I was openly gay. The feeling of exclusion was crushing. Sermons also covered painful territory; one made a throwaway comment that "of course, marriage can only be between a man and a woman," and moments like that caused too many traumatic triggers for me.

A few friends had said, "You must visit my church. It's small, but it's LGBTQ+ friendly, and sometimes we have guitars . . ." Most of those churches were across the city, though, and I was keen to find somewhere close by, so I could get involved in local parish life. After a while I realized part of my problem was deeper: I was afraid to trust a church community again, wary of putting myself in the care of priests and pastors when so many of them in my past had been responsible for causing me so much damage.

I needed to step back and heal before I could plug in to a new congregation, and I needed to choose one carefully when I did start attending. This wasn't "church shopping"—as though I were choosing a new TV set in an electronics store. It wasn't about being picky, but about finding somewhere I'd be genuinely safe.

In the meantime I decided to attend services at cathedrals. They were big and anonymous. I could worship without having to meet anyone else, and the more I went, the more I began to love the stunning architecture, choral music, and incense. It seemed to reflect the themes of mystery and wonder that had resonated with me in my studies at Oxford. Choral Evensong became my favorite service—especially as it allowed me to sleep in on Sunday mornings—and this became my weekly habit, alternating between St. Paul's Cathedral, Southwark Cathedral, and Westminster Abbey.

There was one evangelical-style service I did feel safe attending. It was a bimonthly event run by and for LGBTQ+ Christians and allies. It reminded me of a smaller, but equally great, version of the Gay Christian Network conference in Portland. The services happened on Saturday afternoons and felt like an oasis. A hundred and fifty of us sang songs led by a band with guitars and drums, then listened to an inspiring sermon, and prayed for one another. It was the closest thing I'd found so far to a spiritual home.

As I kept attending those LGBTQ+ Christian worship events in London, it seemed natural that I might want to get back into music again. A few people had said, "We'd love you to lead worship here if you feel able," but something was stopping me. Like the unbreakable Pavlovian link I'd developed between shame and romantic intimacy, there was also a link between singing and the homophobic church environments in which I'd always played.

The Californian sermons that promoted Proposition 8 had left especially deep wounds—having to listen to such degrading comments about gay people, then sing my songs without saying a word. For me, my music had become associated with being silenced and shamed, and it only reminded me of the evangelical environments where I was no longer welcome.

The pain of it crushed my creativity, and I didn't want to even look at my guitars, let alone play them, so despite encouragement to try leading worship again, I just didn't feel able. I kept noticing my three expensive guitars sitting in a corner of my flat. I'd needed high-quality instruments, and they'd been professional workhorses over the years. Now they lay there gathering dust, untouched since my interview had been published. I could hardly believe I hadn't played them for so long.

Money was tight as I tried to build my new career, and every now and then my bank balance dropped below empty. Finally, I made a decision: I would sell all my guitars. *If I ever decide to sing again, I can replace them,* I thought, as I created three eBay listings. I posted the links on Twitter and waited to see if anyone would buy them.

They all sold within hours and went to great homes. My sadness was tinged with happiness, knowing they would be enjoyed in the next chapter of their lives. Mostly, though, I was just relieved to see my bank balance climb out of a deep overdraft.

Maybe I would sing again someday, but if I never did, I had to be okay with that too. The association between music and painful church memories was just too strong. Until that changed, it was important to take that pressure off myself and let the healing process continue.

London's Portobello Road Market was buzzing with activity. I was meeting Wendy there for lunch, but I wasn't feeling well. In fact, I hadn't been feeling well for weeks. We began walking around, but I felt awful.

"I think I'm going to fall over," I said to her suddenly, grabbing hold of a nearby railing. "I feel so exhausted and dizzy."

Adrenaline had carried me through the initial phase of my coming out process: the media mayhem, the vitriol, my keynote at the Gay Christian Network, meeting Westboro Baptist, and my relationship with Mackenzie. Now that those things were over and my calendar was less hectic, I'd hoped my life was just beginning. I'd been healthy and energized throughout all of that, but now, suddenly, all my stamina had disappeared.

"Maybe you have the flu?" Wendy suggested. But it didn't feel like any flu I'd had before. My body wouldn't function, and that day at Portobello Market was a good example; we had to get a taxi after walking around for only ten minutes. The world was swimming, and I'd felt short of breath. Wendy suggested maybe I should see a doctor.

The following day, I went to a medical clinic, and they ran various blood tests. "Let's see if you improve soon," the doctor had said. I knew I needed time off to rest, so I cleared my schedule and slept for a week. But once I stopped, I couldn't get going again.

My strength had totally disappeared, my brain felt slow and foggy, and everything ached. Even with thirteen or fourteen hours of sleep, I still felt exhausted. Trying to resume my usual work, I was dozing off at my laptop, and every muscle in my body hurt. My mobility was rapidly decreasing, and I felt like I was turning into a ninety-year-old woman.

After a couple of months, I was referred to two fatigue specialists. They monitored me and tested for other conditions, and finally at the end of a long series of appointments I was given two diagnoses. I had fibromyalgia, and I had myalgic encephalomyelitis (ME), also known as chronic fatigue syndrome (CFS).

"You have all the symptoms," one doctor explained. "Muscle dysfunction, a vast reduction in normal activities, cognitive slowness, painfully tender joints, sleep that never feels restorative, exhaustion after exercise, swollen glands, slow digestion, and constant immune issues . . . Fibromyalgia is responsible for the majority of your chronic pain and muscle weakness, and ME is responsible for the majority of your fatigue, but it's complex, as they overlap and share symptoms too." I listened, taking it all in.

"Your autoimmune system is in chaos," he told me, "and adrenaline is a prime problem here. You must've been under so much stress during your coming-out process—especially from the vitriol you've faced from people in the church, and losing your career, then needing to rebuild it. It's sent your sympathetic nervous system into high alert, stuck in 'fight or flight.' In your weakened state, some kind of virus may have got in and triggered these conditions. Whatever's happened, you've definitely developed fibromyalgia and ME."

"What's the treatment for these diagnoses?" I asked, hoping something could be done to help me.

"There aren't any cures that we know of," he replied, looking apologetic. "They're complex illnesses, and there's no consensus yet on exactly what causes them. They may be triggered by trauma, or immense stress, or some form of virus. No one knows exactly what kick-starts these diseases into action, but I'm sorry to say that neither has a known cure yet."

He handed me some printouts to take home with me. They were the NICE (National Institute for Health and Care Excellence) guidelines about these conditions. I scanned them, realizing it was not good news at all: "The physical symptoms can be as disabling as multiple sclerosis, systemic lupus erythematosus, or rheumatoid arthritis" and "place a substantial burden on people with the conditions, their families, and carers."

"So there isn't a cure for either?" I asked again, still trying to process it all.

"Sadly not," he replied. "From now on, it's about finding ways to make life as manageable as possible, learning that your capacity is far less than the average person's, and trying to find the right pain medications to help you cope."

The doctor suggested I think of my energy in terms of "spoonfuls." If a healthy person had twenty spoonfuls of energy at their disposal every day, I only had about five. He compared it to being a smartphone with a faulty battery; you can plug it in every night, but it never recharges beyond halfway. He said, "All I can advise fibromyalgia and ME patients is this: plan your days very carefully so that you have enough spoonfuls to do what's essential and you don't overexert yourself. These are very limiting, life-altering conditions, and you're already seeing that."

Walking out of the clinic, I became tearful, thinking: *This is* not *the life I'd planned for myself after coming out*. I'd hoped everything was just beginning for me—it was supposed to be the part in the "movie of life" where I'd come out and the sadness and struggle ended, the moment where I drove off into the sunset to live happily ever after. But clearly it was not going to be that way. My difficult journey, with its shame, anxiety, and adrenal fatigue, had left me with yet more damage and fallout.

I picked up the phone and called Tanya Marlow, a friend I'd known since high school. We'd been in more contact since I'd come out; she'd seen how intense the whole experience had been and wanted to make sure I was doing okay. It was lovely to have her back in my life, and we had many hilarious phone calls reminiscing about our school days.

But that day the call was a tearful one. I knew she'd been diagnosed with ME years earlier. Her illness had begun at the age of seventeen when she'd had glandular fever, or "mono," and her condition worsened substantially in 2010 when she gave birth to her son. Now she was bedbound for most of each day, and her husband, Jon, pushed her around in a wheelchair.

"What did the doctor say?" Tanya asked, knowing I'd just gotten back from my clinic visit.

"They said it's fibromyalgia and ME," I replied. We both paused in sadness and silence.

Tanya had mentioned several times over the last few months that my symptoms seemed similar to hers, and now I had an official answer. I called her a lot in the weeks ahead, as I tried to figure out how to understand these conditions, and if there was anything I could do to improve.

"Go slow and think long-term," she said. "Most people with ME never regain their former energy levels fully, so in part it's about learning a new, much slower pace of life."

Slowing down was the last thing I wanted to do. I had lived all of my life in the closet. Now, after finally coming out, I could be myself. I had a million plans. I wanted to work with churches in the hopes something would change. I wanted to be a visible role model on TV and radio, so teenagers had more examples of being out and proud. I was ready to fly, not to crash to the ground.

Although I had the diagnoses, my doctors were still keeping a constant watch as my symptoms were getting worse not better. CAT scans, ultrasounds, several MRIs, and countless blood tests followed. The sharp decline in my health left me struggling emotionally; I was having to stay home most of the time, and I couldn't see the network of friends I'd been building. I was also worried how this would affect my income, as I needed to work hard to rebuild a new career as a speaker and a writer. I grew increasingly despondent in this isolated environment; it felt like a blanket of sadness fell out of the sky and covered my head and my heart.

My doctor monitored these ups and downs, eventually diagnosing me with depression and anxiety. He suggested I try taking antidepressants. It took trying several different medications for us to find the right one for me, but once we had, I found it helped a great deal. I'd never imagined that I would need antidepressants *after* coming out as gay, but I tried to take it in stride. The tablets continued to help, and I remain on them today, as I've experienced the way they can lift the worst of the sadness and anxiety.

Utterly depleted, I cautiously learned my new limits: initially I was only able to spend three or four hours out of bed per day, and the remainder of the time I had to be flat on my back, asleep or at rest. Every grain of energy was spent trying to do freelance work to keep a roof over my head. I only saw friends once every two or three weeks; other than that, it was just phone calls and Skype. I started eating on plastic disposable plates, as I had no dishwasher and washing dishes by hand was one more task for my weak muscles every evening.

I tried every so-called cure that was recommended for fibromyalgia and ME: dietary changes, acupuncture, colonic irrigation, "lightning" style therapy, increasing exercise, doing no exercise, NSAIDs, muscle testing, iron infusions, CBT, herbal supplements, and antiviral protocols. Every penny I had left in the bank I spent on private treatments, but nothing made more than a minor amount of difference. Barely able to make ends meet financially, and living in a tiny rented room with no space, made things worse.

With a doctor's instructions, I learned to give myself B_{12} injections, despite my lifelong hatred of needles, and these were the one treatment that helped boost my energy. Thanks to the B_{12} injections, my brain fog disappeared, which was a huge breakthrough and one that remains today. But physically, my capacity still stayed way below that of an average person.

Tanya often phoned or Skyped. We tried to keep each other's spirits up about having such debilitating illnesses, and we cried together in the moments that made us despair. It meant so much to have someone else who understood what these complex conditions were like and how misunderstood they seemed to be by mainstream doctors. Chronic illness and disability are things the church rarely speaks about. Tanya felt this needed to change, so she wrote about her experiences with ME in a blog called *Thorns and Gold,* exploring the ways faith persists through the darkest times. I loved reading her reflections on suffering, doubt, hope, and perseverance; they really helped.

Doctors told me one of the toughest things about fibromyalgia and ME was that they seemed like invisible illnesses to other people. If you had a broken leg, everyone could see your leg was in a plaster cast and understood you were injured. But internal illnesses related to the central nervous system, and to muscles and connective tissue, were things people couldn't see at a glance. They couldn't tell that you were unwell.

The strangest thing was that I could almost function at my previous, normal, levels of energy in short bursts. Having chatted with others with the same diagnoses, I discovered that this pattern of having limited energy and then crashing was very common. (I also learned that the most severe fibromyalgia and ME patients were too bedbound to have even one hour of mobility or energy per day, which helped me feel more grateful for my capacity; others had it far worse.)

As months passed, with gradual improvement, I could just about manage a full day of freelance work. Afterward, though, I'd need to go to bed ridiculously early, and the following day needed to be totally empty so I could crash and recharge. It was a strange juggling act, weighing exactly how much energy I could spend per day and per week. I had to plan my calendar with military precision. The toughest part was when people *only* saw me during those limited energy bursts, on days when I appeared to be on "top form," and didn't understand that afterward, I would have a total energy crash, feel awful, and be in bed for twenty-four hours to recuperate. When I couldn't meet people for lunch or coffee, they took it personally, because they'd only seen the briefly energized version of me, and didn't understand how ill I was behind closed doors.

I could manage TV appearances, radio interviews, and giving keynotes, but they all had to be carefully planned: I couldn't overload myself with too much per week, and I needed recovery days to balance out the work days. Learning to pace myself was tough.

When I mentioned my health issues online, some Christians told me these diagnoses were God's judgment on me for pursuing a life of sin. I even received messages saying people had prayed that God would bring a crippling disability into my life when I came out, as proof to everyone that I was promoting a shameful lifestyle. This made it all even harder to handle.

Despite that abuse, I continued my social-media posts because I wanted to speak out about chronic illnesses and what it was like to face them. Interestingly, I heard from an unusually large number of LGBTQ+ people who had autoimmune diseases, fibromyalgia, or ME. I couldn't help thinking that, since many of us had experienced difficult journeys with discrimination, shame, and rejection, perhaps stress had led to a disproportionate level of these illnesses in the LGBTQ+ community.

Doctors told me countless times that all these conditions had somewhat mysterious causes, and that stress and trauma made people susceptible to them. Such a high number of LGBTQ+ people got in touch saying they had these health issues that it seemed perhaps there was a correlation. I had no statistical data beyond my own interactions with people online, but it struck me as unusual and worth further thought.

31

"We're an imprint of HarperCollins, and we'd like to sign you as an author." The words were a wonderful surprise and a bright spot during all the struggles with my health. The San Francisco publishing house wanted me to write a memoir about my life so far: growing up in a faith community knowing I was gay, then everything that had led to my decision to come out, and how life had been since. HarperCollins in London also wanted the rights for the UK and other territories. I said yes and got started.

My work portfolio was shaping up with keynotes, op-eds, radio, TV, and now the book. I paced myself carefully, took pain medications, and ensured I stayed within my energy limits per week. I'd always prided myself on being true to my word, so I was glad that by being fastidious about only saying yes to the right number of commitments, I never canceled a single work booking due to my health (and I never have, to this day).

Campaigning for LGBTQ+ equality was becoming a big part of my life. I was especially passionate about seeing a ban on conversion therapy—the attempt to turn gay or bisexual people straight. Another major focus of my work was mental health awareness, breaking the taboos around depression, anxiety, and other conditions.

I dearly hoped that the church would change its views on same-sex marriage. The most effective way of working toward this, I found, was having one-to-one conversations with pastors and leaders who'd known me for years, encouraging them to rethink their theology. I discovered this quiet method of campaigning seemed to have a lot of impact; pastors in the UK and US were actually shifting their theology as a result of those chats, and I knew grassroots change would be the most likely way to tip the balance of big denominations.

A popular LGBTQ+ magazine saw everything I was doing and asked me to become a monthly columnist. This was a relief, because, combined with the book, I now had reliable money coming in each month and could just about keep a rented roof over my head.

Keynote invitations were also increasing. Corporate executives wanted me to come into their offices and talk about "diversity and inclusion," which was a growing agenda for businesses. Being careful to pace myself, and allow for several rest days each week, I managed to make this work. I spoke at law firms, banks, and insurance companies—they were household names in the business world. In preparation for them, I voraciously researched information on HR diversity protocols and best practice, and my knowledge grew. A couple of firms hired me as a freelance consultant on diversity and as a coach working with staff members who wanted to grow in confidence at work and fulfill their potential.

Portfolio life was a lot to juggle alongside my health issues. Plus, on top of it all, my part-time PhD was still there in the background, although at several points I had to ask the university for a break in my studies because I wasn't able to manage it all.

With the help of my doctors, I mastered the art of making each week work. For every working day, I needed a "crash out" day afterward to balance it. Socializing was minimal, as it took all my energy to earn enough money to survive. I was having to learn a whole new rhythm of life.

"The prime minister requests your company." I read the email again, wondering if it was a joke. *Probably just spam mail,* I thought. But from the sender's address, it looked like a genuine government email. It was for an LGBTQ+ Leaders and Influencers Reception, to be held at Downing Street, the prime minister's residence.

I RSVP'd, saying, "I've love to come," hoping I hadn't just replied to a spambot or an internet weirdo. On Twitter that morning, several of my LGBTQ+ friends were saying they'd been invited too, so I was relieved to discover it was real. I'd had some discouraging doctors' appointments recently, where new supplements for fibromyalgia and ME had made no noticeable difference, and I was feeling low. So the email came at the perfect moment, a ray of sunshine.

How amazing, I thought. *I never would have dreamed, a few years ago when I was still in the closet, that I'd be considered an LGBTQ+ leader.* There weren't many gay women in the UK public eye. We were few and far between, so that seemed to have brought me to people's attention.

The day arrived, and I headed off to No. 10 Downing Street. Everyone smiled as we walked through the famous black door with the number 10 on it. We'd seen it so many times on the news; government officials often made speeches right in front of it. The reception was held out back in a spacious garden area. Looking around, I saw lots of familiar faces from corporate diversity events where I'd spoken or been on discussion panels.

"Hello," said someone, tapping a microphone. "Could you all gather over here, please?"

There was a small stage at one end of the garden and we made our way toward it. A Parliamentary aide gave a welcome speech expressing gratitude for the work each of us did for LGBTQ+ equality in the UK.

Next, the prime minister took the stage and gave an inspiring speech about how diversity makes the UK a better place for everyone. We clapped and cheered. Then, reading out a few people's names, he thanked them individually for their special contribution to this cause. We smiled and nodded as each person's hard work was recognized.

Then, out of the blue, I heard my name. I thought I must be mistaken, but I wasn't. People nearby looked my way and gave me a thumbs-up. I was amazed. I was getting a specific mention by the leader of our country for my contribution to LGBTQ+ equality in the church and the corporate world. It was humbling and healing all at once.

When I saw Christopher for therapy each week, we chatted about how I was navigating my new portfolio career and how I was dealing with fibromyalgia and ME. Careful planning was enabling me to just about juggle both, although my capacity was far lower than that of most healthy people my age, and I had to restrict my social life to almost zero to have the energy I needed for work.

I told him that I felt a strange mixture of weak and strong in this new chapter of life as an openly gay person. My journey had left a lot of scars: first scleroderma, with a literal scar down my forehead, and now fibromyalgia and ME, which seemed to be additional results of the stress that coming out had put on my body and my nervous system. All of these left me physically weakened and less able than I had previously been.

In another sense, though, I felt stronger than I ever had before. My identity was out in the open, and I could be fully authentic at last. I felt more whole and empowered than at any other time in my life. I was happier than I had ever been, even with my health challenges, as I could be *me*. I could campaign for equality in the church. I could speak about LGBTQ+ rights and mental health in corporate environments. I could date and look for a female life partner.

As Christopher and I chatted about this paradox, he asked me if I'd ever heard of kintsugi. I hadn't. He told me it was a Japanese art form in which broken pottery was glued back together with precious metals like gold, silver, or platinum. "The piece looks weaker, because it has been fragmented and shattered," he said, "but it's also stronger than ever, as it is joined together with a valuable, powerful metal. It's not going to crack again easily with gold and silver to bolster its strength. Plus, now it's considered a valuable piece of art, and the places where it was broken have become its greatest beauty."

He pulled up a few pictures online, and I looked at how stunning kintsugi was. The pieces were pricey too, as the gold and silver pushed the value of the pottery up and they became collectibles.

"Maybe you're a bit like kintsugi," he said with a smile. "You've been fractured, but you've also been put back together. And your brokenness is now your strength and your beauty."

"Mmmm . . . I like that," I said, smiling and thinking. "After a lifetime of feeling fragmented by fear and shame, coming out has made me 'undivided.' You're right—it's a lot like kintsugi."

From that day on, I displayed images of those beautiful Japanese art pieces on my laptop wallpaper and my smartphone screensaver. They reminded me, every time I felt weak, that actually my journey had also made me strong. I wasn't the same person I used to be; someone more unique had emerged. My experiences had made me more valuable, not less, despite the fact that they'd left scars and damage in their wake.

In our sessions, we also talked about my Christian faith. Although I'd gone through periods of feeling very angry, I didn't blame God himself for the damage the church inflicted on me. I was able to separate his role from that of his people, which was the only reason my faith survived. My beliefs had been tested to the max, but I'd emerged with a deeper, richer spirituality rooted in mystery and wonder, a more honest faith that had room to breathe.

God still seemed to speak to me through the simplest of things, and in hearing about kintsugi I sensed he was encouraging me again. I felt like he was at work in my life, healing the damage that had been done; his love and kindness were the "gold" and "silver" strengthening my formerly fractured pieces. In my weakness he made me strong—grace was literally holding me together.

Around that time I met a wonderful Jewish rabbi when we were both asked to speak on a panel about faith and mental health. Both of us had dealt with depression, and we wanted to add our voices to breaking the taboo around this topic.

After the event, we stood chatting as we said our good-byes. The rabbi had been deeply moved by hearing my story during the panel discussion. She told me a quick story, and it's one I'll never forget:

> *Rabbi Zusya of Hanipol was an influential eighteenth-century Jewish teacher. As he lay on his deathbed, he couldn't stop crying. His followers stood around him asking, "Rabbi, why are you so sad? After all the good deeds you have done, surely you'll receive a great reward in the afterlife."*
>
> *Rabbi Zusya replied, "I am afraid. When I get to heaven, I know God is not going to ask me, 'Why weren't you more like Moses?' or 'Why weren't you more like King David?' I'm afraid that God will ask, 'Zusya, why weren't you more like Zusya?' And then, what will I say?"*

I loved that she told me that story. It was a powerful reminder that, for those of us who believe in a Creator, we honor that Being by respecting the way they designed us and by allowing our uniqueness to shine. I'd spent a lifetime trying to be someone else. Not only was that damaging me, it was also offensive to the God whom I believed had designed me and woven me together.

The closing line of that powerful Jewish story often echoes around my head: "Zusya, why weren't you more like Zusya?" It's a heartwarming reminder that God longs for us to simply be ourselves.

32

"So, Vicky Beeching, welcome," the host said with a smile. I'd agreed to do a radio interview in London about faith, sexuality, and mental health. They wanted to ask what I'd learned over the years since I'd come out.

"Your songs have been sung in churches around the world and, despite knowing you'd lose that career, you came out as gay. How do you feel about your life now that a few years have passed?" he asked.

I thought for a moment, wanting to be honest. "I'm delighted I took the step—I've never regretted it for a moment. I feel far more comfortable in my own skin. Some things are still difficult, but the good vastly outweighs the bad."

He nodded. "What have been the highlights?"

"Definitely the way other LGBT people of faith came out after reading my article in 2014, and the way that's continued ever since," I said, thinking of the emails and letters that still arrived every week. It seemed like a domino effect; it was bigger and longer lasting than I'd ever imagined.

"Fantastic. What else?" he said.

"I love getting to walk alongside young LGBT people in their journeys—some in person, some by email—seeing them find the courage to be themselves. Also, doing keynote speeches in corporate environments is meaningful to me too; so many organizations are keen to make their work culture more diverse."

"One question that's come in from Twitter," he said with a chuckle. "Have you found Miss Right?!"

I smiled. "Not yet, but I'm open to meeting her someday," I said. Since Mackenzie, I had dated a few women, but none of them had developed into anything serious. "One thing is crucial," I added, laughing, "Miss Right needs to like *Harry Potter* and *Lord of the Rings* movie marathons."

He laughed and followed up with his next question: "What are your hopes for the future of the Church of England? Do you think they will allow same-sex marriage someday?"

"I hope so—and I'm doing all I can to play my part in influencing that change. It's a slow, uphill climb, though. Lots of people are working hard to help that become a reality; there's an increasing number of openly LGBT Christians and we're all vocal about the need for change."

Refilling my water glass, the host posed a new question: "What lessons have you learned from your journey?"

"Well, I've certainly learned what it feels like to move from being an 'insider' to being an 'outsider' in a very short space of time. For me, that's been about the evangelical community closing the door. Previously that part of the church felt like my home. That experience has opened my eyes to the way we turn so many situations in life into 'us versus them' scenarios, where we push away anyone who seems different from us."

He nodded, gesturing for me to keep speaking.

"I've found myself considering who else is made to feel like an 'outsider' by the church. It's a strange feeling when you realize you've been labeled 'unsaved,' yet you know that you are a decent person with a strong personal faith. It's got my brain spinning about who else is la-beled as an outsider by Christians—and whether those people are feeling the way I do."

He looked intrigued.

"Churches provide very narrow boxes in deciding who's in and out when it comes to being a 'true believer.' As a child, my church taught that *only* Pentecostals were truly saved; other Christians were not. I was taught that Catholics definitely weren't true believers—and to be very wary of high church Anglicans, as they were spiritually dead and influenced by religious spirits. It's amazing that even inside the church, we're drawing such offensive lines, based on different kinds of Christians."

He nodded.

"Today," I continued, "there are over thirty-three thousand de-nominations within Christianity and many feel that only their brand of belief is 'the true faith.' Evangelical churches believe only those hold-ing to evangelical theology are 'saved.' Charismatic churches often be-lieve that only Spirit-filled Christians really know God. Many churches consider divorced people to be outsiders, as divorce is seen as going against the teaching of the Bible. Those from other religions are not saved, because they haven't accepted Jesus as their Savior. The general public who hold no views on faith are, likewise, seen as destined for eternal damnation. That's a *lot* of people on the 'outsiders' list."

The host looked thoughtful and said, "Have you come to any conclu-sions about it?"

"Well, I don't believe it's possible to really understand this until you have personally been labeled an outsider. It's far harder to grasp it from the shelter of the inside. I don't know my conclusions yet, but it's left me with a lot to think about . . ."

He nodded. "If they are wrong on you, then there's a high chance they might be wrong about others too, right?"

I smiled. "Exactly."

Thinking for a moment, he asked, "Do you think that theme of insiders and outsiders has relevance outside the church—like in wider society?"

"Absolutely," I replied. "Politics is rife with that culture right now. There's an urgent need for us to build bridges across the great divides in culture and politics. We need to get to know the people we disagree with, to meet as fellow humans and listen to each other's stories. Listening with an open heart is *everything*. That's when prejudices and stereotypes hopefully begin to dissolve, and we realize we have more in common than we imagined."

"Good point," he responded, "especially in US and UK politics at the moment." He pulled a face that expressed the complexity of them both, and I nodded.

"We expect people to fall into such narrow categories," I said. "I was told I could be gay or Christian, but not both. And these *either/or* boxes appear all over the place. Like, being told you can *either* be a boy or a ballerina, but not both. Or you can *either* be a successful career woman or a great mother. I think we need to throw away the *either/or* boxes we place each other in and allow people's uniqueness and diversity to shine."

He looked at the clock, then said, "In the couple of minutes we have left here on the show, tell us about your other passion—mental health awareness."

"Sure," I replied. "I've learned that there are many 'closets' we can feel forced to hide inside. One relates to sexuality, but there are many others—one of them is mental health. When I got diagnosed with depression and anxiety, I realized I was scared to be honest about that in my corporate keynotes, in case people mistakenly thought they made me 'unreliable' and 'unsuitable' to book for freelance work. It slowly dawned on me that I'd put myself in another closet; finally I was openly gay, but I now had a new aspect of myself I didn't feel able to speak about! Since then, I've made the choice to be very open about my mental health issues—and doing so has felt really liberating. Whenever I speak about it publicly, people tell me they also want to 'come out of the mental health closet' and talk about their struggles too, so it's encouraging to see the taboo breaking down."

"Excellent," he replied. "Any final thoughts before we end?"

"I guess, overall, I've learned that life is short and that fear can hold us back from taking the steps we want to. Dreams we were excited about when we were younger get put on the shelf and traded for something safer and more sensible. If we don't pay attention to that now, maybe we never will. I've learned that authenticity is powerful. Not just everyday authenticity—like being a decent person—but a much deeper kind that's raw and costly, a more radical type of authenticity. Vulnerability is powerful too, and equally difficult to practice, as we take down the walls and make ourselves visible and open to people. I hope my story will be a reminder to anyone who hears it that sometimes you've got to leap into the unknown. And often when you do, it turns out better than you thought and a whole new world opens up."

He grinned. Switching off the microphone, he thanked me for being a guest on the show. Leaving the studio, I reflected on how much I'd been through, and how much I'd learned throughout my crazy journey so far. It was hard to sum up my life in a thirty-minute radio program, but interviews like that were a useful chance to step back and consider it all.

Looking at social media, I saw the usual flood of criticism I received every time I went on radio or TV. Christians who opposed LGBTQ+ equality said I wasn't a true follower of Jesus and that I should be ashamed of myself as I championed a "life of sin" and "led a generation into hell." Despite their belief that I was abandoning true faith, I felt God by my side as much as ever before, perhaps even more so. His heartbeat was for justice and equality, and I felt him with me, helping me at every step.

33

My dad had bought a brand-new pair of shoes. Usually, he wore simple black ones, but he'd splurged on some fancy brown leather brogues. "It is a really special occasion," he'd said as he'd laced them up.

It was June 2017, and I was walking into Lambeth Palace, the London residence of the archbishop of Canterbury, with my parents for an award ceremony. To my amazement, I'd been recognized for my contribution to church music and would be receiving a medal from the archbishop himself at this public event at the palace. When the letter had arrived in the mail, I found myself welling up with tears. I'd never thought an openly gay person would get an award of that sort from the archbishop and his team. It felt like a healing moment.

The Church of England remained in difficult tension. It still officially taught that same-sex relationships were sinful, and none of its priests were allowed to conduct marriages for couples of the same gender. But there were also signs of hope.

Discussions were being held about what the future should look like; some LGBTQ+ people were being asked to tell their stories. It was slow progress, but momentum was building. A while back, the archbishop had even acknowledged in an interview that some gay relationships were "stunning" in their quality of love and commitment. Those of us campaigning for same-sex marriage were encouraged by these glimmers of hope, but we also battled exhaustion and heartache, as it seemed so far from being a present reality.

As I walked through the huge wooden doors at Lambeth Palace, the occasion felt even more meaningful because I'd been able to invite my parents. I was glad they could see that my faith was still affirmed by people as senior as Justin Welby, despite the fact that my music career was over and I was no longer welcome to sing in evangelical congregations or at conferences. The award was in recognition of the role I'd played in the past and the fact that my songs had been sung all around the globe. It meant the world to me, and it helped remind me my musical legacy still mattered and hadn't been entirely tossed in the garbage by everyone.

Lots of people were inside, seated in a wood-paneled room, each nominated for something different. To my surprise, at the table opposite us was Kallistos Ware, the Greek Orthodox bishop with the snowy beard who had taught me Contemplative Spirituality at Oxford. He was receiving an award for services to theology—and well deserved it was. I leaned over and said so, enjoying reconnecting after all these years and hearing him speak in his pleasantly booming voice.

Other worship leaders were there too—faces from my past. They were people I used to stand alongside on conference stages. It was good to see them again, although it brought back the painful reminder that coming out had meant I no longer got to do what they did at evangelical conferences, so it was bittersweet.

Mum and Dad looked great in their new outfits; I was so glad we were sharing the experience. When the ceremony began, I watched as the first few people's names were called; each walked to the front of the room where Archbishop Welby stood. He shook their hand, then placed a medal, on a bright blue ribbon, around their neck. I wondered if I'd get tearful when my turn came.

My name was called, and I stood up and walked forward. There were no other openly LGBTQ+ people there nominated for awards, and I worried I might get disapproving looks. Some of the attendees were deeply traditional, and I wondered what they were thinking. I walked ahead as resolutely as I could, looking at the floor.

When I lifted up my eyes, I saw Archbishop Justin in front of me. He placed the ribbon and the medal over my head and around my neck. At that moment, I couldn't keep a tear from escaping. It felt like such a healing and hopeful gesture. But I was also sad. Sad that the church was not yet ready to fully affirm LGBTQ+ people, and aware that my award would generate a lot of criticism from Anglicans around the globe (which it did after the event).

I tried to hold all of this in tension and focus on the positives; standing in Lambeth Palace in that moment, I knew that small steps would lead to bigger change. If the archbishop's team felt able to give an award to someone openly gay and in favor of same-sex marriage, things *were* moving forward.

When I returned to my seat, my parents leaned over and whispered, "Well done. We're so proud of you." They were still on a journey about theology, but their love for me remained unconditional.

Walking out of Lambeth Palace, we strolled over Westminster bridge and looked out across at the river at Big Ben and the setting sun.

"Today was a big moment," my mum said. "It's a reminder that even though your music career is over, it impacted a lot of people. And that some people do still listen to your songs and use them in churches around the world, even if they don't agree with you on LGBTQ+ theology."

I nodded.

"Last week, I played one of your songs at a worship meeting, and people found it so helpful," she added.

"Which one?" I asked.

"'Undivided Heart,'" she replied, "the one about wanting to be totally committed to God. I absolutely love that chorus."

Give me an undivided heart,
I want to love you with every part.
Give me an undivided soul,
I want to be yours alone, yours alone.

"Ah, that one," I said with a smile. That song kept cropping up at significant moments in my journey. Originally the words had been a prayer that I'd be set free from my gay orientation. But since coming out, I'd made my peace with the song and had come to see it in a new way—as a song about wholeness, about holding on to both my faith and my sexuality.

It meant a lot to know my mum had played the song to others and that people had found it inspired them in their faith. As I looked out across the River Thames, I reflected on how the title of that song summed up where my journey had finally brought me after all these years—a place of wholeness where I could be myself, totally undivided.

"Maybe that should be the title of the book I'm writing for Harper-Collins," I joked. "*Undivided Heart* . . . or maybe just *Undivided.*"

"That's not a bad idea," said my dad. "I think *Undivided* would make a very good title. Perhaps it will be."

We stood on the bridge, watching the sunset light up the Westminster skyline. I was still wearing the medal I'd received at the Lambeth Palace awards, and as I touched it I felt a surge of hope for the future of the church.

There were lots of us now, LGBTQ+ Christians and allies, all working to bring change. It was a movement that would keep pressing on, relentlessly, until love won the day. We were all in it together.

As the last traces of pink and red shot across the evening sky, my parents and I stood thinking about the day and all it symbolized. We had been on quite a journey together, and despite our differing views we were still united by a bond of unconditional love.

My life wasn't perfect. Many people in the church still considered me deeply sinful for being gay and campaigning for same-sex marriage, and that was immensely painful. My health was still up and down with fibromyalgia and ME. But there was also a lot to be encouraged by, as the Lambeth ceremony had reminded me.

Minds and hearts were genuinely softening. People were open to hearing about new ways we could understand the Bible. Conversations like the one I'd had with my grandfather had proved to me that it was possible to disagree but still coexist, focusing on a love that crossed ideological divides.

Who knew what other positive steps were just around the corner? We were a generation seeing LGBTQ+ history being made in front of our eyes. I knew someday the church would unanimously support same-sex marriage; it was just a question of time.

The chill of the evening air moved in, and Big Ben chimed as the stars appeared one by one. My parents and I took one last look at the river as it shimmered in the moonlight and walked toward the station to catch our train home.

The Lambeth medal sat on my desk as I worked on the final draft of my book. Each time I saw it, it was a visual reminder that I *was* part of the wider church family, despite the evangelical movement still treating me like an outsider. We needed a title for the book and, chatting with my team at HarperCollins, I suggested the idea of calling it *Undivided*. We all agreed it was a great fit.

Writing the memoir had not been easy. It was hard to revisit all the difficult memories. I knew I had to do it, though; people needed to hear what many LGBTQ+ people of faith still face today. I also wanted to encourage anyone who'd traveled a similar path, reminding them that they weren't alone. So I'd revisited the painful memories, and, armed with lots of Earl Grey tea, I was doing my best to finish the final edit.

To break up those long days of typing, and the emotional ups and downs of what I was writing about, I regularly walked to my post-office box and checked for new mail. Since August 2014 and the publication of my first interview, people had been writing from around the world, and they continue to do so now in 2018. Many said they'd discovered my writing or interviews online, and that my story had been the catalyst they needed to come out too. It was deeply moving to hear it over and over.

Reading those letters inspired me to keep going with the manuscript. When the process felt too hard emotionally, and when fatigue from fibromyalgia and ME was bringing me to my knees, I pulled out those envelopes and read. I loved the colorful stamps and diverse handwriting, all reminders that this is a global issue and that we need each other.

One particular day, I received a card from a teenage girl who I'll rename Sophie to protect her privacy. She was fourteen, living in the US in a traditional religious family, and had been a Christian since childhood.

Sophie told me she'd felt a lot of shame when at the age of thirteen she'd realized she was attracted to girls and not boys. She'd sobbed, asking God to make her straight, because she couldn't cope with the tension of being gay and Christian. Things had felt so bleak that she'd begun self-harming with razor blades, and one night she lined up two bottles of painkillers, planning to take a massive overdose. In a last-ditch attempt to stop herself, she googled, "Can you be gay and Christian?," assuming from her family and church experience that the answer was no.

Her letter explained to me that, in her online search, she'd found my coming-out interview and read it in floods of tears. Hearing that others *were* embracing both their faith and their LGBTQ+ orientation was, she said, like switching on a light. The darkness, she told me, began to fade, and hope crept in. That night she didn't take her own life.

Sophie came out to her parents a few weeks later and, although they disagreed theologically, they were working things through with unconditional love. Her card ended with one final sentence: "Thank you for keeping me alive." I read it with tears running down my face.

I was humbled and touched by her words. I didn't consider myself anyone particularly special; I knew if she hadn't found me in her Google search, she would've found another LGBTQ+ activist, as there were many of us out there sharing the same message. But it meant so much to know my story had helped her.

I couldn't help thinking how similar she'd sounded to my own fourteen-year-old self, battling with darkness, pain, and thoughts of suicide. It meant more than I could express to know Sophie's life would play out so differently from mine. She hadn't waited until the age of thirty-five to come out of the closet. She had her teens and twenties ahead of her to enjoy. She could experience dating and relationships alongside all her straight peers. She could grow into a person confident in her identity. She could be happy and fully alive.

None of us can go back and change our own regrets, but we can help others have a brighter future.

I closed Sophie's card and saw it had a quote written on the front. It was from St. Catherine of Siena, a fourteenth-century Catholic theologian who had a passion for speaking truth to power. Sophie had scribbled a sentence above it saying: "This sums up how I'll live my life from now on." I read the Catherine of Siena quote and smiled. It said: "Be the person you were created to be, and you will set the world on fire."

Sophie was, I could tell, one of many young people who were going to take the world by storm. I knew she represented a younger generation of LGBTQ+ people who would start their journey of self-acceptance far earlier than many my age had done. As a result, they would be even more courageous and dream even bigger. They would live to see the church and wider society move to places of inclusion that would roll on far beyond my lifetime. If this was a glimpse of the future, then things were headed in a hopeful direction indeed.

I placed her card on my window ledge, and it still sits there today, reminding me why I'm here and what matters most. It spurs me on, to keep going with my campaigning work, even when my health is up and down and when vitriol continues to pour in from those who oppose LGBTQ+ equality. I want to see lives helped and made whole, and I will never give up on that quest. It's all totally worth it—Sophie and countless others remind me of that.

Wherever I find myself these days, whether at corporate conferences giving keynotes on diversity or in one-to-one conversations with pastors helping them embrace LGBTQ+ equality, my message is the same: *We become our most beautiful, powerful, irreplaceable selves when we allow our diversity to shine.*

This can only happen when we refuse to feel shame about the things that make us unique and different, when we gather together the fragmented pieces of who we are and boldly unite them into a self that is congruent and in harmony. Vulnerability is difficult, but crucial. Radical, raw, heartfelt authenticity is tough, but worth it.

Freed from shame and fear, we are finally able to live, and love, from a place of wholeness. We find peace. We become complete. We become people who are, at our deepest core, undivided.

APPENDIX

Although I no longer write songs, sometimes I write spoken liturgy for use in churches. The benediction below is one I created on the topic of faith and diversity. It's part prayer, part blessing, part commission—a free-form thought, without any fixed rhythm or meter, that found its way onto paper. It sums up my hope for a church that will someday make all LGBTQ+ people feel welcome.

A BENEDICTION FOR INCLUSIVE WORSHIP

Words create worlds.
God spoke in Genesis, his language distilling into stars, oceans, planets.
And God still speaks today,
Always innovating and constantly creative.

He does not bend to cultural progress, rather he leads the way.
Not innovation for innovation's sake,
But the plan of an upside-down kingdom where the last are first,
And the dinner table is set for the unlikeliest of guests.

His magnetic love draws in the outsider
And swings wide the doors for any and for all.
Religious elites look on, shaking their heads,
At this lavish outpouring of outrageous grace.

Words create worlds.
God spoke in Genesis, his language distilling into stars, oceans, planets.
And God still speaks today.

As his voice echoes and new constellations dance into view,
May we have minds that stretch wide enough,
To perceive the vastness of his imagination.
And may we have ears to hear,
Unoffended by the greatness of his grace,
Even when its boundaries venture farther than our own.

AUTHOR'S NOTE

RESOURCES AND DISCLAIMERS

To stay in touch with me and to support the work I'm doing, find me online here:

www.vickybeeching.com
www.twitter.com/vickybeeching
www.instagram.com/vickybeeching
www.facebook.com/vickybeeching/

If you've finished this book and are interested in reading more about LGBTQ+ equality, I'd love to help. Visit my website for a list of recommended books that explore what the Bible does and doesn't say about same-sex relationships and marriage, that tell other people's stories of reconciling their faith and their LGBTQ+ orientation, and that promote LGBTQ+ equality in wider society: www.vickybeeching .com/LGBTresources.

A few quick disclaimers: I do not claim to represent all gay people or all gay Christians—everyone's journey is totally unique, and many will have had very different experiences.

I am aware that, despite my difficult journey, I am still a person with much privilege; I am white, educated, and living in the UK. Others face much greater hardships.

I acknowledge that evangelical churches are not a denomination or even a homogenous group. Rather, evangelicalism is a movement, and the expression of its values varies from church to church; some churches are, thankfully, more progressive than others, but these are still a small minority.

This is not a theology book or an academic essay; it's a memoir. Because of that, my explanations of how to understand the Bible had to be extremely limited in word count. They are simply a light-touch, narrative introduction to what LGBTQ+ theology might cover, and are not intended to be substantial or academic.

I acknowledge that fibromyalgia and ME are very complex illnesses, as is scleroderma. Nervous breakdowns, likewise, are complicated and multifaceted. In this book I have only shared my personal experiences and have explained the conditions to the best of my understanding. This is not a medical textbook; other patients will have their own varying symptoms and experiences, and their own views on causation and treatment.

All the stories and memories in this book are remembered to the best of my ability. To protect other people's identities, I've changed names where appropriate. Some of the timelines referenced in this book have been stretched or compressed to enable chapters to flow. Some of the interviews, letters, or meetings have been amalgamated into overall representative examples for brevity. Fitting a lifetime into a book is not easy, but I've done my absolute best.

A theological disclaimer: In this book, I refer to God solely with male pronouns. Personally, I prefer to alternate between male and female pronouns for God or to use something gender neutral, as God is beyond gender. I had to choose how many battles to fight in this book, and that battle felt like one too many: for traditional Christians, seeing "she" or "they" in reference to God would only have increased the difficulties of engaging with my story, so I chose to stick with masculine pronouns.

Referring to God in the feminine is not a recent invention. The English anchoress and mystic Julian of Norwich, writing during the Middle Ages, described God as "Mother." For biblical examples of God's feminine nature and genderlessness, see Genesis 1:27; Hosea 11:3–4; Isaiah 66:13; Psalm 131:2; and Matthew 23:37.

ACKNOWLEDGMENTS

Writer and professor Askhari Johnson Hodari said, "If everyone helps to hold up the sky, then one person does not become tired." I love that imagery; it's certainly been true in the writing of this book. I'm grateful to everyone who has played a part!

First, thank you to my publishers on both sides of the pond. To everyone at HarperOne in San Francisco: thank you to Katy Hamilton, my amazing and infinitely patient editor, and to Mark Tauber for pursuing and signing me; to Anna Paustenbach, Suzanne Quist, Jenn Jensen, Courtney Nobile, Adrian Morgan, Ann Moru, Yvonne Chan, and Trina Hunn—you are all phenomenal.

To everyone at William Collins in London: thank you to Carlos Darby, Katherine Patrick, Matt Clacher, Myles Archibald, Caroline Bovey, and Fliss Porter—you have all been incredible to work with; and to Andrew Lyon for getting the book's journey started in the UK. I'm also grateful to Gail Ross, Howard Yoon, Dara Kaye, and Anna Sproul-Latimer for help with the book during my stay in Washington, DC.

To my family and relatives: thank you for your support and love, especially my mum and dad, who have always wanted the best for me and made many sacrifices to give me a great start in life; my amazing sister, Jo; my ninety-three-year-old grandad Ron (and "Nanny" Dorothy Davies, whom we all miss so much); Stan, Hilda, and Mary Beeching (who still live on in our hearts); the Van der Lindens, Linsells, and all my other relatives—your unconditional love means so much.

To my wonderful circle of friends: thank you for keeping my spirits up and sharing the journey. Wendy Beech-Ward, for so many years of being best friends, for brilliant memories through the highs and lows, and for playing a big role in me finding the courage to come out; Jo Squire, for being so honest, authentic, and supportive—you inspire me to be unapologetically myself; Tanya Marlow, for a friendship that's lasted since we were eleven and for helping me understand ME/CFS and learn to cope with it. Brandan Robertson, Matthew Vines, Kevin Garcia, Matthias Roberts, Eliel Cruz, Amelia Markham, Justin Lee, Dianna Anderson, Jeremiah Stanley, Sarah Gallagher, and my many other LGBTQ+ Christian friends across the pond: it means the world to be able to talk about faith and sexuality with people who face the same issues!

Here in the UK, thank you to Katharine Welby-Roberts, Leena Norms, Natalie Burwell, Nuala O'Sullivan, Claire Harvey, Helen Semple, Dave Erasmus, Abi Barrett, Stephen Dixon, Heather Staff, Ruth Hunt, Jane Czyzselska, Gabe Stoutimore, and Helen Austin—every one of you makes my life brighter and I'm grateful for our chats! Thank you to Robert Song, Margaret Masson, Becca Dean, Maeve Sherlock, and Simon McMurtary (the wonderful Durhamites!).

Thank you to Patrick Strudwick for doing my 2014 coming-out interview and for your friendship and support ever since. Thanks to Jan Oakley (and Oscar the cat!) for the retreat in Devon. Thank you to Jonathan Merritt for your friendship and your help with my health. Thanks to Seven Graham for so much wisdom and support.

I will forever be grateful to my insightful team of beta readers: Wendy Beech-Ward, Natalie Burwell, Leena Norms, Professor Robert

Song, Bishop Alan Wilson, Matthew Vines, Brandan Robertson, Peter Tatchell, Abi Barrett, Canon Mark Oakley, Gabe Stoutimore, Jane Czyzselska, and Brett Farrell.

Tanya Marlow—your role started as a beta reader and transcended into something way beyond that; you became a "book coach" throughout the entire process! You read the entire manuscript at least six times in its different stages and gave endless feedback, line by line, all of which made a huge difference; I've learned so much about writing from you.

Thank you to Matthias Roberts for both the US and UK book cover designs; you did an awesome job. Thank you to Nicholas Dawkes for the photo shoot, and to Baxter the "studio dog," who made me laugh in the photos! Thank you to Micah J. Murray for the excellent book-related web design.

Thank you to everyone who showed me care and kindness during my music career in the US. There are too many to name, but I'm grateful to so many of you, including Bec Fink, Michelle York, David Smallbone and family, Matt Smallbone, Reid McNulty, Chris Nichols, Jen Scoggins, Mel Campbell-Goodson, and Edie Spain.

Thank you to everyone who has provided an endorsement for this book and to all who will help spread the word when the book launches.

My final thanks go to the amazing gang of people in my social media community! Your messages bring me so much joy, and I love that we are journeying through life as a giant group, scattered around the globe but brought together in our digital conversations. We are all in this together.

NOTES

CHAPTER 7

1. Peter Tatchell, "Don't Fall for the Myth that It's 50 Years Since We Decriminalised Homosexuality," *The Guardian*, May 23, 2007, https://www.theguardian.com/commentisfree/2017/may/23/fifty-years-gay-liberation-uk-barely-four-1967-act.

CHAPTER 9

1. Richard Reddie, "The Church: Enslaver or Liberator?" *BBC History*, last updated February 17, 2011, http://www.bbc.co.uk/history/british/abolition/church_and_slavery_article_01.shtml.
2. Felicia R. Lee, "From Noah's Curse to Slavery's Rationale," *New York Times*, November 1, 2003, http://www.nytimes.com/2003/11/01/arts/from-noah-s-curse-to-slavery-s-rationale.html.
3. The Canons of the Holy Fathers Assembled at Gangra, Canon III (340 CE), http://www.tertullian.org/fathers2/NPNF2-14/Npnf2-14-40.htm#P2117_423984.
4. St. Augustine, *The City of God*, Christian Classics Ethereal Library, https://www.ccel.org/ccel/schaff/npnf102.iv.XIX.15.html.
5. St. Thomas Aquinas, *The Summa Theologica*, Christian Classics Ethereal Library, https://www.ccel.org/a/aquinas/summa/SS/SS057.html.
6. Leandri de Santisimo Sacramento, *Quaestiones Morales Theologicae*, vol. 4, https://play.google.com/books/reader?id=W0FFAAAAcAAJ&printsec=frontcover&output=reader&hl=en&pg=GBS.PP1.
7. Pope Pius IX, "Instruction of the Holy Office in Response to Questions from the Vicar Apostolic of the Galla Tribe in Ethiopia on the Legitimacy of Participation

of Catholics in the Slave Trade," June 20, 1866, in *Collectanea Sacra Congregationis de Propaganda Fide* (1866).

8. Maurice W. Armstrong, Lefferts A. Loetscher, and Charles A. Anderson, eds., *The Presbyterian Enterprise* (Eugene, OR: Wipf & Stock Publishers, 2001), 214.
9. Armstrong, Loetscher, and Anderson, *The Presbyterian Enterprise*, 215.
10. Armstrong, Loetscher, and Anderson, *The Presbyterian Enterprise*, 215.
11. Armstrong, Loetscher, and Anderson, *The Presbyterian Enterprise*, 214.
12. C. S. Lewis, *Surprised by Joy: The Shape of My Early Life* (New York: Harcourt Brace, 1955), 215.

CHAPTER 11

1. Rev. Justin D. Fulton, *The True Woman: A Series of Discourses, to Which Is Added Woman vs. Ballot* (Boston: Lee and Shepard, 1869), https://www.loc.gov/item/93838311.
2. J. B. Sanford, "Reasons Why Senate Constitutional Amendment No. 8 Should Not Be Adopted," *The California Outlook*, vol. 11, September 16, 1911.
3. Susan Fenimore Cooper, "Female Suffrage: A Letter to the Christian Women of America," *Harper's New Weekly Magazine*, vol. 41 (June–November 1870).
4. Cooper, "Female Suffrage."
5. Jerry Falwell, "Segregation or Integration: Which?," sermon preached in 1958.
6. Falwell, "Segregation or Integration: Which?"

CHAPTER 12

1. Bishop Kallistos Ware, *The Orthodox Way* (New York: St. Vladimir's Seminary Press, 1979).
2. Peter Enns, *The Sin of Certainty: Why God Desires Our Trust More Than Our "Correct" Beliefs* (San Francisco: HarperOne, 2016).
3. Bishop Kallistos Ware, *The Inner Kingdom: The Collected Works*, vol. 1 (New York: St. Vladimir's Seminary Press, 2000), 9.
4. Bishop Kallistos Ware, *The Inner Kingdom*, 9.
5. Bishop Kallistos Ware, *The Orthodox Way*.

CHAPTER 15

1. Jennifer Knapp, *Facing the Music: My Story* (New York: Simon & Schuster, 2014).

CHAPTER 21

1. Jane Williams, "Acts of Apostles, Part 6: The Gentile Mission," *The Guardian*, January 19, 2009, https://www.theguardian.com/commentisfree/belief/2009/jan/19/christianity-religion-acts-gentiles.